VALIDITY IN INTERPRETATION

VALIDITY IN INTERPRETATION

E. D. HIRSCH, JR.

NEW HAVEN AND LONDON, YALE UNIVERSITY PRESS, 1967

Copyright © 1967 by Yale University.

Designed by Anne Rajotte,
set in Times Roman type,
and printed in the United States of America by
the Carl Purington Rollins Printing-Office of the
Yale University Press, New Haven, Conn.
Distributed in Canada by McGill University Press.
Library of Congress catalog card number: 67–13438

For Ronald S. Crane
and William K. Wimsatt

Aristotle's idea that each discipline has its own distinct and autonomous method has been widely and inappropriately applied to the various disciplines of textual interpretation. History, of course, has been on Aristotle's side. The quasi-theoretical fields of legal, biblical, and literary hermeneutics have evolved for the most part in relative isolation. Probably this independent development of local hermeneutic theories can be accounted for by the simple fact that lawyers are not usually professional literary critics nor literary critics qualified interpreters of law, but it does not follow from this that statutory and literary interpretation require autonomous and distinct methods. No methods of legal, biblical, or literary construction have ever been devised which are not in some instances either misleading or useless. A lawyer usually interprets the law better than a literary critic not because he applies special canons of statutory construction but because he possesses a wider range of immediately relevant knowledge. The accurate form of Aristotle's conception, as applied to hermeneutics, is that each interpretive problem requires its own distinct context of relevant knowledge.

Classifications of texts, as Croce rightly argued, correspond to no distinct essences or Aristotelian entelechies. They refer instead to vague family groupings which overlap one another within the vast continuum of recorded speech. No matter how narrow the class becomes (law, civil law, criminal law; or poetry, epic poetry, lyric poetry) the borderlines between the groupings remain fuzzy. Consequently, no interpretive method can be consistently appropriate to any narrow class of texts, and it follows a fortiori that the application of broad legal, literary, or biblical canons to texts classed under those names is a splendid example of misplaced confidence and premature generalization. The proper sphere of generalization is the domain of principles, not methods, and the determination of general principles is properly the concern of general hermeneutic theory.

This book has been conceived as a contribution to general hermeneutic theory with special emphasis on the problem of validity. The problem has been neglected in recent years largely because the very conception of absolutely valid interpretation has come to be regarded with profound skepticism. In law, for example, a so-called pragmatism prevails which holds that the meaning of a law is what present judges say the meaning is. Similarly, in biblical exegesis, the Bultmannians hold that the meaning of the Bible is a new revelation to each succeeding generation. In literary theory the most familiar form of the analogous doctrine holds that the meaning of a literary text is "what it means to us today." I have given the name "radical historicism" to such theories, and have taken arms against them in Chapter 2 and Appendix II, where I also discuss a similar but still more radical form of skepticism which I have called "psychologism." Finally, I discuss throughout the book, though chiefly in Chapter 1, a third type of theory which I have called "autonomism"—the doctrine that literary texts belong to a distinct ontological realm where meaning is independent of authorial will. All three views implicitly deny the possibility of validity in any absolute or normative sense of the word.

The wider implications of such hermeneutical skepticism are usually overlooked by its adherents. At stake ultimately is the right of *any* humanistic discipline to claim genuine knowledge. Since all humane studies, as Dilthey observed, are founded upon the interpretation of texts, valid interpretation is crucial to the validity of all subsequent inferences in those studies. The theoretical aim of a genuine discipline, scientific or humanistic, is the attainment of truth, and its practical aim is agreement that truth has probably been achieved. Thus the practical goal of every genuine discipline is consensus—the winning of firmly grounded agreement that one set of conclusions is more probable than others—and this is precisely the goal of valid interpretation. It must not be dismissed as a futile goal simply because the subject matter of interpretation is often ambiguous and its conclusions uncertain. Certainty is not the same thing as validity, and knowledge of ambiguity is not necessarily ambiguous knowledge.

The most distressing consequence of hermeneutical skepticism is a version of what Yvor Winters calls "the fallacy of imitative form," which, transferred to hermeneutics, consists in the notion that part of the interpreter's task is to be mysterious about mysterious texts and to write mythically about myths. One venerable literary theory holds, for example, that literature turns from the real world to build up a "second nature" nearer the heart's desire, and I have heard it argued with wondrous logic that literary interpretation should do the same: since literature does not accurately convey reality, literary interpretation need not accurately convey the reality which is literature.

> Some people will say these are little things; they are not; they are of bad example. They tend to spread the baneful notion that there is no such thing as a high correct standard in intellectual matters; that every one may as well take his own way; they are at variance with the severe discipline necessary for all real culture; they confirm us in habits of willfulness and eccentricity, which hurt our minds, and damage our credit with serious people.

Arnold speaks of severe discipline, yet an equally compelling writer reminds us that wisdom lies in "negative capability"—the capacity to be "in uncertainties, Mysteries, doubts, without any irritable reaching after fact and reason." Severe discipline in interpretation would seem to require just this irritable reaching after fact and reason, even when the text is a poem by Keats. Yet negative capability and severe discipline are not really antithetical impulses in interpretation. They correspond to two distinct moments in knowledge which Whitehead aptly calls "the stage of romance" and "the stage of precision." To understand a poem by Keats a reader must imaginatively re-enact the doubts, glories, and mysteries which inform Keats' sense of life, but afterwards the reader can subject his imaginative construction to a severe discipline which tests whether his supposed understanding of Keats was just an illusion; in interpretation the divinatory moment can be followed by the critical. The divinatory moment is unmethodical, intuitive, sympathetic; it is an imaginative guess without which nothing can begin. The second, or critical, moment of interpretation submits the first moment to a "high intellectual standard" by testing it against all the relevant knowledge available. Thus, although the critical moment is dependent and secondary, it has the indispensable function of raising interpretive guesses to the level of knowledge.

The following pages are mainly concerned with the second moment in interpretation. Since there are no methods for making imaginative guesses, the reader will be disappointed if he expects to discover in these pages a new interpretive program or "approach." The only methods advocated in this book are those for weighing evidence. Nor can the reader expect to find complete and exemplary demonstrations of the validating process. The few random examples in the book are presented en passant and not as substantial parts of the argument, since all textual examples are themselves interpretive problems rather than brute givens. The argument of the book is unabashedly and I think necessarily theoretical. Of course a theoretical essay on validity ought to have practical implications for achieving valid interpretations, and I hope this will turn out to be so, but I recognize that the practical consequences of a book like this are bound to be largely indirect. It would be unfeasible and undesirable to publicize all the evidence relevant to every interpretive problem; consensus does not foreclose common sense. My hope is that the principles set forth in this book will help other interpreters gain confidence that consensus can be reached by mastering the relevant evidence—whether or not all of it is laid out in print. Only rarely can an editor, for example, describe in his notes every consideration that has led him to a textual decision, but obviously he should base his decision on all the relevant evidence available, and the serious interpreter should do no less in his own domain. The principles set forth and the distinctions drawn in this book (particularly the crucial distinction between meaning and significance) serve to support the conclusion that valid interpretation can indeed be achieved. To the extent that these principles, distinctions, and conclusions are accepted, the practical implications of the book will, I believe, take care of themselves.

Some of the intellectual debts I have incurred in writing this book are so heavy and pervasive that mere reference to them in occasional footnotes would be an inadequate acknowledgment. While no one can keep an accurate account of his intellectual obligations, I believe that the writers to whom I chiefly owe my fundamental ideas are Ferdinand de Saussure, Wilhelm Dilthey, Edmund Husserl, John Maynard Keynes, Karl Popper, Hans Reichenbach, and Friedrich Schleiermacher. Yet this list is bound to be arbitrary. Probably the best way to indicate the extent of my many obligations to other writers would be to append a bibliography. Indeed, persuaded that a list of essays and books would be highly useful to others interested in the subject, I had always intended to append a bibliography and had been writing titles on filing cards for several years. By one of those misfortunes that inhabit the nightmares of scholars this collection of cards was lost in Rome some months ago when my family was preparing for a very hasty return to the United States. The lost titles are gradually reappearing on another set of cards, and it is my intention to publish in due course a bibliographical essay on hermeneutic theory which will in part make up for this regrettable omission.

Other obligations both intellectual and personal cannot be

recorded on filing cards nor obliterated by chance accidents. To René Wellek I am deeply indebted for his generosity over many years. His conversation and letters, his unstinting interest and inexhaustible erudition have been continually helpful to me. I also record my thanks to Wayne Booth, Klaus Hartmann, Louis Martz, and Frederick Pottle for their criticisms of the manuscript; Emilio Betti for many stimulating hours in Rome among the *circolo ermeneutico,* and for his monumental *Teoria generale della interpretazione;* John Hobbs for his help in typing and improving the manuscript; Sir Peter Medawar for his essays and his kind permission to quote from them; and *PMLA* and *The Review of Metaphysics* for permission to reprint Appendixes I and II, first published in their pages. (Although these essays repeat some of the conceptions in the book, they also discuss other relevant issues, and I have found it useful to refer the reader to these discussions in the notes.) I am also very grateful to the John Solomon Guggenheim Memorial Foundation for a grant which made possible the writing of this book.

The two scholars for whom this book is inscribed have enriched me both by precept and example. Their intellectual rigor and integrity have exemplified an ideal to which the book has all too falteringly aspired, while their unfailing personal encouragement has steeled me to persevere in the writing of it. It was my good fortune to be in London with them several months in 1960 when all three of us had leisure to pursue conversation as well as research. My first distinct conception of this book dates from that time, and since then I have been continually buoyed up by their friendship and encouragement. Finally I record my profound gratitude to my wife, who has read or listened to every word of this book at every stage of its composition and made many suggestions for its improvement.

E. D. H., Jr.

Charlottesville, Virginia
November 1966

TABLE OF CONTENTS

Contents

1.

IN DEFENSE OF THE AUTHOR

*It has been said of Boehme that his books are
like a picnic to which the author brings the words
and the reader the meaning. The remark may
have been intended as a sneer at Boehme, but it
is an exact description of all works of literary art
without exception.*

Northrop Frye

A. BANISHMENT OF THE AUTHOR

It is a task for the historian of culture to explain why there has
been in the past four decades a heavy and largely victorious
assault on the sensible belief that a text means what its author
meant. In the earliest and most decisive wave of the attack
(launched by Eliot, Pound, and their associates) the battle-
ground was literary: the proposition that textual meaning is
independent of the author's control was associated with the
literary doctrine that the best poetry is impersonal, objective,
and autonomous; that it leads an afterlife of its own, totally
cut off from the life of its author.[1] This programmatic notion
of what poetry should be became subtly identified with a notion
of what all poetry and indeed all forms of literature necessarily
must be. It was not simply desirable that literature should de-
tach itself from the subjective realm of the author's personal
thoughts and feelings; it was, rather, an indubitable fact that
all written language remains independent of that subjective
realm. At a slightly later period, and for different reasons, this
same notion of semantic autonomy was advanced by Heidegger

1. The classic statement is in T. S. Eliot, "Tradition and the Individual Talent," *Selected Essays* (New York, 1932).

and his followers.[2] The idea also has been advocated by writers who believe with Jung that individual expressions may quite unwittingly express archetypal, communal meanings. In some branches of linguistics, particularly in so-called information theory, the semantic autonomy of language has been a working assumption. The theory has found another home in the work of non-Jungians who have interested themselves (as Eliot did earlier) in symbolism, though Cassirer, whose name is sometimes invoked by such writers, did not believe in the semantic autonomy of language.[3] As I said, it is the job of the cultural historian to explain why this doctrine should have gained currency in recent times, but it is the theorist's job to determine how far the theory of semantic autonomy deserves acceptance.

Literary scholars have often contended that the theory of authorial irrelevance was entirely beneficial to literary criticism and scholarship because it shifted the focus of discussion from the author to his work. Made confident by the theory, the modern critic has faithfully and closely examined the text to ferret out its independent meaning instead of its supposed significance to the author's life. That this shift toward exegesis has been desirable most critics would agree, whether or not they adhere to the theory of semantic autonomy. But the theory accompanied the exegetical movement for historical not logical reasons, since no logical necessity compels a critic to banish an author in order to analyze his text. Nevertheless, through its historical association with close exegesis, the theory has liberated much subtlety and intelligence. Unfortunately, it has also frequently encouraged willful arbitrariness and extravagance in academic criticism and has been one very important cause of the prevailing skepticism which calls into doubt the possibility of objectively valid interpretation. These disadvan-

2. See, for example, Martin Heidegger, *Unterwegs zur Sprache* (Pfullingen, 1959).
3. See Ernst Cassirer, *The Philosophy of Symbolic Forms:* Vol. 1, *Language,* trans. R. Manheim (New Haven, 1953), particularly pp. 69, 178, 213, 249–50, and passim.

tages would be tolerable, of course, if the theory were true. In intellectual affairs skepticism is preferable to illusion.

The disadvantages of the theory could not have been easily predicted in the exciting days when the old order of academic criticism was being overthrown. At that time such naïvetés as the positivistic biases of literary history, the casting about for influences and other causal patterns, and the post-romantic fascination with the habits, feelings, and experiences surrounding the act of composition were very justly brought under attack. It became increasingly obvious that the theoretical foundations of the old criticism were weak and inadequate. It cannot be said, therefore, that the theory of authorial irrelevance was inferior to the theories or quasi-theories it replaced, nor can it be doubted that the immediate effect of banishing the author was wholly beneficial and invigorating. Now, at a distance of several decades, the difficulties that attend the theory of semantic autonomy have clearly emerged and are responsible for that uneasiness which persists in the academies, although the theory has long been victorious.

That this state of academic skepticism and disarray results largely from the theory of authorial irrelevance is, I think, a fact of our recent intellectual history. For, once the author had been ruthlessly banished as the determiner of his text's meaning, it very gradually appeared that no adequate principle existed for judging the validity of an interpretation. By an inner necessity the study of "what a text says" became the study of what it says to an individual critic. It became fashionable to talk about a critic's "reading" of a text, and this word began to appear in the titles of scholarly works. The word seemed to imply that if the author had been banished, the critic still remained, and his new, original, urbane, ingenious, or relevant "reading" carried its own interest.

What had not been noticed in the earliest enthusiasm for going back to "what the text says" was that the text had to represent *somebody's* meaning—if not the author's, then the critic's. It is true that a theory was erected under which the meaning of the text was equated with everything it could plausibly be taken to mean. (I have described in Appendix I the fallacies of this and other descriptions of meaning that were contrived to escape the difficulties of authorial irrelevance.[4]) The theory of semantic autonomy forced itself into such unsatisfactory, ad hoc formulations because in its zeal to banish the author it ignored the fact that meaning is an affair of consciousness not of words. Almost any word sequence can, under the conventions of language, legitimately represent more than one complex of meaning.[5] A word sequence means nothing in particular until somebody either means something by it or understands something from it. There is no magic land of meanings outside human consciousness. Whenever meaning is connected to words, a person is making the connection, and the particular meanings he lends to them are never the only legitimate ones under the norms and conventions of his language.

One proof that the conventions of language can sponsor different meanings from the same sequence of words resides in the fact that interpreters can and do disagree. When these disagreements occur, how are they to be resolved? Under the theory of semantic autonomy they cannot be resolved, since the meaning is not what the author meant, but "what the poem means to different sensitive readers."[6] One interpretation is as valid as another, so long as it is "sensitive" or "plausible." Yet the teacher of literature who adheres to Eliot's theory is also by profession the preserver of a heritage and the conveyor of knowledge. On what ground does he claim that his "reading" is more valid than that of any pupil? On no very firm ground.

4. See particularly pp. 224–35.
5. The random example that I use later in the book is the sentence: "I am going to town today." Different senses can be lent to the sentence by the simple device of placing a strong emphasis on any of the six different words.
6. The phrase is from T. S. Eliot, *On Poetry and Poets* (New York, 1957), p. 126.

A. Banishment of the Author

This impasse is a principal cause of the loss of bearings sometimes felt though not often confessed by academic critics.

One ad hoc theory that has been advanced to circumvent this chaotic democracy of "readings" deserves special mention here because it involves the problem of value, a problem that preoccupies some modern literary theorists. The most valid reading of a text is the "best" reading.[7] But even if we assumed that a critic did have access to the divine criteria by which he could determine the best reading, he would still be left with two equally compelling normative ideals—the best meaning and the author's meaning. Moreover, if the best meaning were not the author's, then it would have to be the critic's—in which case the critic would be the author of the best meaning. Whenever meaning is attached to a sequence of words it is impossible to escape an author.

Thus, when critics deliberately banished the original author, they themselves usurped his place, and this led unerringly to some of our present-day theoretical confusions. Where before there had been but one author, there now arose a multiplicity of them, each carrying as much authority as the next. To banish the original author as the determiner of meaning was to reject the only compelling normative principle that could lend validity to an interpretation. On the other hand, it might be the case that there does not really exist a viable normative ideal that governs the interpretation of texts. This would follow if any of the various arguments brought against the author were to hold. For if the meaning of a text is not the author's, then no interpretation can possibly correspond to *the* meaning of the text, since the text can have no determinate or determinable mean-

7. It would be invidious to name any individual critic as the begetter of this widespread and imprecise notion. By the "best" reading, of course, some critics mean the most valid reading, but the idea of bestness is widely used to embrace indiscriminately both the idea of validity and of such aesthetic values as richness, inclusiveness, tension, or complexity—as though validity and aesthetic excellence must somehow be identical.

ing. My demonstration of this point will be found in Appendix I and in the sections on determinacy in Chapter 2.[8] If a theorist wants to save the ideal of validity he has to save the author as well, and, in the present-day context, his first task will be to show that the prevailing arguments against the author are questionable and vulnerable.

B. "THE MEANING OF A TEXT CHANGES— EVEN FOR THE AUTHOR"

A doctrine widely accepted at the present time is that the meaning of a text changes.[9] According to the radical historicistic view, textual meaning changes from era to era; according to the psychologistic view, it changes from reading to reading. Since the putative changes of meaning experienced by the author himself must be limited to a rather brief historical span, only the psychologistic view need concern us here. Of course, if any theory of semantic mutability were true, it would legitimately banish the author's meaning as a normative principle in interpretation, for if textual meaning could change in any respect there could be no principle for distinguishing a valid interpretation from a false one. But that is yet another problem that will be dealt with in a suitable place.[10] Here I need not discuss the general (and insoluble) normative problems that would be raised by a meaning which could change, but only the conditions that have caused critics to accuse authors of such fickleness.

8. See pp. 44–48, 225–30.
9. See René Wellek and Austin Warren, *Theory of Literature* (New York, 1948), Chap. 12.
10. I have discussed it in Appendix I, pp. 212–16. For the sake of clarity I should, however, quickly indicate to the reader that verbal meaning can be the same for different interpreters by virtue of the fact that verbal meaning has the character of a type. A type covers a range of actualizations (one example would be a phoneme) and yet in each actualization remains (like a phoneme) the identical type. This last point is explained in Chap. 2, Sec. D, and in Appendix III, pp. 266–70.

B. *"The Meaning of a Text Changes"*

Everyone who has written knows that his opinion of his own work changes and that his responses to his own text vary from reading to reading. Frequently an author may realize that he no longer agrees with his earlier meaning or expression and will revise his text. Our problem, of course, has nothing to do with revision or even with the fact that an author may explain his meaning differently at different times, since the authors are sometimes inept explainers of their meanings, as Plato observed. Even the puzzling case of the author who no longer understands his own text at all is irrelevant to our problem, since his predicament is due to the fact that an author, like anyone else, can forget what he meant. We all know that sometimes a person remembers correctly and sometimes not, and that sometimes a person recognizes his mistakes of memory and corrects them. None of this has any theoretical interest whatever.

When critics assert that the author's understanding of his text changes, they refer to the experience that everybody has when he rereads his own work. His response to it is different. This is a phenomenon that certainly does have theoretical importance—though not of the sort sometimes allotted to it. The phenomenon of changing authorial responses is important because it illustrates the difference between textual meaning and what is loosely termed a "response" to the text. Probably the most extreme examples of this phenomenon are cases of authorial self-repudiation, such as Arnold's public attack on his masterpiece, *Empedocles on Etna,* or Schelling's rejection of all the philosophy he had written before 1809. In these cases there cannot be the slightest doubt that the author's later response to his work was quite different from his original response. Instead of seeming beautiful, profound, or brilliant, the work seemed misguided, trivial, and false, and its meaning was no longer one that the author wished to convey. However, these examples do not show that the meaning of the work had changed, but precisely the opposite. If the work's meaning had changed (instead of the author himself and his attitudes), then the author would not have needed to repudiate his meaning and could have spared himself the discomfort of a public recantation. No doubt the *significance* of the work to the author had changed a great deal, but its meaning had not changed at all.

This is the crux of the matter in all those cases of authorial mutability with which I am familiar. It is not the meaning of the text which changes, but its significance to the author. This distinction is too often ignored. *Meaning* is that which is represented by a text; it is what the author meant by his use of a particular sign sequence; it is what the signs represent. *Significance,* on the other hand, names a relationship between that meaning and a person, or a conception, or a situation, or indeed anything imaginable. Authors, who like everyone else change their attitudes, feelings, opinions, and value criteria in the course of time, will obviously in the course of time tend to view their own work in different contexts. Clearly what changes for them is not the meaning of the work, but rather their relationship to that meaning. Significance always implies a relationship, and one constant, unchanging pole of that relationship is what the text means. Failure to consider this simple and essential distinction has been the source of enormous confusion in hermeneutic theory.

If we really believed that the meaning of a text had changed for its author, there could be only one way that we could know it: he would have to tell us. How else could we know that his understanding had changed—understanding being a silent and private phenomenon? Even if an author reported that his understanding of his meaning had changed, we should not be put off by the implausibility of the statement but should follow out its implications in a spirit of calm inquiry. The author would have to report something like this: "By these words I meant so and so, but now I observe that I really meant something different," or, "By these words I meant so and so, but I insist that from now on they shall mean something different." Such an event is unlikely because authors who feel this way usually undertake a revision of their text in order to convey their new meaning more effectively. Nevertheless, it is an event that *could* occur, and its very possibility shows once again that the same sequence of linguistic signs can represent more than one complex of meaning.

Yet, even though the author has indeed changed his mind about the meaning he wants to convey by his words, he has not managed to change his earlier meaning. This is very easily proved by his own report. He could report a change in his understanding only if he were able to compare his earlier construction of his meaning with his later construction. That is the only way he could know that there is a difference: he holds both meanings before his mind and rejects the earlier one. But his earlier meaning is not thereby changed in any way. Such a report from an author would simply force a choice on the interpreter, who would have to decide which of the author's two meanings he is going to concern himself with. He would have to decide which "text" he wanted to interpret at the moment. The critic is destined to fall into puzzlement if he confuses one text with the other or if he assumes that the author's will is entirely irrelevant to his task.

This example is, as I said, quite improbable. I do not know of a single instance where an author has been so eccentric as to report without any intention to deceive that he now means by his text what he did not mean. (Deliberate lies are, of course, another matter; they have no more theoretical interest than failures of memory.) I was forced into this improbable example by the improbability of the original thesis, namely that an author's meaning changes for himself. What the example showed on the contrary was that an author's original meaning *cannot* change—even for himself, though it can certainly be repudiated. When critics speak of changes in meaning, they are usually referring to changes in significance. Such changes are, of course, predictable and inevitable, and since the primary object of criticism, as distinct from interpretation, is significance, I shall have more to say about this distinction later, particularly in Chaper 4. For the moment, enough has been said to show that the author's revaluation of his text's significance does not change its meaning and, further, that arguments which rely on such examples are not effective weapons for attacking either the stability or the normative authority of the author's original meaning.

C. "IT DOES NOT MATTER WHAT AN AUTHOR MEANS— ONLY WHAT HIS TEXT SAYS"

As I pointed out in section A, this central tenet in the doctrine of semantic autonomy is crucial to the problem of validity. If the tenet were true, then any reading of a text would be "valid," since any reading would correspond to what the text "says"— for that reader. It is useless to introduce normative concepts like "sensitive," "plausible," "rich," and "interesting," since what the text "says" might not, after all, be any of those things. Validity of interpretation is not the same as inventiveness of interpretation. Validity implies the correspondence of an interpretation to a meaning which is represented by the text, and none of the above criteria for discriminating among interpretations would apply to a text which is dull, simple, insensitive, implausible, or uninteresting. Such a text might not be worth interpreting, but a criterion of validity which cannot cope with such a text is not worth crediting.

The proponents of semantic autonomy in England and America can almost always be relied on to point to the example of T. S. Eliot, who more than once refused to comment on the meanings of his own texts. Eliot's refusals were based on his view that the author has no control over the words he has loosed upon the world and no special privileges as an interpreter of them. It would have been quite inconsistent with this view if Eliot had complained when someone misinterpreted his writings, and, so far as I know, Eliot with stoical consistency never did complain. But Eliot never went so far as to assert that he did not mean anything in particular by his writings. Presumably he did mean something by them, and it is a permissible task to attempt to discover what he meant. Such a task has a determinate object and therefore could be accomplished correctly or incorrectly. However, the task of finding out what a text says has no determinate object, since the text can say different things to different readers. One reading is as valid or invalid as another. However, the decisive objection to the theory of semantic autonomy is not that it inconveniently fails to provide an adequate criterion of validity. The decisive objection must be sought within the theory itself and in the faultiness of the arguments used to support it.

One now-famous argument is based on the distinction between a mere intention to do something and the concrete accomplishment of that intention. The author's desire to communicate a particular meaning is not necessarily the same as his success in doing so. Since his actual performance is presented in his text, any special attempt to divine his intention would falsely equate his private wish with his public accomplishment. Textual meaning is a public affair. The wide dissemination of this argument and its acceptance as an axiom of recent literary criticism can be traced to the influence of a vigorous essay, "The Intentional Fallacy," written by W. K. Wimsatt and Monroe Beardsley and first published in 1946.[11] The critic of the arguments in that essay is faced with the problem of distinguishing between the essay itself and the popular use that has been made of it, for what is widely taken for granted as established truth was not argued and could not have been successfully argued in the essay. Although Wimsatt and Beardsley carefully distinguished between three types of intentional evidence, acknowledging that two of them are proper and admissible, their careful distinctions and qualifications have now vanished in the popular version which consists

11. *Sewanee Review, 54* (1946). Reprinted in William K. Wimsatt, Jr., *The Verbal Icon: Studies in the Meaning of Poetry* (Lexington, Ky., 1954).

in the false and facile dogma that what an author intended is irrelevant to the meaning of his text.

The best way to indicate what is fallacious in this popular version is to discuss first the dimension in which it is perfectly valid—evaluation. It would be absurd to evaluate the stylistic felicity of a text without distinguishing between the author's intention to convey a meaning and, on the other hand, his effectiveness in conveying it. It would be similarly absurd to judge the profundity of a treatise on morality without distinguishing between the author's intention to be profound and his success in being so. Evaluation is constantly distinguishing between intention and accomplishment. Take this example: A poet intends in a four-line poem to convey a sense of desolation, but what he manages to convey to some readers is a sense that the sea is wet, to others that twilight is approaching. Obviously his intention to convey desolation is not identical with his stylistic effectiveness in doing so, and the anti-intentionalists quite justly point this out. But the intentional fallacy is properly applicable *only* to artistic success and to other normative criteria like profundity, consistency, and so on. The anti-intentionalist quite properly defends the right and duty of the critic to judge freely on his own criteria and to expose discrepancies between wish and deed. However, the intentional fallacy has no proper application whatever to verbal meaning. In the above example the only universally valid meaning of the poem is the sense of desolation. If the critic has not understood that point, he will not even reach an accurate judgment—namely, that the meaning was ineptly expressed and perhaps was not worth expressing in the first place.[12]

Beneath the so-called intentional fallacy and, more generally, the doctrine of semantic autonomy lies an assumption which if true would at least render plausible the view that the meaning of a text is independent of its author's intention. I refer to the concept of a public consensus. If a poet intended his poem to

12. For a definition of verbal meaning see Chap. 2, Sec. A.

convey desolation, and if to every competent reader his poem conveyed only a sense that twilight is approaching, then such public unanimity would make a very strong case (in this particular instance) for the practical irrelevance of the author's intention. But when has such unanimity occurred? If it existed generally, there would not be any problems of interpretation.

The myth of the public consensus has been decisive in gaining wide acceptance for the doctrine that the author's intention is irrelevant to what the text says. That myth permits the confident belief that the "saying" of the text is a public fact firmly governed by public norms. But if this public meaning exists, why is it that we, who are the public, disagree? Is there one group of us that constitutes the true public, while the rest are heretics and outsiders? By what standard is it judged that a correct insight into public norms is lacking in all those readers who are (except for the text at hand) competent readers of texts? The idea of a public meaning sponsored not by the author's intention but by a public consensus is based upon a fundamental error of observation and logic. It is an empirical fact that the consensus does not exist, and it is a logical error to erect a stable normative concept (i.e. *the* public meaning) out of an unstable descriptive one. The public meaning of a text is nothing more or less than those meanings which the public happens to construe from the text. Any meaning which two or more members of the public construe is ipso facto within the public norms that govern language and its interpretation. Vox populi: vox populi.

If a text means what it says, then it means nothing in particular. Its saying has no determinate existence but must be the saying of the author or a reader. The text does not exist even as a sequence of words until it is construed; until then, it is merely a sequence of signs. For sometimes words can have homonyms (just as, by analogy, entire texts can), and sometimes the same word can be quite a different word. For example, when we read in Wordsworth's *Intimations Ode* the phrase "most worthy to be blessed," are we to understand

13

"most" as a superlative or merely an intensifier like "very"? Even on this primitive level, signs can be variously construed, and until they are construed the text "says" nothing at all.

D. "THE AUTHOR'S MEANING IS INACCESSIBLE"

Since we are all different from the author, we cannot reproduce his intended meaning in ourselves, and even if by some accident we could, we still would not be certain that we had done so. Why concern ourselves, therefore, with an inherently impossible task when we can better employ our energies in useful occupations such as making the text relevant to our present concerns or judging its conformity to high standards of excellence? The goal of reproducing an inaccessible and private past is to be dismissed as a futile enterprise. Of course, it is essential to understand some of the public facts of language and history in order not to miss allusions or mistake the contemporary senses of words, but these preliminary tasks remain squarely in the public domain and do not concern a private world beyond the reach of written language.

Before touching on the key issue in this argument—namely, that the author's intended meaning cannot be known—I would like to make an observation about the subsidiary argument respecting the public and private dimensions of textual meaning. According to this argument, it would be a mistake to confuse a public fact—namely, language—with a private fact—namely, the author's mind. But I have never encountered an interpretation that inferred truly private meanings from a text. An interpreter might, of course, infer meanings which according to our judgment could not possibly under any circumstances be implied by the author's words, but in that case, we would reject the interpretation not because it is private but because it is probably wrong. That meaning, we say, cannot be implied by those words. If our skepticism were shared by all readers of the interpretation, then it would be reasonable to say that the interpretation is private. However, it is a rare interpretation that does not have at least a few adherents, and if it has any at all, then the meaning is not private; it is at worst improbable. Whenever an interpretation manages to convince another person, that in itself proves beyond doubt that the author's words *can* publicly imply such a meaning. Since the interpreted meaning *was* conveyed to another person, indeed to at least two other persons, the only significant interpretive question is, "Did the author really intend that public meaning by his words?" To object that such a meaning is highly personal and ought not to have been intended is a legitimate aesthetic or moral judgment, but is irrelevant to the question of meaning. That meaning—if the author did mean it—has proved itself to be public, and if the interpreter manages to do his job convincingly, the meaning can become available to a very large public. It is simply a self-contradiction for a member of the public to say, "Yes, I see that the author did mean that, but it is a private not a public meaning."

The impulse that underlies this self-contradictory sort of argument is a sound insight that deserves to be couched in terms more suitable than "public" and "private." The issue is first of all a moral and aesthetic one. It is proper to demand of authors that they show consideration for their readers, that they use their linguistic inheritance with some regard for the generality of men and not just for a chosen few. Yet many new usages are bound to elude the generality of men until readers become habituated to them. The risk of resorting to semi-private implications—available at first only to a few—is very often worth taking, particularly if the new usage does finally become widely understood. The language expands by virtue of such risky innovations. However, the soundest objection to so-called private meanings does not relate to moral and aesthetic judgment but to the practice of interpretation. Those interpreters who look for personal implications in such formalized utterances as poems very often disregard genre conventions and limitations of which the author was very well aware. When an author composes a poem, he usually intends it as an utterance whose implications are not obscurely autobiographical. There may be exceptions to this rule of thumb, and poetic kinds are too various to warrant any unqualified generalizations about the conventions of poetry and the intentions of authors, but too many interpreters in the past have sought autobiographical meanings where none were meant. Such interpreters have been insensitive to the proprieties observed by the author and to his intentions. The fallacy in such interpretations is not that the inferred meanings are private, but that they are probably not the author's meanings. Whether a meaning is autobiographical is a neutral and by itself irrelevant issue in interpretation. The only thing that counts is whether the interpretation is probably right.

The genuine distinction between public and private meaning resides in the first part of the argument, where it is asserted that the author's intended meaning cannot be known. Since we cannot get inside the author's head, it is useless to fret about an intention that cannot be observed, and equally useless to try to reproduce a private meaning experience that cannot be reproduced. Now the assertion that the author's meaning cannot be reproduced presupposes the same psychologistic theory of meaning which underlies the notion that an author's meaning changes even for himself. Not even the author can reproduce his original meaning because nothing can bring back his original meaning experience. But as I suggested, the irreproducibility of meaning experiences is not the same as the irreproducibility of meaning. The psychologistic identification of textual meaning with a meaning experience is inadmissible. Meaning experiences *are* private, but they are not meanings.[13]

The most important argument to consider here is the one which states that the author's intended meaning cannot be *certainly* known. This argument cannot be successfully met

13. See Chap. 2, Sec. B, and Chap. 4, Sec. A and B.

because it is self-evidently true. I can never know anot.
person's intended meaning with certainty because I cannot ,
inside his head to compare the meaning he intends with t
meaning I understand, and only by such direct comparis(
could I be certain that his meaning and my own are identica
But this obvious fact should not be allowed to sanction th
overly hasty conclusion that the author's intended meaning i
inaccessible and is therefore a useless object of interpretation
It is a logical mistake to confuse the impossibility of certainty
in understanding with the impossibility of understanding. It is a
similar, though more subtle, mistake to identify knowledge with
certainty. A good many disciplines do not pretend to certainty,
and the more sophisticated the methodology of the discipline,
the less likely that its goal will be defined as certainty of knowledge. Since genuine certainty in interpretation is impossible,
the aim of the discipline must be to reach a consensus, on the
basis of what is known, that correct understanding has *probably*
been achieved. The issue is not whether certainty is accessible
to the interpreter but whether the author's intended meaning
is accessible to him. Is correct understanding possible? That is
the question raised by the thesis under examination.

Most of us would answer that the author's meaning is only
partially accessible to an interpreter. We cannot know all the
meanings the author entertained when he wrote down his text,
as we infer from two familiar kinds of evidence. Whenever I
speak I am usually attending to ("have in mind") meanings that
are outside my subject of discourse. Furthermore, I am always
aware that the meanings I can convey through discourse are
more limited than the meanings I can entertain. I cannot, for
example, adequately convey through words many of my visual
perceptions—though these perceptions are meanings, which is
to say, objects of consciousness. It is altogether likely that no
text can ever convey all the meanings an author had in mind as
he wrote.

But this obvious fact is not decisive. Why should anyone
with common sense wish to equate an author's textual meaning

17

with all the meanings he happened to entertain when he wrote? Some of these he had no intention of conveying by his words. Any author knows that written verbal utterances can convey only verbal meanings—that is to say, meanings which can be conveyed to others by the words he uses. The interpretation of texts is concerned exclusively with sharable meanings, and not everything I am thinking of when I write can be shared with others by means of my words. Conversely, many of my sharable meanings are meanings which I am not directly thinking of at all. They are so-called unconscious meanings.[14] It betrays a totally inadequate conception of verbal meaning to equate it with what the author "has in mind." The only question that can relevantly be at issue is whether the *verbal* meaning which an author intends is accessible to the interpreter of his text.

Most authors believe in the accessibility of their verbal meaning, for otherwise most of them would not write. However, no one could unanswerably defend this universal faith. Neither the author nor the interpreter can ever be certain that communication has occurred or that it can occur. But again, certainty is not the point at issue. It is far more likely that an author and an interpreter can entertain identical meanings than that they cannot. The faith that speakers have in the possibility of communication has been built up in the very process of learning a language, particularly in those instances when the actions of the interpreter have confirmed to the author that he has been understood. These primitive confirmations are the foundation for our faith in far less primitive modes of communication. The inaccessibility of verbal meaning is a doctrine that experience suggests to be false, though neither experience nor argument can prove its falsity. But since the skeptical doctrine of inaccessibility is highly improbable, it should be rejected as a working assumption of interpretation.

Of course, it is quite reasonable to take a skeptical position that is less sweeping than the thesis under examination: certain

14. See Chap. 2, Secs. D and E.

E. "The Author Often Does Not Know What He Means"

texts might, because of their character or age, represent authorial meanings which are now inaccessible. No one would, I think, deny this reasonable form of skepticism. However, similar versions of such skepticism are far less acceptable, particularly in those theories which deny the accessibility of the author's meaning whenever the text descends from an earlier cultural era or whenever the text happens to be literary. These views are endemic respectively to radical historicism and to the theory that literary texts are ontologically distinct from nonliterary ones. Both of these theories are challenged in subsequent chapters. However, even if these theories were acceptable, they could not uphold the thesis that an author's verbal meaning is inaccessible, for that is an empirical generalization which neither theory nor experience can decisively confirm or deny. Nevertheless, with a high degree of probability, that generalization is false, and it is impossible and quite unnecessary to go beyond this conclusion.

E. "THE AUTHOR OFTEN DOES NOT KNOW
WHAT HE MEANS"

Ever since Plato's Socrates talked to the poets and asked them with quite unsatisfactory results to explain "some of the most elaborate passages in their own writings," it has been a commonplace that an author often does not really know what he means.[15] Kant insisted that not even Plato knew what he meant, and that he, Kant, could understand some of Plato's writings better than Plato did himself.[16] Such examples of

15. Plato, *Apology,* 22b–c.
16. Immanuel Kant, *Critique of Pure Reason,* trans. N. K. Smith (London, 1933), A 314, B 370, p. 310: "I shall not engage here in any literary enquiry into the meaning which this illustrious author attached to the expression. I need only remark that it is by no means unusual, upon comparing the thoughts which an author has expressed in regard to his subject, whether in ordinary conversation or in writing, to find that we understand him better than he has understood himself."

19

authorial ignorance are, no doubt, among the most damaging weapons in the attack on the author. If it can be shown (as it apparently can) that in some cases the author does not really know what he means, then it seems to follow that the author's meaning cannot constitute a general principle or norm for determining the meaning of a text, and it is precisely such a general normative principle that is required in defining the concept of validity.

Not all cases of authorial ignorance are of the same type. Plato, for instance, no doubt knew very well what he meant by his theory of Ideas, but it may have been, as Kant believed, that the theory of Ideas had different and more general implications than those Plato enunciated in his dialogues. Though Kant called this a case of understanding the author better than the author understood himself, his phrasing was inexact, for it was not Plato's meaning that Kant understood better than Plato, but rather the subject matter that Plato was attempting to analyze. The notion that Kant's understanding of the Ideas was superior to Plato's implies that there is a subject matter to which Plato's meaning was inadequate. If we do not make this distinction between subject matter and meaning, we have no basis for judging that Kant's understanding is better than Plato's.[17] Kant's statement would have been more precise if he had said that he understood the Ideas better than Plato, not that he understood Plato's meaning better than Plato. If we do not make and preserve the distinction between a man's meaning and his subject matter, we cannot distinguish between true and false, better and worse meanings.

This example illustrates one of the two main types of authorial ignorance. It has greatest importance in those genres of writing that aspire to tell the truth about a particular subject matter. The other principal type of authorial ignorance pertains not to the subject matter but to the author's meaning itself, and

17. The distinction between meaning and subject matter is discussed in Chap. 2, Sec. F, and is one foundation for my objections to Gadamer's identification of meaning with *Sache*. See Appendix II, pp. 247–49.

E. "*The Author Often Does Not Know What He Means*"

can be illustrated whenever casual conversation is subjected to stylistic analysis:

> "Did you know that those last two sentences of yours had parallel constructions which emphasized their similarity of meaning?"
>
> "No! How clever of me! I suppose I really did want to emphasize the similarity, though I wasn't aware of that, and I had no idea I was using rhetorical devices to do it."

What this example illustrates is that there are usually components of an author's intended meaning that he is not conscious of. It is precisely here, where an interpreter makes these intended but unconscious meanings explicit, that he can rightfully claim to understand the author better than the author himself. But here again a clarification is required. The interpreter's right to such a claim exists only when he carefully avoids confusing meaning with subject matter, as in the example of Plato and Kant. The interpreter may believe that he is drawing out implications that are "necessary" accompaniments to the author's meaning, but such necessary accompaniments are rarely unavoidable components of someone's *meaning*. They become necessary associations only within a given *subject matter*.[18] For example, although the concept "two" necessarily implies a whole array of concepts including those of succession, integer, set, and so on, these may not be implied in a given usage of the word, since that usage could be inadequate or misconceived with respect to the subject matter in which "two" falls. Only within that subject matter does there subsist necessity of implication. Thus, by claiming to perceive implications of which the author was not conscious, we may sometimes distort and falsify the meaning of which he was conscious, which is not "better understanding" but simply misunderstanding of the author's meaning.

18. This distinction was not observed in the interesting essay by O. Bollknow, "Was heisst es einen Verfasser zu verstehen besser als er sich selber verstanden hat?" in *Das Verstehen, Drei Aufsätze zur Theorie des Geisteswissenschaften* (Mainz, 1949).

But let us assume that such misunderstanding has been avoided and that the interpreter really has made explicit certain aspects of an author's undoubted meaning of which the author was unconscious—as in stylistic analysis of casual conversation. The further question then arises: How can an author mean something he did not mean? The answer to that question is simple. It is not possible to mean what one does not mean, though it is very possible to mean what one is not conscious of meaning. That is the entire issue in the argument based on authorial ignorance. That a man may not be conscious of all that he means is no more remarkable than that he may not be conscious of all that he does. There is a difference between meaning and consciousness of meaning, and since meaning is an affair of consciousness, one can say more precisely that there is a difference between consciousness and self-consciousness. Indeed, when an author's meaning is complicated, he cannot possibly at a given moment be paying attention to all its complexities. But the distinction between attended and unattended meanings is not the same as the distinction between what an author means and what he does not mean.[19] No example of the author's ignorance with respect to his meaning could legitimately show that his intended meaning and the meaning of his text are two different things.

Other varieties of authorial ignorance are therefore of little theoretical interest. When Plato observed that poets could not *explain* what they meant, he intimated that poets were ineffectual, weak-minded, and vague—particularly with respect to their "most elaborate passages." But he would not have contended that a vague, uncertain, cloudy, and pretentious meaning is not a meaning, or that it is not the poet's meaning.[20] Even when a poet declares that his poem means whatever it is taken to mean (as in the case of some modern writers who

19. For a discussion of so-called conscious and unconscious meanings see Chap. 2, Sec. D and E.

20. Or at least that of the muse who temporarily possesses him—the muse being, in those unseemly cases, the real author.

believe in the current theory of public meaning and authorial irrelevance), then, no doubt, his poem may not mean anything in particular. Yet even in such a limiting case it is still the author who "determines" the meaning.

One final illustration of authorial ignorance, a favorite among literary critics, is based on an examination of an author's early drafts, which often indicate that what the author apparently intended when he began writing is frequently quite different from what his final work means. Such examples show how considerations of style, genre, and local texture may play a larger part in his final meaning than that played by his original intention, but these interesting observations have hardly any theoretical significance. If a poet in his first draft means something different than he means in his last, it does not imply that somebody other than the poet is doing the meaning. If the poet capitalizes on a local effect which he had not originally intended, so much the better if it makes a better poem. All this surely does not imply that an author does not mean what he means, or that his text does not mean what he intends to convey.

If there is a single moral to the analyses of this chapter, it is that meaning is an affair of consciousness and not of physical signs or things. Consciousness is, in turn, an affair of persons, and in textual interpretation the persons involved are an author and a reader. The meanings that are actualized by the reader are either shared with the author or belong to the reader alone. While this statement of the issue may affront our deeply in-grained sense that language carries its own autonomous meanings, it in no way calls into question the power of language. On the contrary, it takes for granted that all meaning communicated by texts is to some extent language-bound, that no textual meaning can transcend the meaning possibilities and the control of the language in which it is expressed. What has been denied here is that linguistic signs can somehow speak their own meaning—a mystical idea that has never been persuasively defended.

2.

MEANING AND IMPLICATION

> *"The question is," said Alice, "whether you*
> *can make words mean so many different things."*
> *"The question is," said Humpty Dumpty, "which*
> *is to be master—that's all."*
>
> *Lewis Carroll*

Since it is very easy for a reader of any text to construe meanings that are different from the author's, there is nothing in the nature of the text itself which requires the reader to set up the author's meaning as his normative ideal. Any normative concept in interpretation implies a choice that is required not by the nature of written texts but rather by the goal that the interpreter sets himself. It is a weakness in many descriptions of the interpretive process that this act of choice is disregarded and the process described as though the object of interpretation were somehow determined by the ontological status of texts themselves. The argument, for example, that changing cultural conditions change the meaning of a text assumes that the object of interpretation necessarily changes under changed conditions. Similarly, the defense of re-cognitive interpretation often assumes that something in the nature of a text requires the meaning to be the stable and determinate meaning of an author.[1] But the object of interpretation is precisely that which

1. I borrow the term "re-cognitive interpretation" from Emilio Betti. A re-cognition implies, of course, the cognition of what the author had cognized (i.e. meant)—Boeckh's "Erkennen des Erkannten." Although the term here embraces wider domains than are usually included under "cognition" (i.e. unconscious and emotive domains), the

cannot be defined by the ontological status of a text, since the distinguishing characteristic of a text is that from it not just one but many disparate complexes of meaning can be construed. Only by ignoring this fact can a theorist attempt to erect a normative principle out of a neutral and variable state of affairs—a fallacy that seems endemic to discussions of hermeneutics. Bluntly, no necessity requires the object of interpretation to be determinate or indeterminate, changing or unchanging. On the contrary, the object of interpretation is no automatic given, but a task that the interpreter sets himself. *He* decides what he wants to actualize and what purpose his actualization should achieve.

Thus, while it is a fallacy to claim that a particular norm for interpretation is necessarily grounded in the nature of this or that kind of text, rather than in the interpreter's own will, it is quite another matter to claim that there can be only one sort of norm when interpretation is conceived of as a corporate enterprise. For it may very well be that there exists only one norm that can be universally compelling and generally sharable. In the previous chapter I argued that no presently known normative concept other than the author's meaning has this universally compelling character. On purely practical grounds, therefore, it is preferable to agree that the meaning of a text is the author's meaning.

Usually it is true that the defense of the old ideal of recognitive interpretation is carried out on a different front. It is pointed out that the main reason for studying texts, particularly old ones, is to expand the mind by introducing it to the immense possibilities in human actions and thoughts—to see and feel what other men have seen and felt, to know what they have known. Furthermore, none of these expansive benefits comes to the man who simply discovers his own meanings in

---

sympathetic reader will make the appropriate adjustment. See Emilio Betti, *Teoria generale della interpretazione* (2 vols. Milan, Giuffrè, 1955), *1,* 343–432.

someone else's text and who, instead of encountering another person, merely encounters himself. When a reader does that, he finds only his own preconceptions, and these he did not need to go out and seek. Finally, the defender of re-cognitive interpretation adds that the knowledge of what has been thought and felt is also, after all, a form of knowledge and, as such, worth gaining for its own sake.

There is nothing despicable in this argument, nor can any considerable objection be raised against it, except that the knowledge sought may be, for various reasons, impossible to achieve. Some of these skeptical objections I have already answered in principle, and in this chapter I shall deal with the two root forms of all such skepticism—psychologism and radical historicism. However, I shall not repeat at length the moral arguments in favor of viewing interpretation as a re-cognition of the author's meaning.

It is, of course, quite true that the choice of a norm for interpretation is a free social and ethical act. Any reader can adopt or reject any norm, and he is justified in thinking that there is no absolute necessity for his choosing one or another. Furthermore, he may or may not accept the idea that all uses of language carry moral imperatives which derive from the double-sided, interpersonal character of linguistic acts. All this he may reject as unconvincing, and nothing in the mute signs before him will compel him to change his mind or bring him ill fortune if he does not. Partly for this reason, I have chosen a different sort of defense—one that appeals not to the ethics of language but to the logical consequences that follow from the act of public interpretation. As soon as anyone claims validity for his interpretation (and few would listen to a critic who did not), he is immediately caught in a web of logical necessity. If his claim to validity is to hold, he must be willing to measure his interpretation against a genuinely discriminating norm, and the only compelling normative principle that has ever been brought forward is the old-fashioned ideal of rightly understanding what the author meant. Consequently, my case rests not on the powerful moral arguments for re-cognitive interpretation, but on the fact that it is the only kind of interpretation with a determinate object, and thus the only kind that can lay claim to validity in any straightforward and practicable sense of that term.

While the problem of validity is consistently circumvented by those who attack the ideal of re-cognitive interpretation, the substantial elements in their attack cannot be ignored. Even though only one compelling normative principle exists, it is still necessary to show that it is a viable principle. Thus, I shall have to show that the author's verbal meaning is determinate, that it is reproducible, and finally that it provides a means for coping with the knottiest problem of interpretation, the problem of implication.

Such an account of the authorial meaning that is sought by re-cognitive interpretation should serve as a foundation for all other interpretive goals as well. For even when the original author is rejected or disregarded, any construction of a text still constitutes a meaning that must have an author—though he be merely the critic himself. All forms of written interpretation and all interpretive goals that transcend private experience require that some author's meaning be both determinate and reproducible. In discussing the nature of verbal meaning, I shall pay particular attention to these two universal requirements.

A. DEFINING VERBAL MEANING

Although verbal meaning requires the determining will of an author or interpreter, it is nevertheless true that the norms of language exert a powerful influence and impose an unavoidable limitation on the wills of both the author and interpreter. Alice is right to say that Humpty Dumpty cannot successfully make words mean just anything he wants them to. Therefore, any discussion of verbal meaning should define in principle the way in which linguistic norms exert this codetermining influence.

Is language always constitutive of verbal meaning or is it sometimes merely a controlling factor that sets limits to possible verbal meanings? This problem has been much discussed, and like many others in the purview of hermeneutics, it probably cannot be solved with certainty, since no satisfactory way of testing either hypothesis has been devised. Nevertheless, it is very probable that neither hypothesis is true for all instances and sorts of verbal meaning. Sometimes a use of language is uniquely constitutive of meaning; sometimes, apparently, a particular choice of words merely imposes limitations and is not uniquely required for the meaning that is actually willed. This is suggested by the example of translation. Some utterances, particularly of a technical sort, can be perfectly translated, while others, particularly lyric poems, are never perfectly carried over into another language. It seems to follow that the language-bound quality of utterances, that is, the degree to which language is constitutive of meaning, can vary from null to somewhere in the vicinity of 100 per cent.

Certainly the claims of the meta-linguists and the proponents of Muttersprache seem to be far too absolute. They have given convincing and impressive examples of the way language can constitute thought and meaning and have reminded us that Humboldt's conception of language as *energeia* was an epoch-making insight. But these observations do not compel the unprovable and improbable conclusion that a unique use of language is always constitutive of a unique meaning.[2] The argument that a Muttersprache imposes an inescapable Weltanschauung on its speakers seems to overlook the remarkable variety in the assumptions and attitudes of speakers who have the same Muttersprache. On this point the sagest comment I have encountered is by Manfred Sandmann:

> It would be wrong to infer from the absence of an adequate linguistic sign an ignorance of the corresponding thing-meant (German has no word for bully, English

2. See Chap. 3, Sec. E.

no word for Schadenfreude); it would be equally wrong to conclude that an English-speaking person could not see that *dew, rain, ice, water, mist,* etc., were only different states of the same thing simply because there is no word for that thing in the English language.[3]

An amusing illustration of Sandmann's very sensible position is found in a contest set by Paul Jennings in *The Observer* of 20 December 1964. The contestant was to invent a word for each of ten definitions, such as "to make a sound like escaping bath water," "to pursue an excessive standard of living or 'keep up with the Joneses,' " and "having the appearance of affluence but living on credit." Obviously meanings such as these frequently exist before individual words become generally available to express them, and it is, of course, true that when such words do become available they may alter (i.e. partly constitute) the meanings they were devised to express. For example, a single word, by virtue of its compactness, may have quite a different effect than the definition it was designed to support. This concentrating and hypostatizing effect may be very important in some utterances but may carry no meaning value at all in others. No absolute, a priori pronouncement is warranted, since the effect may or may not be operative in a particular utterance. This rejection of absolute, a priori generalizations with regard to linguistic effects that are variable and local is one of the main points of this book.[4]

On the other hand, it obviously is warranted to say that linguistic norms at the very least always impose limitations on verbal meaning. In the first place, there exist limitations which are intrinsic to all linguistic media. For example, it is impossible to express in language meanings that are constituted by a medium that is not linguistic, such as music or painting.[5] How-

3. Manfred Sandmann, *Subject and Predicate: A Contribution to the Theory of Syntax* (Edinburgh, 1954), p. 73.
4. See particularly Chap. 3, Secs. B–E.
5. Of course language often *refers* to meanings constituted by other media, though it cannot accurately translate those meanings.

ever, this general limitation on the possibilities of language is not of great significance in textual interpretation, since it merely states the tautology that what is constituted by another medium is constituted by it and therefore cannot be separated from it. Of far greater importance in hermeneutical theory are those meanings excluded from language not by their nature but by the linguistic norms that actually obtain. The operation of these limitations may be called for convenience the Humpty-Dumpty effect. Although Saussure is convincing when he argues that the potentialities of a language are finite at any moment in time, these linguistic limitations can never be legislated in advance. The most important version of the Humpty-Dumpty effect is the one that Alice pointed out: when somebody does in fact use a particular word sequence, his verbal meaning cannot be anything he might wish it to be. This very general restriction is the single important one for the interpreter, who always confronts a particular sequence of linguistic signs.

Yet even in confronting a particular word sequence the interpreter must recognize that "the norms of language" are not a uniform set of restrictions, requirements, and patterns of expectation, but an immense number of different ground rules that vary greatly with respect to different utterances. This point has been made with great clarity and concreteness by Wittgenstein.[6] The generalization that "mind reading" is not the duty of the interpreter, who is obliged to understand only those meanings which "the public norms of language" permit, may plausibly apply to many kinds of formal discourse, but it would not apply to a parent's interpretation of a child's elliptical statements or to the frequent ellipses of ordinary conversation. Since these utterances do carry verbal meaning under the particular norms that obtain for such speech acts, the principle that verbal meaning is limited by the norms of language does not constitute any easy a priori narrowing of the interpreter's

6. In *Philosophical Investigations,* trans. G. E. M. Anscombe (New York, 1953), p. 26, and passim.

task. The norms of language are neither uniform nor stable but vary with the particular sort of utterance that is to be interpreted. A single principle underlies what we loosely call "the norms of language." It is the principle of sharability. Because sharability is the decisive element in all linguistic norms, it is important to conceive of them, despite their complexity and variability, on this fundamental level. We thereby place emphasis not on the structural characteristics of the linguistic medium, but on the function of speech, which is our central concern. Theory of interpretation need not and ought not describe linguistic norms merely in terms of syntax, grammar, meaning kernels, meaning fields, habits, engrams, prohibitions, and so on, all of which are extremely variable and probably incapable of adequate description. It is more important to emphasize the huge and unencompassable areas of meaning—including emotional and attitudinal meanings—that language actually does represent. Considering this immensity taken as a whole, the restrictions imposed by all the different varieties of linguistic ground rules do not require special emphasis. It is by no means a denial of those restrictions to say that the capacity of language to represent all conceivable meanings is ultimately limited only by the overarching principle of sharability.

On these grounds I offer the following as a provisional, concise definition of verbal meaning, to be expanded and explored later in this chapter: Verbal meaning is whatever someone has willed to convey by a particular sequence of linguistic signs and which can be conveyed (shared) by means of those linguistic signs.

B. REPRODUCIBILITY: PSYCHOLOGISTIC OBJECTIONS

The reproducibility (and thus the sharability) of verbal meaning depends on there being something to reproduce. For the moment I will assume that any verbal meaning as defined above is a determinate entity with a boundary that discriminates what it is from what it is not. I shall discuss the nature of that boundary in the last part of this chapter, but first I shall consider the objections raised by those who deny the possibility of re-cognitive interpretation on the grounds that verbal meaning is never perfectly reproducible. The most widespread objection is that an interpreter by necessity must understand a meaning that is different from the author's meaning because the interpreter is different from the author. This objection holds even when the interpreter is the author himself, since no man is precisely the same at different times.

The argument that an interpreter's understanding is necessarily different because he is different assumes a psychologistic conception of meaning which mistakenly identifies meaning with mental processes rather than with an object of those processes. Since (the argument runs) an interpreter's experiences, feelings, attitudes, habitual responses are all different from the author's, so therefore must be the meanings that he construes from the words before him. Since one man's conception of and response to a rainbow is always different in subtle ways from another man's, so therefore must be his understanding of the word "rainbow." I say that this view equates meaning with mental processes because the undoubted fact that one man's mental life is not the same as another's is thought to be a sufficient ground for concluding that he understands different meanings. If something different is going on in his head, then what he understands has to be different. Thus, under this conception, meaning is in effect identified with a particular complex of mental acts.

That an interpreter can and often does fail to understand exactly what an author means by a word like "rainbow" is not in dispute. Nor would a sensible man deny that such misunderstandings are frequently caused by the fact that one man's conception of and response to a rainbow are different from another's. The crucial question is, Must such misunderstandings necessarily occur? But to this question, like so many others in

B. Reproducibility: Psychologistic Objections

hermeneutics, no decisive answer can possibly be given. The psychologistic notion that one man's meaning is always different from another's is not an empirical theory that can ever be falsified by an empirical test, since no one can ever be certain precisely what meaning another man entertains.

Nevertheless, the psychologistic conception can be shown to be inadequate as a theory of meaning, because it is not capable of explaining how quite different mental processes can produce an identical meaning, and that is an experience which occurs consistently in the mental processes of one and the same person at different moments of time. Thus, while it could never be shown that two different persons entertained identical meanings, it can be shown that the psychologistic theory of meaning is wrong. A far better argument is required to uphold the view that an interpreter's meaning is always necessarily different from an author's. The inadequacy of that argument was exposed centuries ago in a Platonic dialogue which I reproduce in its entirety, being convinced that Socrates' irony points up the issue far more effectively than my sober exposition ever could.

THE PSYCHOLOGUS

Characters:

Socrates   *Psychologus*

S. Here he comes now. Hello, Psychologus. We were just talking about you.

P. Well, if it isn't Socrates! How have you been after all this time? You're looking well. Haven't changed a bit since we last met some months ago—though you really have changed, of course, since everybody does. Take me, for example. I'm not the same as I was when we last met. My feelings and experiences are different, and frankly I'm older.

S. You *are* a philosopher, Psychologus. I hadn't been thinking of such high things at all. In fact, I was saying that you were able to perceive the subtlest differences in meaning every time you encountered the same words. We had been talking about the word "rainbow."

P. Absolutely right. I'm sure you understand that my only interest in making that point is to get the matter straight and help people to get rid of their naïve illusions. Actually there is a little poem about a rainbow— you know: "My heart leaps up," and so on—and I can tell you quite frankly, Socrates, that for me it is a different poem every time I read it.

S. It means something different to you every time?

P. Precisely. As I was saying, I'm different myself every time, and I have different associations and responses. Entre nous, I used to like it but now more often than not it leaves me cold.

S. It is not now as it hath been of yore?

P. Ah! I see you read poetry too. That's quite a change for you, Socrates.

S. Yes, I think that's your point about people changing. But I am troubled by something—though I'm not sure precisely what it is. It has to do with your saying that it's a different poem every time you read it, while I thought I also understood you to say that it was always the same poem that you read.

P. Socrates, it's hard to decide sometimes whether you are being sly or just simpleminded. When we say it's the same poem, that is just a loose manner of speaking. The *poem* isn't the same at all. We call it the same for convenience because the *words* are the same every time even though the meaning isn't.

S. You mean the physical signs stay the same, though what they mean changes?

P. Precisely.

S. No, I don't think that's quite the way to put it, because I'm wondering whether we really ought to call the signs the same.

B. Reproducibility: Psychologistic Objections

P. Why not?

S. Well, sometimes I might read the poem in another book or even in a manuscript, so the physical signs would be different even though I called the poem the same. I don't think it can be the physical signs that are the same.

P. You do like to stretch things out. I am trying to explain why the *meaning* is always different and you are still fretting with the letters and words. After all, letters and words are not just marks on paper; they are signs. The physical marks may be different, but the signs are the same.

S. I see. We can solve our problem by not talking about physical signs but about physical marks that represent signs?

P. Frankly, Socrates, you are trying my patience. If you will forget about the marks, we can go on to talk about meaning.

S. You must forgive a slow old man, Psychologus. As you said, we are all getting older every minute. But I was under the impression that we were talking about meaning all the time.

P. What do you mean?

S. Psychologus, I admit that I'm thinking of a much simpler kind of meaning than rainbows and hearts leaping up. Those matters are far too complicated for a person like me to describe. They are so complicated that I can never quite remember whether they meant the same to me at two different times. I've a very poor memory, you know, which is why I like philosophy. In a philosopher it can even be an advantage to forget his old ideas. Now where were we?

P. You said we were talking about meaning all the time.

S. Well, I think so—if meaning is something that is represented by marks and sounds and the like.

P. That's right.

S. Well, since all those different marks represent signs, I was wondering if what you called the signs and words of that little poem aren't meanings just as much as rainbows and hearts leaping up?

P. Of course not.

S. Well then, what name should we give to the sort of thing that is represented by the different physical marks in those different books?

P. I've already said they are signs. You could call them words or phonemes or whatever you like, so long as you don't call them meanings. My friend Seispers calls them "types." The different physical marks are "tokens," and what they represent is a "type."

S. And a type is not a meaning?

P. It is certainly not what I call a meaning.

S. Well, let us by no means call it that. But still something troubles me.

P. About meaning—at last?

S. Well, about how a type can be the same when the physical marks that represent it can be so different.

P. What is so strange about that?

S. I was wondering how I could think that a type was the same when each of my experiences of it, my attitudes toward it, my responses to it are so different. You know, whether I am hungry or sleepy, or happy or in pain, whenever I encounter those different tokens I still think that they represent the same type.

P. That is precisely what I am getting at. The words of the poem are always the same, though their meaning is always different.

S. Ah, thank you, Psychologus. You have clarified my thoughts on these matters.

P. Not at all, Socrates. It is a pleasure to talk to a man who can still continue to learn at such an advanced age.

End of Dialogue

B. Reproducibility: Psychologistic Objections

Meaning is an affair of consciousness, and the fundamental characteristic of consciousness, as Hume, for all his psychologism, acutely observed, is that it is always consciousness of something.[7] One of the most brilliant passages in Coleridge's *Biographia Literaria* is his use of this insight to attack the empirico-psychologistic notion of perception, according to which the thing that one sees when one looks at a table is one's perception of a table. How odd, observed Coleridge, when we always supposed that we were seeing a table![8] To speak of perceptions instead of "tables" is precisely the sort of misplaced sophistication that is found in the psychologistic account of meaning, according to which what one understands is really one's perception of or response to a meaning. But the remarkable fact of consciousness is that the objects of its awareness are not the same as the subjective "perceptions," "processes," or "acts" which are directed toward those objects. My perception of a visible object like Coleridge's table or of a nonvisible object like a phoneme can vary greatly from occasion to occasion, and yet what I am conscious of is nevertheless the same table, the same phoneme. This universal fact of consciousness cannot be explained in ordinary psychologistic terms.[9] Either it must be ignored, or its existence, by some circumlocution, denied.

The goal-directedness of mental acts, by virtue of which something can remain the same for consciousness even though one's perspective, emotion, state of health may vary, is par-

7. See *Treatise of Human Nature,* Bk. I, Sec. 6: "When I enter most intimately into what I call *myself,* I always stumble on some particular perception or other, of heat or cold, light or shade, love or hatred, pain or pleasure. I never can catch *myself* at any time without a perception, and never can observe anything but the perception."

8. *Biographia Literaria,* ed. J. Shawcross (2 vols. London, 1907), *1,* 179.

9. See Hume, *Treatise,* Bk. I, Appendix: "If perceptions are distinct existences, they form a whole only by being connected together. But no connexions among distinct existences are ever discoverable by human understanding."

ticularly important in a consideration of meaning. This distinction between what is "going on in the mind" on the one hand, and what the mind is averted to on the other, is not, however, a special conception devised for its convenience in defending the self-identity of verbal meanings. It is a characteristic element in all acts of consciousness.

In phenomenology, the philosophical tradition that has most fully explored the distinction between mental objects and mental acts, this object-directedness of consciousness has been called "intentionality"—a word that must be accepted for want of a better.[10] In the standard phenomenological vocabulary the basis for my criticism of the psychologistic conception of meaning would be stated as follows: An unlimited number of different intentional acts can intend (be averted to) the very same intentional object. Since meaning, like anything else that consciousness is averted to, is an intentional object (that is, something there for consciousness), and since verbal meaning is a meaning like any other, the point can be made more specific by saying that *an unlimited number of different intentional acts can intend the same verbal meaning.* This is, of course, the crucial point in deciding whether it is possible to reproduce a verbal meaning. Like any other intentional object, it is in principle reproducible. The psychologistic denial of this does not stand up to experience.

What led to this denial in the first place was, I think, a consideration that really had no connection with the inadequate tenets of the psychologistic position. The kind of psychologism that prevails among skeptical interpreters usually amounts to a confusion of verbal meaning with significance—a confusion that I have already tried to unravel.[11] When someone says, "My response to a text is different every time I read it," he is certainly speaking the truth; he begins to speak falsely when he identifies his response with the meaning he has construed. Furthermore, he is wrong when he identifies his response with

10. For a definition of intentionality see Appendix I, pp. 217–21.
11. See Chap. 1, Sec. B, and Chap. 4, Sec. C.

subjective acts alone. As soon as he makes his own response an object of consideration, he is concerned with another kind of meaning (i.e. significance) that is potentially as determinate and reproducible as verbal meaning itself. The fact that he can discuss, remember, describe, and even write about his response proves this point beyond doubt.

This is not to deny that an interpreter's response—that is, the more or less personal significance he attaches to a verbal meaning—cannot actually alter the character of the verbal meaning he construes. Of course this can happen, and it may in fact happen very frequently. However, it generally does so precisely because the interpreter has not troubled to distinguish between his response and what he is responding to—an illustration of the way interpretive theories tend to confirm themselves. If a reader cannot distinguish between what someone's text means and what it means to himself, then obviously for such a reader the distinction could have no empirical confirmation. It is therefore of some practical value to remember that neither in fact nor in logic is a verbal meaning the same as any of the countless relational complexes within which it can form a part.

If this distinction is made, there is no important reason for anyone to insist on the unlikely and untestable hypothesis that one man's verbal meaning is always necessarily different from another's, for the primary cause of the insistence has been a confusion of verbal meaning with significance. It is true that the significance of a text for one person is not altogether the same as for another, because the men themselves and therefore their personal relationships to a particular verbal meaning are different. But this undoubted fact cannot legitimately be extended to verbal meaning as well as personal significance. If, as experience shows, the same meaning can be intended by different intentional acts of one person at different moments in time, then that is a reasonable warrant for the hypothesis that the same meaning can be intended by the different intentional acts of different persons. And if verbal meaning is, by definition, meaning that can be shared, then it is reasonable to believe that verbal meaning exists. Obviously, its very existence depends upon its reproducibility. At the last ditch few would, I think, be so eccentric as to deny the sharability of meaning. To whom and to what purpose would they address their denial?

C. REPRODUCIBILITY: HISTORICISTIC OBJECTIONS

It is one thing to say blankly that we can never "truly" understand the texts of a past age; it is quite another thing to venture the less absolute and no doubt true conception that we sometimes cannot possibly acquire all the cultural givens necessary for understanding an old text. This second stricture obviously applies to many texts from cultures about which we know very little and also to some from cultures about which we know a great deal. The absolute form of historical skepticism should not be confused with this healthy consciousness of the limitations under which every interpreter sometimes works. Only the absolute form of radical historicism threatens the enterprise of re-cognitive interpretation by holding that the meanings of the past are intrinsically alien to us, that we have no "authentic" access to those meanings and therefore can never "truly" understand them.

By one of those typical ironies in intellectual history (ironies which support Hegel's theory that human thought evolves by negating itself) it has been a development of historicism itself which in the present day has raised the most persistent objections to the possibility of historical knowledge. Historicism began with the belief that all human cultures were immediate to God; that was its root concept in its inaugural years from Herder to Ranke. Every cultural era was, to use Herder's metaphor, another melody in the divine symphony, and every melody had its own divine individuality.[12] Thus historicism

12. J. G. Herder, *Sammtliche Werke*, ed. B. Suphan (33 vols. Berlin, 1877–1913), *8,* 314 f.; *18,* 282 f.

C. Reproducibility: Historicistic Objections

first insisted that every culture was worth knowing for its own sake, "as it really was," but with Hegelian and Lovejovian inevitability this emphasis on the individuality of different cultures has now evolved into an emphasis on the unbridgeable gulf between one culture and another. From Dilthey's conception that human consciousness was constituted by its historical givens[13]—an idea that was implicit in Herder—it was not a very long step to Heidegger's conception of the temporality and historicity of human being. The earlier emphasis on individuality which had given significance to the study of other cultures in their own right became, by one or two turns of the Hegelian gyre, an emphasis on the impossibility of studying other cultures in their own right. The past became "ontically alien" to us.

This philosophical form of radical historicism lent intellectual respectability to a prevalent and popular form of historical self-consciousness which had already created an atmosphere of skepticism regarding the genuine knowability of past cultures. By popular historicism I mean the kind of assumptions underlying, for example, all the recurrent magazine articles that gravely describe the latest portentous peculiarities of the latest "younger generation," or those assumptions underlying the cult of the new and the feeling that one can or cannot think or act in a particular way "in this day and age." The possible examples are so numerous and the assumptions so widely spread and so deeply engrained in the popular mind that such historicism is capable of making itself true. For in the realm of culture a belief or opinion is as real as an empirical fact and, given enough currency, becomes itself an empirical fact that must be reckoned with. Consequently, the popular emphasis on the radical differentness of cultural eras—or even on the radical differentness between one decade and another—has

13. G. Misch and others, eds., *Wilhelm Diltheys Gesammelte Schriften* (8 vols. Leipzig and Berlin, 1913–36), *7,* 38: "Denn man stösst hier eben an die Geschichtlichkeit des menschlichen Bewusstseins als eine Grundeigenschaft desselben."

41

tended to obliterate sensitivity to sameness amid historical change and has lent broad credence to the view that we cannot "truly" understand the texts of another age.

This kind of historicism, like the psychologism to which it is intimately related, is not a theory that is capable of empirical confirmation or falsification. That its tenets are highly unlikely to be true I argue in some detail in Appendix II, where I criticize the only substantial defense of radical historicism in the field of hermeneutics—that of H. G. Gadamer. Here I shall simply develop a few brief distinctions that will isolate the general dogma of historical skepticism from the more limited and reasonable doubts that any interpreter might entertain in a particular case with respect to understanding a particular complex of verbal meanings from the past.

In the first place, radical historicism should be distinguished from the popular, indeed nearly universal, conviction that every age must reinterpret for itself the texts of the past. This doctrine is as much a description of fact as a moral imperative: Every past age has done just that, and every future age will no doubt continue to do so. However, it is a mistake to view this doctrine as equivalent to the radical historicist dogma that every age *understands* the texts of the past differently, and that no age truly understands them as they were, for it is not true that a "reinterpretation" is the same as a "different understanding." To think so is to identify an understanding of a text with the peculiarities and complexities of written interpretation; it is to confuse the *subtilitas intellegendi* with the *subtilitas explicandi*. This distinction is laid out at greater length in Chapter 4, but I have mentioned it briefly here because failure to be aware of it would reinforce the plausibility of radical historicism.[14]

Another distinction that should be drawn is that between the general probability that we can understand a contemporary better than a predecessor, and the particular probability that

14. See Chap. 4, Secs. A and B.

may obtain in a particular case. It is generally probable that a woman will live longer than a man, but this general probability is a useless abstraction when we confront a healthy man of fifty and a woman of the same age who has lung cancer. It is altogether possible, for example, that Lucan was better understood by Housman than by many of Lucan's contemporary readers, and it is even more probable that Blake is better understood by scholars today than he was understood by any of his contemporaries. It should be remembered that the language and assumptions within a culture can be highly variable, so that it might easily be the case that a modern reader could have learned the particular language of a particular author more intimately than any contemporary who spoke the "same" language.

This last point discloses one of the most vulnerable conceptions in radical historicism. The radical historicist is rather sentimentally attached to the belief that only our own cultural entities have "authentic" immediacy for us. That is why we cannot "truly" understand the texts of the past, such "true" understanding being reserved for contemporary texts, and all understanding of the past being "abstract" and "constructed." But, in fact, all understanding of cultural entities past or present is "constructed." The various languages of a culture (taking "language" in the broadest possible sense) are acquired through learning, and not inborn. Furthermore, since all the various languages of a culture are learned by more than one person, they can, implicitly, be learned by any person who takes the trouble to acquire them. And once a person has truly acquired a language it does not matter how he managed to do so—whether by rote and constant exposure like a three-year-old or by disciplined application and self-conscious design. There is no immediacy in understanding either a contemporary or a predecessor, and there is no certainty. In all cases, what we understand is a construction, and if the construction happens to be unthinking and automatic, it is not necessarily more vital and authentic for that.

One can make distinctions, present examples, expose misconceptions, but one can never prove or disprove the dogma of radical historicism.[15] We can never be sure that we have "truly" understood a text from the past any more than we can be sure we have understood one from our own time. Generally, we are more likely to get a contemporary text right, but this general likelihood does not automatically hold in any particular instance (where factors of temperament, knowledge, diligence, and luck are decisive), and interpretation is always concerned with particular texts. But while the position of radical historicism is very probably false, one must acknowledge that its adherents, particularly those of a Heideggerian cast, hold to its tenets as to a religion—and the claims of a religion are absolute. Ultimately one simply accepts them or rejects them.

D. DETERMINACY: VERBAL MEANING AND TYPIFICATION

Reproducibility is a quality of verbal meaning that makes interpretation possible: if meaning were not reproducible, it could not be actualized by someone else and therefore could not be understood or interpreted. Determinacy, on the other hand, is a quality of meaning required in order that there *be* something to reproduce. Determinacy is a necessary attribute of any sharable meaning, since an indeterminacy cannot be shared: if a meaning were indeterminate, it would have no boundaries, no self-identity, and therefore could have no identity with a meaning entertained by someone else. But determinacy does not mean definiteness or precision. Undoubtedly, most verbal meanings are imprecise and ambiguous, and to call them such is to acknowledge their determinacy: they are what they are—namely ambiguous and imprecise—and they are not univocal and precise. This is another way of saying that an ambiguous meaning has a boundary like any other verbal meaning, and that one of the frontiers on this

15. See Appendix II, pp. 256–58.

D. *Determinacy: Verbal Meaning and Typification*

boundary is that between ambiguity and univocality. Some parts of the boundary might, of course, be thick; that is, there might at some points be a good many submeanings that belonged equally to the meaning and not to it—borderline meanings. However, such ambiguities would, on another level, simply serve to define the character of the meaning so that any overly precise construing of it would constitute a misunderstanding. Determinacy, then, first of all means self-identity. This is the minimum requirement for sharability. Without it neither communication nor validity in interpretation would be possible.

But by determinacy I also mean something more. Verbal meaning would be determinate in one sense even if it were merely a locus of possibilities—as some theorists have considered it. However, this is a kind of determinacy that cannot be shared in any act of understanding or interpretation. An array of *possible* meanings is no doubt a determinate entity in the sense that it is not an array of *actual* meanings; thus, it too has a boundary. But the human mind cannot entertain a possible meaning; as soon as the meaning is entertained it is actual. "In that case, then," the proponent of such a view might argue, "let us consider the text to represent an array of different, *actual* meanings, corresponding to different actual interpretations." But this escape from the frying pan leads right into the amorphous fire of indeterminacy. Such a conception really denies the self-identity of verbal meaning by suggesting that the meaning of the text can be one thing, and also another, different thing, and also another; and this conception (which has nothing to do with the ambiguity of meaning) is simply a denial that the text means anything in particular. I have already shown that such an indeterminate meaning is not sharable. Whatever it may be, it is not verbal meaning nor anything that could be validly interpreted.

"Then," says the advocate of rich variousness, "let us be more precise. What I really mean is that verbal meaning is historical or temporal. It is something in particular for a span of time, but it is something different in a different period of time." Certainly the proponent of such a view cannot be reproached with the accusation that he makes verbal meaning indeterminate. On the contrary, he insists on the self-identity of meaning at any moment of time. But, as I have pointed out in my critique of Gadamer's theory (Appendix II), this remarkable, quantum-leap theory of meaning has no foundation in the nature of linguistic acts nor does it provide any criterion of validity in interpretation.[16] If a meaning can change its identity and in fact does, then we have no norm for judging whether we are encountering the real meaning in a changed form or some spurious meaning that is pretending to be the one we seek. Once it is admitted that a meaning can change its characteristics, then there is no way of finding the true Cinderella among all the contenders. There is no dependable glass slipper we can use as a test, since the old slipper will no longer fit the new Cinderella. To the interpreter this lack of a stable normative principle is equivalent to the indeterminacy of meaning. As far as his interests go, the meaning could have been defined as indeterminate from the start and his predicament would have been precisely the same.

When, therefore, I say that a verbal meaning is determinate I mean that it is an entity which is self-identical. Furthermore, I also mean that it is an entity which always remains the same from one moment to the next—that it is changeless. Indeed, these criteria were already implied in the requirement that verbal meaning be reproducible, that it be always the same in different acts of construing. Verbal meaning, then, is what it is and not something else, and it is always the same. That is what I mean by determinacy.

A determinate verbal meaning requires a determining will. Meaning is not made determinate simply by virtue of its being represented by a determinate sequence of words. Obviously, any brief word sequence could represent quite different com-

16. See pp. 249–50.

D. Determinacy: Verbal Meaning and Typification

plexes of verbal meaning, and the same is true of long word sequences, though it is less obvious. If that were not so, competent and intelligent speakers of a language would not disagree as they do about the meaning of texts. But if a determinate word sequence does not in itself necessarily represent one, particular, self-identical, unchanging complex of meaning, then the determinacy of its verbal meaning must be accounted for by some other discriminating force which causes the meaning to be *this* instead of *that* or *that* or *that,* all of which it could be. That discriminating force must involve an act of will, since unless one particular complex of meaning is *willed* (no matter how "rich" and "various" it might be), there would be no distinction between what an author does mean by a word sequence and what he could mean by it. Determinacy of verbal meaning requires an act of will.

It is sometimes said that "meaning is determined by context," but this is a very loose way of speaking. It is true that the surrounding text or the situation in which a problematical word sequence is found tends to narrow the meaning probabilities for that particular word sequence; otherwise, interpretation would be hopeless. And it is a measure of stylistic excellence in an author that he should have managed to formulate a decisive context for any particular word sequence within his text. But this is certainly not to say that context determines verbal meaning. At best a context determines the guess of an interpreter (though his construction of the context may be wrong, and his guess correspondingly so). To speak of context as a determinant is to confuse an exigency of interpretation with an author's determining acts.[17] An author's verbal meaning is limited by linguistic possibilities but is determined by his actualizing and specifying some of those possibilities. Correspondingly, the verbal meaning that an interpreter construes is determined by *his* act of will, limited by those same possibilities. The fact that a particular context has led the inter-

17. On the nature of a context see Chap. 3, Sec. B, pp. 86–88.

47

preter to a particular choice does not change the fact that the determination is a choice, even when it is unthinking and automatic. Furthermore, a context is something that has itself been determined—first by an author and then, through a construction, by an interpreter. It is not something that is simply there without anybody having to make any determinations.

While the author's will is a formal requirement for any determinate verbal meaning, it is quite evident that will is not the same as meaning. On the other hand, it is equally evident that verbal meaning is not the same as the "content" of which an author is conscious. That point has already been made in Chapter 1.[18] An author almost always means more than he is aware of meaning, since he cannot explicitly pay attention to all the aspects of his meaning. Yet I have insisted that meaning is an affair of consciousness. In what sense is a meaning an object of consciousness even when one is not aware of it? Consider the example given in the earlier passage just referred to, in which a speaker admits he meant something he was not aware of meaning. Such an admission is possible because he conceived his meaning as a whole, and on reflection later perceived that the unattended meaning properly falls within that whole. That is, in fact, the only way the speaker's admission could be true.

What kind of whole is it that could contain a meaning even though the meaning was not explicitly there? And how can such a generous sort of entity still have very stern barriers which exclude other meanings that the author might actually have been attending to, as well as countless others that he was not? Clearly this remarkable characteristic of verbal meaning is the crucial one to examine.

Suppose I say, in a casual talk with a friend, "Nothing pleases me so much as the Third Symphony of Beethoven." And my friend asks me, "Does it please you more than a swim

18. Sec. E. See also this chapter, Sec. E.

D. Determinacy: Verbal Meaning and Typification

in the sea on a hot day?" And I reply, "You take me too literally. I meant that no *work of art* pleases me more than Beethoven's Third." How was my answer possible? How did I know that "a swim in the sea" did not fall under what I meant by "things that please me"? (The hyperbolic use of "nothing" to stand for "no work of art" is a common sort of linguistic extension and can constitute verbal meaning in any context where it is communicable. My friend could have understood me. He misunderstands for the sake of the example.) Since I was not thinking either of "a swim in the sea" or "Brueghel's *Hay Gathering,"* some principle in my meaning must cause it to exclude the first and include the second. This is possible because I meant a certain *type* of "thing that pleases me" and willed all possible members belonging to that type, even though very few of those possible members could have been attended to by me. Thus, it is possible to will an et cetera without in the least being aware of all the individual members that belong to it. The acceptability of any given candidate applying for membership in the et cetera depends entirely on the type of whole meaning that I willed. That is to say, the acceptability of a submeaning depends upon the *author's* notion of the sub-suming type whenever this notion is sharable in the particular linguistic circumstances.

The definition of verbal meaning given earlier in this chapter can now be expanded and made more descriptive. I said before that verbal meaning is whatever an author wills to convey by his use of linguistic symbols and which can be so conveyed. Now verbal meaning can be defined more particularly as a *willed type* which an author expresses by linguistic symbols and which can be understood by another through those symbols. It is essential to emphasize the concept of type since it is only through this concept that verbal meaning can be (as it is) a determinate object of consciousness and yet transcend (as it does) the actual contents of consciousness.

A type is an entity with two decisive characteristics. First, it is an entity that has a boundary by virtue of which something belongs to it or does not. In this respect it is like a class, though it has the advantage of being a more unitary concept: a type can be entirely represented in a single instance, while a class is usually thought of as an array of instances. The second decisive characteristic of a type is that it can always be represented by more than one instance. When we say that two instances are of the same type, we perceive common (identical) traits in the instances and allot these common traits to the type. Thus a type is an entity that has a boundary by virtue of which something belongs to it or does not, and it is also an entity which can be represented by different instances or different contents of consciousness. It follows that a verbal meaning is always a type since otherwise it could not be sharable: If it lacked a boundary, there would be nothing in particular to share; and if a given instance could not be accepted or rejected as an instance of the meaning (the representational character of a type), the interpreter would have no way of knowing what the boundary was. In order that a meaning be determinate for another it must be a type. For this reason, verbal meanings, i.e. shared meanings, are always types and can never relinquish their type character.[19]

Thus verbal meaning can never be limited to a unique, concrete content. It can, of course, refer to unique entities, but only by means that transcend unique entities, and this transcendence always has the character of a typification. This is so even when a verbal meaning has reference to something that is obviously unique, like "the death of Buonaparte." "Death," "the," and "of" all retain their type character even though their combination might effect a particular new type. The same is true of "Buonaparte," for a name is a type, and the particular name "Buonaparte" could not relinquish its type character without thereby ceasing to be a name, in which case it would be incomprehensible and unsharable. No doubt this particular name in a particular use would not have a meaning identical to

19. See Appendix III, pp. 266–69.

E. Determinacy: Unconscious and Symptomatic Meanings

"Buonaparte" in another usage. But that would simply mean that they are different types as well as, on another level, instances of the same type. However, they could never be merely concrete instances. The determinacy and sharability of verbal meaning resides in its being a type. The particular type that it is resides in the author's determining will. *A verbal meaning is a willed type.* The rest of this chapter and most of the next will be concerned with the ramifications of this concept and with its capacity to clarify the nature of verbal meaning and textual interpretation.

E. DETERMINACY: UNCONSCIOUS AND SYMPTOMATIC MEANINGS

The fact that verbal meaning has to have some kind of boundary in order to be communicable and capable of valid interpretation does not exclude so-called unconscious meaning. The only requisite is that an unconscious meaning, whatever its character, must lie within the boundary that determines the particular verbal meaning that is being considered. In other words, the principle for excluding or accepting unconscious meanings is precisely the same as for conscious ones. In many cases it is impossible to be sure whether a meaning was conscious or unconscious to an author, and in these cases, therefore, the distinction is irrelevant. However, it is nevertheless serviceable to clarify the concept of unconscious meaning in order to avoid confusing an author's verbal meaning with his personality, mentality, historicity, and so on, interesting and relevant as these may be to the legitimate concerns of criticism.

The one negative characteristic common to all varieties of unconscious meanings is that the author was not aware of them. Obviously, this definition is not very reassuring since there is no limit to what an author may not be aware of. Usually the term "unconscious meaning" refers to those meanings which are not attended to by the author but which are nevertheless present in another region of his mind—a lower region as it were, which is generally called the subconscious. The term is normally restricted still further to those meanings in the author's subconscious mind which are indicated by characteristics of his text. While this last very sensible limitation approaches the criteria for verbal meaning as defined in this chapter, it disregards one crucial element of the definition, the element of will.

While it is possible to will a great many things of which one is not directly aware (for example, the continuation of an et cetera), it is not possible to will something against one's will. That is a verbal contradiction which discloses a contradiction in fact. Will can extend into unknown and unnoticed regions as far as it likes, but it cannot relinquish its connection with that aspect of itself which is conscious. For will involves not merely choices and goals, but *voluntary* choices and goals, and again our habits of language remind us of the conscious element in will. A "tendency" or "impulse" that is totally subconscious, that has no strands tying it directly to a conscious impulse, is not willed in the ordinary sense of the term, nor in the sense I allot to the word. Such an impulse would be, precisely, involuntary. And even if such an involuntary impulse were disclosed in speech, that would not in itself make it a constituent of verbal meaning.

One obvious example is stuttering. The fact that a person stutters when he speaks certain words may indicate a great deal about him, but these indications are not part of his verbal meaning. They are, rather, involuntary accompaniments to meaning, that is, *symptoms* of meaning, not linguistic signs representing meaning. The difference between a sign and a symptom consists precisely in this: a sign is voluntary (arbitrary) and conventional, a symptom involuntary and independent of convention. A linguistic sign is able to represent a range of verbal meanings precisely by virtue of its arbitrary character, while a linguistic symptom is a nonarbitrary indication of something else, just as a fever is a symptom or involun-

E. Determinacy: Unconscious and Symptomatic Meanings

tary indication of a disease.[20] Symptomatic meanings may be of immense interest, but they should not be confused with verbal meanings, because verbal meaning thereby loses its determinacy. There is no limit to the different things a text can be symptomatic of, and there is no intrinsic reason to limit symptomatic meanings simply to those inhabiting the author's subconscious mind.

On the other hand, it would be a mistake to draw the line between a sign and a symptom by a simple and crude discrimination that ignores the variability and latitude of verbal meanings. If, for example, a husband comes home to his wife, sighs deeply, and says, "I'm very tired tonight," his verbal meaning might contain, in addition to information about his physical state, a plea for sympathy and praise. Even if this plea were largely unconscious it might still be part of the verbal meaning if the conventions established by habitual usage between the husband and wife made it possible for the words "I'm very tired tonight" to convey such an implicit plea. Part of the convention might be that the phrase must be uttered with a shake of the head and a deep sigh, that it must not be stated with reference to particular plans for the evening, but only à-propos des bottes, and that it must be said only when the husband is known to have been working hard. Once these conventions have become established (and all verbal meaning requires analogous generic conventions, as I point out in the next chapter), then it is not necessary that the husband always attend explicitly to all the implications of his utterance, though he must consciously will a particular type of meaning in order for the meaning to exist at all. Verbal meanings of this sort are like icebergs: the larger part may be submerged, but the submerged part has to be connected with the part that is exposed.

The iceberg metaphor presents the image of a visible shape connected to a larger invisible shape below the level of conscious awareness. Even though the visible mass is the smaller

20. See Charles Bally, "Qu'est-ce-qu'un signe?" *Journal de Psychologie normale et pathologique, 36* (1939), 161–74.

part, it determines, from the standpoint of anyone examining the iceberg, what belongs to the iceberg as a whole and what does not belong. Any part of the whole that is not continuous with the mass above the surface cannot be part of the iceberg. If there is something down below which is separate and discontinuous, then it must either be independent or belong to something else. Physical analogies are dangerous, but in this case the analogy holds. The self-identity of a verbal meaning depends on a coherence that is at least partly analogous to physical continuity. If a text has traits that point to subconscious meanings (or even conscious ones), these belong to the verbal meaning of the text only if they are coherent with the consciously willed type which defines the meaning as a whole. If such meanings are noncoherent with the willed type, then they do not belong to verbal meaning which is by definition willed. As soon as *unwilled* meaning is admitted, then anything under the surface of the vast sea could be considered part of the iceberg, and verbal meaning would have no determinacy.

But can the distinction between a sign and a symptom be made in practice? How is one to judge whether a particular meaning is coherent or noncoherent with the willed type? The principle of coherence is precisely the same as the principle of a boundary. Whatever is continuous with the visible part of an iceberg lies inside its boundaries, and whatever lies within these falls under the criterion of continuity. The two concepts are codefining, and I have already shown that the boundary principle depends on the concept of a type. Any meaning that has the trait or traits by which a type is defined belongs to that type, and any meaning which lacks these traits does not belong. The principle of continuity is that of membership in a type. In other words, as I stated at the beginning of this section, the principle for accepting or rejecting unconscious meanings is precisely the same as for conscious ones.

The adequacy of the conception can be illustrated by the example of lying. Does the verbal meaning of a lie consist in the meaning that a speaker wills to convey, or does it also carry the additional meaning that what is willed is deliberately false?

E. Determinacy: Unconscious and Symptomatic Meanings

If a lie did carry this additional meaning, which is antagonistic to the usual purpose of lying, then on most occasions there would be no point in telling a lie. In other words, if part of the verbal meaning of a lie were that it is false, then there would really be no such thing as a lie, since one part of the meaning would rectify the falsity of the other part. We do not say that someone has misunderstood a lie when he is taken in by it. He has understood it only too well; the liar's verbal meaning has been successfully communicated.

But consider the case of the unsuccessful lie or, shall we say, the stylistically inept lie. A boy plays hookey. His mother asks him later to tell her what happened that day at school. The boy blushes deeply and hesitates: "Oh, er, just the usual thing. I had arithmetic and er geography. Oh, no, that's wrong; we didn't have geography today. It was English and er," and this is broken off with a gesture of uncertainty. We might suppose that the story had been insufficiently rehearsed or, better, that subconsciously the boy did not want to lie. But whatever conclusion we might draw, the fact remains that the boy did lie. His verbal meaning was false. His stylistic incompetence was not part of his verbal meaning but was symptomatic of his conscious or subconscious unwillingness to lie.

I choose this extreme example because borderline cases are often the most informative ones. If verbal meaning is determined by will and if, as in this case, a text seems to disclose antithetical impulses, how can the principle of a willed type provide a criterion of coherence? Are there not two disjunctive willed types, and therefore is the meaning not much more complex than the simple conceptual model would suggest? I think the proper answer is that the conceptual model shows precisely how to clarify such complexities. As long as the boy continued to lie, the willed type represented by his words included the meaning that he had been at school and excluded the meaning that he had not been at school. The truth-telling impulse that he might also have willed lay outside his *verbal* meaning because it could not be communicated by his words. If he suddenly broke off and confessed, then the meaning of his second statement would contradict that of the first, and the meaning of the second statement would be a contrary willed type. Thus his ineptitude may have been symptomatic of a divided will, but his verbal meaning, limited as it was by the linguistic signs he employed, was a unity.

This insistence on the unity of verbal meaning does not exclude the notion of a divided will when it is expressed as a sign rather than as a symptom. For example, if the boy had said, "Well, er, maybe I was at school today," then his unwillingness either to lie or to tell the truth would have been expressed verbally in an ambiguous willed type, and his verbal meaning would be ambiguous, since the word "maybe" functions as a verbal sign rather than a symptomatic accompaniment. Furthermore, since the ambiguity of the boy's will is now directly part of his verbal meaning, his halting hesitancies of speech cease to be merely symptomatic accompaniments and become stylistic reinforcements of meaning. The reason that the hesitancies should no longer be considered "involuntary" symptoms lying outside the boundary of verbal meaning is that they are now expressions of a will that lies within the verbal willed type instead of an accompanying impulse that lies outside its boundary.

However, it would be very foolish to say that symptomatic, involuntary meanings are not a proper and legitimate concern of criticism. In fact, they are one of the most interesting subjects of critical inquiry. Obviously the most profitable thing to know about a lie is that it is a lie—an act of judgment that entirely depends on distinguishing a man's verbal meaning from the symptoms and facts that may betray him. When Blake said that Milton wrote in fetters when he spoke of angels and at liberty when he spoke of devils, because he was of the devil's party without knowing it, his entirely legitimate critical comment was not necessarily a comment on the verbal meaning of *Paradise Lost.*[21] It was primarily a symptomatic inference.

21. *The Marriage of Heaven and Hell,* Pl. 6.

F. *Determinacy: Meaning and Subject Matter*

Of course, it is a far more interesting critical observation than a mere interpretation of verbal meaning usually is—interesting because it is a comment on Milton, and on poets, and because it implicitly asserts the superiority of Books I and II over Book III of *Paradise Lost,* a kind of critical judgment that no one would want to exorcise from literary criticism.

Thus, when I make the point that symptomatic inferences are not interpretations of verbal meaning, my purpose is not to suggest that such inferenecs are in some way impure or illegitimate, but to clarify the distinction made in Chapter 1 between meaning and significance. Symptomatic, involuntary meaning is part of a text's significance, just as its value or its present relevance is. But significance is the proper object of criticism, not of interpretation, whose exclusive object is verbal meaning. It is a charter of freedom to the critic, not an inhibition, to insist on this distinction, for the liberty of the critic to describe the countless dimensions of a text's significance is closely dependent on his not being constricted by a confusion between significance and meaning. No responsible critic wants to pervert and falsify the meaning of a text, yet at the same time he does not want to be inhibited from pursuing whatever seems most valuable and useful.[22] If he recognizes that verbal meaning is determinate, whereas significance and the possibilities of legitimate criticism are boundless, he will have overcome a confusion that has, ironically, inhibited critical freedom. At the same time, he will not dismiss lightly the modest, and in the old-fashioned sense, philological effort to find out what an author meant—the only proper foundation of criticism.

F. DETERMINACY: MEANING AND SUBJECT MATTER

When discussing Kant's claim to understand Plato better than Plato himself, I observed that Kant failed to distinguish between Plato's meaning and the subject matter to which that

22. See Chap. 4, Sec. E.

57

meaning referred. This apparently simple distinction is, however, far from easy to grasp, and if it eluded Kant, it is only fair to confess that it quite thoroughly eluded me in my previous essay on hermeneutic theory (Appendix I). It is also a distinction that Husserl failed to observe in what is, nonetheless, the most detailed, penetrating, and convincing account of meaning that I am acquainted with (*Logische Untersuchungen,* Part II). Probably the first methodological, though not totally satisfactory, approximation of the distinction was made by De Morgan in his brilliant essay "On the Structure of the Syllogism."[23] In De Morgan's influential terminology the distinction was stated as one between the universe as a whole and a particular "universe of discourse." De Morgan's vocabulary is in this context less serviceable than his ideas, and I have found it more useful in describing the determinacy of verbal meaning to define the distinction as one between meaning and subject matter.

The distinction arises from the observable fact that not all uses of a word like "tree" carry the same implications. If someone heard the word "tree" spoken by a child, a woodsman, a botanist, or a poet, he would very reasonably guess that in each instance the word probably carried different implications. Specifically, he might infer that the botanist implied not only the part of the tree that is above ground, but the root system as well. A child, on the other hand, though he could be aware that a tree has roots, might mean simply the part of the tree that is visible. Yet it is a fact about trees that they have roots. Does this mean that roots are implied willy-nilly when somebody uses the word "tree"? Apparently not, since people do entertain and communicate implications that are inadequate or faulty. If the implications of a verbal meaning were invariably

23. Augustus De Morgan, "On the Structure of the Syllogism, and on the Application of the Theory of Probabilities to Questions of Argument and Authority," *Cambridge Philosophical Transactions* (Nov. 9, 1846). See also F. Rossi-Landi, *Significato, communicazione e parlare comune?* (Padua, 1961), pp. 249–61.

determined by the "objective" character of what it refers to, then nobody could ever communicate a conceptual mistake! There is, therefore, a distinction between meaning and subject matter.

To define the distinction is, however, no simple task since subject matter is a concept that apparently makes absolute epistemological claims. There is, on the one hand, what someone implies by "tree" and, on the other, what "tree" in fact really implies. But who is to say what "tree" really implies? To assume that there is some independent and universal ground of implication that transcends and controls what any individual might mean by "tree" is to fall into the fallacy of the public consensus, under which a use of the word would have the same implications to all, regardless of the author's meaning. I shall not repeat the arguments of Chapter 1 which deny the existence of such public unanimity but, instead, shall consider the quite relative character of subject matter as a discriminating concept.

When someone's meaning is incomplete or false, we are able to say that it is inadequate to its subject matter only if we have or believe that we have a more complete and truer conception of the subject matter than the author has. But suppose we in turn express our superior conception of the subject matter and are judged by a further critic who believes he has a still truer or broader conception than our own. He in turn will say that our meaning is inadequate, and he will do so on the basis of a still different conception of the subject matter. Now, in each case the judgment of the two critics might be correct. The first critic might have a conception that is truly more adequate than the original author, and the second critic might have a conception more adequate than the first. On the other hand, one or both of the critics might be wrong. Obviously, the notion of subject matter is in practice entirely relative to the knowledge or presumed knowledge of the critic.

Thus, while it may be the case that a critic has once and for all reached a totally adequate conception of a subject matter, it is also true that this is not always so, and in practice subject matter is a variable conception. It would be highly presumptive of any critic to claim that he had attained absolute knowledge, although he might very reasonably claim a broader knowledge than the author's. It follows that, in any particular instance of criticism, subject matter is an ideal pole of knowledge which is in fact represented by the present conception of the critic. To say that meaning may be different from subject matter is to say that an author's conception of something may be different from a critic's—which is a self-evident proposition.

But this reduction of the distinction to something self-evident does not altogether resolve the very real problem of determining the difference, if any, between meaning and subject matter in a particular case. If we believe that any author or any person would agree that a tree has roots, is it not reasonable to assume that roots are implied by the word "tree" in any usage? The author might not have considered this necessary implication, but on reflection he would surely agree that he had to imply roots when he said "tree." This argument is, however, misleading. It may be true that any reasonable man might be brought to admit that he *should* have implied "roots" when he said "tree," and a persuasive critic might even convince him that his meaning did in fact carry that implication. But there is a distinction between what an author admits he should have meant in order to embrace a true conception of a tree, and what he might actually have meant.

Furthermore, if the critic's conception of a subject matter is made the ground for determining the implications of an utterance, then it also becomes the ground for determining their interrelationships and relative emphases. But a subject matter is surely neutral with respect to these things. If the meaning "roots" is implied by "tree," that still does not indicate whether "roots" is a vague or highly precise meaning, whether the nutritional function of the roots is implied, whether the roots have a central emphasis or trail off into a dim penumbra of meaning. None of this could be answered simply with reference to subject matter, and consequently subject matter cannot *determine* implications. With respect to a subject matter the implications of an utterance remain indeterminate just as they do with respect to a putative public consensus. The proper ground for determining implications is now to be considered.

G. DETERMINACY: MEANING AND IMPLICATION

Most of the practical problems of interpretation are problems of implication. There are, of course, a good many instances where the most primitive and "literal" meanings of a text can come under dispute, but these are far rarer than controversies which turn on the "unsaid" meanings of a text. In the loose terminology of some literary critics such meanings have been called "connotations"—that is, implications "meant-with" the manifest or "denotative" content of a text. This use of "denotation" and "connotation" is, of course, at variance with their use in logic, and I have abandoned the words altogether because they have lost their precision and because there is not and could not be a universally applicable distinction between primary or manifest, and secondary or nonmanifest meanings. No meaning represented by a verbal sign is manifest; all meanings must be construed, and what is "manifest" in a particular construction may not even have been directly noticed by the author. (That is why I placed the words "literal" and "unsaid" in quotation marks above.) Of course, some meanings are necessarily dependent on prior or primary meanings, and consequently the words "denotation" and "connotation" do correspond to a distinction whose application to a *particular* text everyone might be in agreement about. However, for the purpose of adequate theoretical description, it is more useful to find terms that have both precision and generality. I think the commonly used term "implication" has both qualities. To say that a particular meaning is implied by an utterance is not to insist that it is always "unsaid" or "secondary," but only that it is a component within a larger whole. The distinction is between a submeaning of an utterance and the whole array of submeanings that it carries. This array, along with the principles for generating it, I call the "meaning" of the utterance, and any submeaning belonging to the array I call an "implication."

Few would deny that the crucial problem in the theory and practice of interpretation is to distinguish between possible implications that do belong to the meaning of a text and those that do not belong.[24] I have argued that if such a principle of determinacy did not exist (a principle under which we accept or reject possible implications) communication and interpretation would be impossible. The determinacy of verbal meaning is entirely dependent on the determinacy of implications— that is, on the existence of a principle for including or excluding them. Undoubtedly, the most important preliminary principle of discrimination is that which distinguishes verbal meaning from significance. That distinction, widely overlooked and almost entirely unpublicized since the time of Boeckh, is worth recapitulating before turning to the general problem of implication.

If, as I have argued, verbal meaning necessarily has the character of a willed type that can be conveyed through linguistic signs, then significance would be any meaning which has a relation to the verbal meaning so defined—no matter how neutral, descriptive, or tame the related meaning might be. Thus, if it is said that Gibbon's comments on superstition reflect the common attitudes of his own time, that would point out a meaning of Gibbon's work *to* historical generalities, but not a meaning *in* the work itself. The difference between these

24. Classic examples of the problem are found in William Empson, *Seven Types of Ambiguity* (3d ed. New York, 1955), which demonstrates on almost every page what happens to interpretation when a text is self-consciously conceived to be a "piece of language," and the problem of validity is ignored. Anyone desiring further concrete examples of the issues probed in this book is advised to consult Empson.

tiny prepositions is highly important and too often ignored. Significance is always "meaning-to," never "meaning-in." Significance always entails a relationship between what is in a man's verbal meaning and what is outside it, even when that relationship pertains to the author himself or to his subject matter. If Milton really was of the devil's party without knowing it, that would be part of the meaning of *Paradise Lost to* Milton's personality, part of the work's significance, and no doubt such observations do call attention to characteristics of meaning *in Paradise Lost.* (Criticism and interpretation are not, as I point out in a subsequent chapter, autonomous.) If such instances of significance are not distinguished from instances of meaning the result is bound to be a now familiar state of confusion, for there is literally no limit to the significance of the shortest and most banal text. Not only can its verbal meaning be related to all conceivable states of affairs—historical, linguistic, psychological, physical, metaphysical, personal, familial, national —but it can also be related at different times to changing conditions in all conceivable states of affairs. Not that such exercises would be very often useful or interesting, but they could be performed, and that which is interesting or useful to somebody varies considerably with different men and different times. When, in the preceding two sections, I distinguished verbal meaning both from symptomatic meaning and from subject matter, I simply selected for examination the two kinds of significance that have been most often confused with verbal meaning. However, there are innumerable varieties of significance beyond these, and plenty of breathing space for all conceivable exercises of criticism so long as it emancipates itself from the inhibitions of a state of confusion.

While significance is by nature limitless, the crucial feature of implication is that it is not, and the nature of its limits is indicated by the useful, though not completely adequate, metaphor of its etymological derivation. To be "folded in" is to be inside, ready to be folded out or explicated. The metaphor is not quite adequate because it suggests that an implication is always hidden, lurking behind or between the folds of more obvious or primary meanings. This is very frequently the case, of course, but not always, since, as I have indicated, it is not always possible to distinguish what is primary or obvious from what is secondary and hidden. Nevertheless, the metaphor is useful insofar as it suggests that implications lie within the meaning as a whole and are circumscribed by some kind of boundary which delimits that meaning. Thus the etymological metaphor suggests a more general and, I think, quite indispensable conceptual model—that of part and whole. An implication belongs within a verbal meaning as a part belongs to a whole.

A merely spatial conception of the part-whole relationship is inadequate, however, because it suggests an articulated physical object whose parts have the same physical character as the whole which they constitute. The peculiarity of a whole meaning is that it retains its integrity and completeness even if all its implications have not been articulated. In other words, the whole meaning is not simply an array of parts but is also a principle for generating "parts," a principle by virtue of which the meaning is somehow complete or whole even though the actual job of generating all the parts remains incomplete. What is this remarkable principle? I have suggested that it is the principle which characterizes a type.[25] The special potency of a type is precisely the same as the generative potency possessed by a meaning. A type stands independent and complete, yet at the same time it contains a principle by virtue of which it is possible to judge whether any conceivable entity belongs to or embodies the type. This type principle requires elaboration.

A type is an entity that can be embodied in or represented by more than one instance. Anything that is unique cannot, with respect to those aspects which are unique, be a type. Precisely because a type can be embodied in more than one instance, it has the apparently magical potency of containing and generat-

25. Chap. 2, Sec. D.

ing parts of itself which it does not explicitly contain. For example, if we consider a very simple type such as a right triangle, we can say that the type contains the implication stated in the Pythagorean theorem. (For the sake of simplicity in exposition, I am assuming that the type is in this case equivalent to subject matter, though it is perfectly possible to have a willed type of right triangle which sharply excludes some of its geometrical properties.) But why is it that the type "right triangle" contains the implication, the square of the hypotenuse equals the summed squares of the other two sides? If one answers, "Because that is the nature of a right triangle," one simply begs the question. If one answers, "Because part of the meaning of a right triangle is the Pythagorean theorem," that would be more descriptive, but it would not explain how "right triangle" can contain "Pythagorean theorem," particularly if one did not explicitly attend to the theorem when one intended the type. "But the theorem applies to *all* right triangles so it must apply here." This begins to be more illuminating, though we may still wonder how one meaning "contains" the other. "Since I have learned, thanks to Pythagoras, that his theorem applies to all right triangles, and since almost everybody else has learned this too, it is possible to mean 'Pythagorean theorem' as *part* of what I mean when I say 'right triangle.' *If nobody had ever heard of the theorem it would not be possible to have it as part of my verbal meaning.* Not only does the theorem apply to all members of the type, making it a characteristic that belongs to the type, but it is also something that is known by others to belong. Because of *their* knowledge, the theorem is contained in the meaning 'right triangle.' They are able to fill out the implications because they are familiar with the type. If they were not familiar with it they could not do so, and I could not convey the implication."

We have finally managed to arrive at a satisfactory explanation. Since a type is something that can be embodied in more than one instance, it is something whose determining characteristics are common to all instances of the type. Furthermore, since the type can be represented in more than one instance, it can be shared or known by more than one person. When another person has learned the characteristics of the type, he can "generate" those characteristics without their being given to him explicitly. It is sufficient merely to give him a decisive clue as to the particular type that is meant.

An implication belongs to a meaning as a trait belongs to a type. For an implication to belong to verbal meaning, it is necessary that the type be shared, since otherwise the interpreter could not know how to generate implications; he would not know which traits belonged to the type and which did not. And there is only one way the interpreter can know the characteristics of the type; he must learn them. (For these characteristics are not usually "syncategorematic" or absolutely necessary comeanings like color and extension. Even the Pythagorean theorem is a learned characteristic of a right triangle, no matter how "necessary" it may seem once it is learned.) Implications are derived from a shared type that has been learned, and therefore *the generation of implications depends on the interpreter's previous experience of the shared type.* The principle for generating implications is, ultimately and in the broadest sense, a learned convention.

The reader will notice that I have deliberately made a small alteration in my description of verbal meaning. Instead of calling it a "willed type," I have used the expression "shared type." In doing so I have shifted emphasis from the type willed by the author to a type experience that is common to author and reader. This is the other side of the coin. If verbal meaning is a willed type that can be conveyed through linguistic signs, it follows that the possibility of conveying the willed type depends on the interpreter's prior experience of the willed type. Otherwise, the interpreter could not generate implications; he would not know which implications belonged to the meaning and which did not. The willed type must be a shared type in order for communication to occur. This is another way of saying that the willed type has to fall within known conventions in order to be shared—an exigency that was implicit from the start in the concept of sharability.

My emphasis in this chapter has been on the author's will, because my central topic has been the determinacy of verbal meaning, and authorial will is a formal requirement for determinacy. Of equal importance is the sharability of verbal meaning, and for this the necessary requirement is the existence of shared conventions. Verbal meaning is both a willed type and a shared type. This second characteristic is the main subject of my next chapter.

3.

THE CONCEPT OF GENRE

But how many different kinds of sentence are there?
Say, assertion, question, and command? There are
countless *such kinds: countless different kinds of*
use of what we call "signs," "words," "sentences."
And this multiplicity is not something fixed, given
once for all, but new types of language, new lan-
guage-games, as we may say, come into existence,
and others become obsolete and get forgotten.
                                    Ludwig Wittgenstein

For the sake of clarity, I have been emphasizing one side of a complex process that is by nature two-sided and reciprocal. Speech is not simply the expression of meaning but also the interpretation of meaning, each pole existing through and for the other, and each completely pointless without the other. When interpretation is the main subject of consideration, a theorist is likely to leap into categories like "public norms," "traditions," "contexts," and "linguistic necessities." On the other hand, when meaning is the primary subject, he is driven to recognize the necessity of the author's determining will. Furthermore, when his primary concern is interpretation, he very naturally focuses on the starting point of interpretation, which is a sequence of linguistic signs and a context, and by starting there he is led to emphasize the independent, determinant power of these two givens. But when his primary concern is the nature of meaning, he very naturally assumes that the signs do represent something, and he is led to emphasize the determinant power of the authorial will that is required in order to make the signs represent *something*. In each case the theorist could qualify his overemphasis by acknowledging that interpretation must have reference to somebody's meaning, or that meaning must defer to the communicative limitations and the canalizations of language, but these qualifications do not remove the misleading emphases that inevitably arise from focusing primarily on interpretation or on meaning alone. The critical reader probably feels that I have laid altogether too much stress on authorial will and have neglected the independent channeling power of language. But overemphasis is sometimes needed to redress an underemphasis. Having made what seems to be an absolutely essential preliminary point which has been much neglected, I now propose to examine the double-sidedness of speech in a balanced way that duly attends to the exigencies both of meaning and of interpretation.

The great and paradoxical problem that must be confronted in considering the double-sidedness of speech is that the general norms of language are elastic and variable while the norms that obtain for a particular utterance must be definitive and determinate if the determinate meaning of the utterance is to be communicated. I have repeatedly insisted that a word sequence cannot, under the general norms of language, delimit a determinate meaning, and I have also said that these norms are not sufficiently narrowed merely by reference to a context.[1] Something more is needed, and that additional dimension can be hinted at by referring to the work of Saussure and Wittgenstein.

When I pointed out the difference between the norms of language in general and the norms that obtain for a particular utterance,[2] I was calling attention to one aspect of Saussure's epoch-making distinction between *langue* and *parole*. Saussure revealed the supreme importance in speech of the simple distinction between a possibility and an actuality.[3] The "norms of language" is a variable concept because it refers to the possibilities, not the actualities of language. The "norms of an utter-

1. For discussions of context see Chap. 2, Sec. D, and this chapter, Sec. B.
2. See Chap. 1, Sec. C.
3. Ferdinand de Saussure, *Course in General Linguistics*, eds. C. Bally and A. Sechehaye, trans. W. Baskin (New York, 1959), pp. 14, 19.

ance," on the other hand, is quite a different conception. It refers to something actualized from those possibilities— namely, the norms that do control and define the utterance, not the vast, uncertain array that could do so.

Although Wittgenstein's seminal meditations on language do not take cognizance of Saussure's work, they cover some of the same ground and extend some of the same insights. Coming to understand the meaning of an utterance is like learning the rules of a game.[4] To play the game properly you must have learned the rules. But since there are a great many games (*langue*), and since it is necessary to know the rules that apply to a particular game (*parole*), a problem arises. How does one know which game is being played? To have mastered all the rules—that is, to have learned the norms of language—is not to know which norms apply in a particular case. That problem is certainly the origin of many disagreements between well-qualified interpreters. Even when they know all the games, they may still disagree about which game they are playing.

The problem is in one sense absolutely unsolvable. We can never be sure which game is being played, because we never have a rulebook. We must learn, as Wittgenstein insists, by playing. But the interpreter may still very properly ask, In the absence of a rulebook how can anybody learn the rules for a game that has never been played before and will be played only once? The answer is that nobody could learn the rules under those conditions, and there is clearly something wrong with a description which implies that he can. It was therefore mis-leading when I said that an interpreter has to learn "the norms that obtain for a particular utterance." Nobody could learn them just by experiencing that utterance alone. One has to play a game several times before he really understands it and thereby learns the rules. The game, therefore, must be asso-ciated not with just one utterance, but with a type of utterance —that is, with several utterances having, in Wittgenstein's

4. Wittgenstein, *Philosophical Investigations,* p. 26 and passim.

terms, a "family resemblance."[5] For language games (utterances) that are entirely unique there could be no public norms, no shared rules.

Here again the concept of type proves to be indispensable. Since a type can be represented by more than one instance, it is a bridge between instances, and only such a bridge can unite the particularity of meaning with the sociality of interpretation. Certainly a communicable meaning can have aspects that are unique—indeed, every meaning does. But it must also belong to a recognizable type in order to *be* communicable.

I have already argued that every particular linguistic meaning like "the death of Buonaparte" is type-bound, and that an implication belongs to an utterance as a trait belongs to a type. I called these submeanings or traits "implications," in contradistinction to the larger type they belong to, which I called "the meaning of the utterance." But since these implications are not only traits of a type but also types themsclves, it will be convenient to call that type which embraces the whole meaning of an utterance by the traditional name "genre," a term which I shall try to make precise in this chapter. Using this term, the paradox regarding the individuality of meaning and the variability of interpretation can be resolved by saying that a speaker and an interpreter must master not only the variable and unstable norms of language but also the particular norms of a particular genre.

A. GENRE AND THE IDEA OF THE WHOLE

The central role of genre concepts in interpretation is most easily grasped when the process of interpretation is going badly or when it has to undergo revision: "Oh! you've been talking about a book all the time. I thought it was about a restaurant," or "I thought I understood you, but now I'm not so sure." Such flashes of insight or accessions of puzzlement

5. Ibid., p. 32.

always follow a common pattern. The meaning that is being understood has been revealing itself normally, more or less according to expectations, until quite unexpected types of words or locutions begin to occur. When that happens an interpreter can either revise everything he has understood thus far and grasp a new and different type of meaning or he can conclude that, whatever the meaning might be, he has not understood it. Such experiences, in which a misunderstanding is recognized during the process of interpretation, illuminate an extremely important aspect of speech that usually remains hidden. They show that, quite aside from the speaker's choice of words, and, even more remarkably, quite aside from the context in which the utterance occurs, the details of meaning that an interpreter understands are powerfully determined and constituted by his meaning expectations. And these expectations arise from the interpreter's conception of the type of meaning that is being expressed.

By "type of meaning" I do not, of course, intend to imply merely a type of message or theme or anything so simple as a mere content. The interpreter's expectations embrace far more than that. They include a number of elements that may not even be explicitly given in the utterance or its context, such as the relationship assumed to exist between the speaker and interpreter, the type of vocabulary and syntax that is to be used, the type of attitude adopted by the speaker, and the type of inexplicit meanings that go with the explicit ones. Such expectations are always necessary to understanding, because only by virtue of them can the interpreter make sense of the words he experiences along the way. He entertains the notion that "this is a certain type of meaning," and his notion of the meaning as a whole grounds and helps determine his understanding of details. This fact reveals itself whenever a misunderstanding is suddenly recognized. After all, how could it have been recognized unless the interpreter's expectations had been thwarted? How could anything surprising or puzzling occur to force a revision of his past understanding unless the interpreter had expectations that could be surprised or thwarted? Furthermore, these expectations could have arisen only from a genre idea: "In this type of utterance, we expect these types of traits." Since the expectations do not arise out of nowhere, they must, for the most part, arise from past experience: "In this type of utterance, we expect these types of traits because we know from experience that such traits go with such utterances."

The decisive function of generic expectations can be illustrated by a very simple example in which the interpretation of a poem was controlled not only by a subtle mistake in identifying a particular type of simile but also by a genre mistake in confusing one type of farewell with another. What struck me very forcibly when I encountered this misconstruction in a classroom was the difficulty I had in convincing students that their construction was wrong. They remained convinced that Donne's "A Valediction Forbidding Mourning" was being spoken by a dying man, and that it concerned spiritual communion in death and after death. The opening lines of the poem are:

> As virtuous men pass mildly away,
> And whisper to their souls to go,
> Whilst some of their sad friends do say,
> 'Now his breath goes,' and some say 'No,'
>
> So let us meet and make no noise,
> No tear-floods nor sigh-tempests move.

In the center of the poem, the theme of union-in-absence does nothing to dispel the thought that death is a main theme:

> Our two souls therefore, which are one,
> Though I must go, endure not yet
> A breach.

And the idea of death is further confirmed in the final lines:

> Thy firmness makes my circle just,
> And makes me end where I begun.

Many readers will no doubt remain convinced that death is a principal theme of the poem, though it is almost certainly about a temporary physical absence, and the speaker is almost certainly not a dying man.

My students remained convinced of the contrary because there was nothing in the text which compelled them to change their minds. Everything they found was legitimately capable of supporting their construction. Having begun with a faulty conception of the type of meaning being expressed, they found all their expectations fulfilled. They had assumed that the word "mourning" in the title must apply to death. Subsequently, the image of a dying man in the first lines confirmed that assumption, as did everything else in the poem. Needless to say, when the poem is interpreted under a less mortuary conception, the various images, similes, and arguments take on different meanings, and these are also legitimately supported by the text. This experience strongly suggested to me that an interpreter's preliminary generic conception of a text is constitutive of everything that he subsequently understands, and that this remains the case unless and until that generic conception is altered.[6]

This phenomenon should not be regarded as a special pitfall limited to the interpretations of untrained readers. That is the comforting but delusive faith of some interpreters who believe in the semantic autonomy of texts. A self-critical interpreter knows better. Emil Staiger once made a public confession of the way a faulty generic conception of a poem had caused him for a long period subtly to misconstrue it. He had been preparing to include a short text in a collection of poems under the assumption that it was an old folksong, and it was only after some research that he discovered it to be a mid-nineteenth-century love poem. This changed his understanding of the text considerably: "Now, subsequently, I find that even the first line is far too weak and mood-ridden for an old folksong. The

6. See Chap. 5, Sec. A.

sweet and mild wind that carries the complaint touches the very boundary of late Romantic tendermindedness. . . . Having found out where the poem belongs, I have, as it were amplified its sound by historical resonances. Now I hear every detail exactly."[7]

This point was systematically demonstrated in a book which undertook to defend quite a different thesis—I. A. Richards' *Practical Criticism.* When Richards, in order to show the inadequacies of literary schooling in England, asked a number of undergraduates to write interpretations of some unfamiliar poems given to them without titles or attributions, the results were, naturally enough, widely divergent. Richards believed that better trained students would not disagree so absurdly, but the results of a new *Practical Criticism* containing interpretations by better trained students would very probably disappoint Professor Richards. The vocabulary of the interpretations would be different but the divergences and discrepancies would be much the same. For *Practical Criticism* really demonstrated that without helpful orientations like titles and attributions, readers are likely to gain widely different generic conceptions of a text, and these conceptions will be constitutive of their subsequent understanding. Since their interpretations will substantially depend on their guesses about the type of meaning expressed, and since in the absence of guideposts these guesses will vary widely, it is inevitable that Richards' experiment will always produce similar results. An interpreter's notion of the type of meaning he confronts will powerfully influence his understanding of details. This phenomenon will recur at every level of sophistication and is the primary reason for disagreements among qualified interpreters.

This seems to suggest that an interpretation is helplessly dependent on the generic conception with which the interpreter happens to start, but such a conclusion would be mis-

7. Emil Staiger, *Die Kunst der Interpretation* (Zurich, 1955), pp. 15–16.

leadingly simple and despairing, as the occasional recognition of misunderstandings proves. If the generic idea of the meaning as a whole could not be defeated and baffled by the experience of subsequent details, then we would never recognize that we had misunderstood. On the other hand, it is essential to notice that in most cases our expectations are not baffled and defeated. We found the types of meanings we expected to find, because what we found was in fact powerfully influenced by what we expected. All along the way we construe *this* meaning instead of *that* because *this* meaning belongs to the type of meaning we are interpreting while *that* does not. If we happen to encounter something which can only be construed as *that,* then we have to start all over and postulate another type of meaning altogether in which *that* will be at home. However, in the very act of revising our generic conception we will have started over again, and ultimately everything we understand will have been constituted and partly determined by the new generic conception. Thus, while it is not accurate to say that an interpretation is helplessly dependent on the generic conception with which an interpreter happens to start, it is nonetheless true that his interpretation is dependent on the last, unrevised generic conception with which he starts. All understanding of verbal meaning is necessarily genre-bound.

This description of the genre-bound character of understanding is, of course, a version of the hermeneutic circle, which in its classical formulation has been described as the interdependence of part and whole: the whole can be understood only through its parts, but the parts can be understood only through the whole. This traditional formulation, however, clouds some of the processes of understanding in unnecessary paradox. It is true that an idea of the whole controls, connects, and unifies our understanding of parts. It is also true that the idea of the whole must arise from an encounter with parts. But this encounter could not occur if the parts did not have an autonomy capable of suggesting a certain kind of whole in the first place. A part—a word, a title, a syntactical pattern—is frequently autonomous in the sense that some aspect of it is the same no matter what whole it belongs to. A syntactical inversion such as "Fair stands the wind for France" is perceived as an inversion no matter where it occurs, and knowing that such an inversion belongs in a certain type of utterance and not in another, we experience the invariant aspect of the part as a trait which characterizes one type of meaning rather than another. Then, having experienced that trait, we come to expect others belonging to the same type, and this system of expectations, at first vague, later more explicit, *is* the idea of the whole that governs our understanding. Of course, we may make a wrong guess, and, of course, it is true that our guess does control and constitute many of the traits we subsequently experience, but not all traits are genre-dependent (the same ones can belong to different genres), and not everything in verbal understanding is variable. Understanding is difficult, but not impossible, and the hermeneutic circle is less mysterious and paradoxical than many in the German hermeneutical tradition have made it out to be.

Consequently, to define the hermeneutic circle in terms of genre and trait instead of part and whole not only describes more accurately the interpretive process but also resolves a troublesome paradox. This description does, however, raise problems of its own—the most important one being that "genre" still represents an imprecise and variable concept. A generic conception is apparently not something stable, but something that varies in the process of understanding. At first it is vague and empty; later, as understanding proceeds, the genre becomes more explicit, and its range of expectations becomes much narrower. This later, more explicit and narrow generic conception is, to be sure, subsumed under the original, broad generic conception, just as a variety is subsumed under a species. Nevertheless, a term that is so variable in its application is not yet a theoretically useful term. In the next section one of my chief concerns will be to define the word "genre" more closely.

B. INTRINSIC GENRES

The variability of the genre conception is entirely a feature of interpretation, not of speaking. The interpreter has to make a guess about the kind of meaning he confronts, since without this guess he possesses no way of grounding and unifying his transient encounters with details. An individual trait will be rootless and meaningless unless it is perceived as a component in a whole meaning, and this idea of the whole must be a more or less explicit guess about the kind of utterance being interpreted. Genre ideas, then, have a necessary heuristic function in interpretation, and it is well known that heuristic instruments are to be thrown away as soon as they have served their purpose. Nevertheless, a generic conception is not simply a tool that can be discarded once understanding is attained, because, as I pointed out in the preceding section, understanding is itself genre-bound. The generic conception serves both a heuristic and a constitutive function. It is because of this that the genre concept is not hopelessly unstable. For if correct understanding has in fact been achieved, and if understanding is genre-bound, it follows that verbal meaning must be genre-bound as well. A genre conception is constitutive of speaking as well as of interpreting, and it is by virtue of this that the genre concept sheds its arbitrary and variable character.

In what sense is verbal meaning genre-bound? First of all, it is obvious that not only understanding but also speaking must be governed and constituted by a sense of the whole utterance. How does a speaker manage to put one word after another unless his choices and usages are governed by a controlling conception? There must be some kind of overarching notion which controls the temporal sequence of speech, and this controlling notion of the speaker, like that of the interpreter, must embrace a system of expectations. For the words that are to be said are not yet present before the speaker's mind, and the words he has already said have gone by. No one has better described this marvel of consciousness and speech than St. Augustine:

> I am about to repeat a psalm that I know. Before I begin, my expectation alone reaches over the whole: but so soon as I shall have once begun, how much so ever of it I shall take off into the past, over so much my memory also reaches: thus the life of this action of mine is extended both ways: into my memory, so far as concerns that part which I have repeated already, and into my expectation too, in respect of what I am about to repeat now; but all this while is my marking faculty present at hand through which that which was future is conveyed over that it may become past: which the more it progresses forward, so much more the expectation being shortened is the memory enlarged; till the whole expectation be at length vanished quite away, when namely, that whole action being ended, shall be absolutely passed into the memory. What is now done in this whole psalm, the same is done also in every part of it, yea and in every syllable of it; the same order holds in a longer action too, whereof perchance this psalm is but a part. (Conf. XI, 28)

Augustine chose as his example a psalm he already knew because ultimately he wanted to make an analogy with God's foreknowledge. But his observation holds true for all utterances, even those for which the system of expectations is far less rigid than that of a memorized utterance.

Is it warranted to call the speaker's controlling idea of the whole a generic conception? Could it not simply be a notion confined to "this particular, unique meaning"? It cannot be so confined for two reasons. First, the controlling conception has a dimension of inexplicitness because the details of the utterance are not present to consciousness all at once. The system of expectations which controls the speaker's sequence of words has at first a range of possible fulfillments. Everyone has noticed that he does not always tell the same story precisely

79

the same way, for even though each telling might be controlled by the same generic conception, the sentences and meanings are usually not precisely the same. The second reason that the speaker's controlling conception must be generic rather than unique is more fundamental. Even when the meaning which the speaker wishes to convey is unusual (and some aspects of his conveyed meaning will almost always be unique) he knows that in order to convey his meaning he must take into account his interpreter's probable understanding. If his interpreter's system of expectations and associations is to correspond to his own, he must adopt usages which will fulfill not only his own expectations but also those of his interpreter. This imaginative transference from the speaker to the interpreter parallels that from the interpreter to the speaker and is called by Bally *dédoublement de la personalité.*[8]

The speaker can achieve this socializing of his expectations only if he is familiar with typical past usages and experiences common to himself and his interpreter. By virtue of these shared past experiences, the type of meaning he expects to convey will be the type of meaning his interpreter will also be led to expect. Obviously, these expectations must belong to a type of meaning rather than merely to a unique meaning, because otherwise the interpreter would have no way of expecting them. Thus, the speaker knows that his type of meaning must be grounded in a type of usage, since it is only from traits of usage, i.e. vocabulary range, syntactical patterns, formulaic invariants, and so on, that the interpreter can expect the speaker's type of meaning. Consequently, types of meaning are always necessarily wedded to types of usage, and this entire, complex system of shared experiences, usage traits, and meaning expectations which the speaker relies on is the generic conception which controls his utterance. Understanding can occur only if the interpreter proceeds under the same system of expectations, and this shared generic conception, constitutive

8. Charles Bally, *Linguistique générale et linguistique française* (2d ed. Bern, 1944), p. 37.

both of meaning and of understanding, is the intrinsic genre of the utterance.

The problem of defining an "intrinsic genre" more fully still remains, and obviously the most difficult aspect of this problem is to discover whether there consistently exists such an entity. Is there really a stable generic concept, constitutive of meaning, which lies somewhere between the vague, heuristic genre idea with which an interpreter always starts and the individual, determinate meaning with which he ends? At first glance the answer seems to be no, since apparently the interpreter's idea of the whole becomes continuously more explicit until the genre idea at last fades imperceptibly into a particularized and individual meaning. If this is so, and if the intrinsic genre is defined as a conception shared by the speaker and the interpreter, it would seem that what I have called the "intrinsic genre" is neither more nor less than the meaning of the utterance as a whole. Obviously, it is a useless tautology to assert that the interpreter must understand the speaker's meaning in order to understand the speaker's meaning. That is a circularity no more helpful than the paradox of the hermeneutic circle as promulgated by Heidegger. If we cannot preserve a distinction between the particular *type* of meaning expressed and the particular meaning itself, then the intrinsic genre becomes simply the meaning as a whole. Nothing but confusion is achieved by calling a particular meaning a "genre."

Yet we seem forced into this paradox by requirements that look powerfully coercive. The interpreter cannot give up his generic idea, since to do so would be to give up everything he has understood by virtue of it. We cannot escape this conclusion by saying that the interpreter first conceives the whole meaning as a type, then subsequently as a particular. That conception fails to consider that a particular meaning must always remain for him a meaning of a particular type, and that this type idea cannot be relinquished without giving up the particular meaning as well. No one can understand "these particular raindrops" without understanding "raindrops." To discard the generic idea "raindrops" by virtue of which "these particular raindrops" was understood in the first place is necessarily to throw away "these particular raindrops" as well.

Could we say, by way of analogy, that "raindrops" is the intrinsic genre of "these particular raindrops"? Such an analogy, which makes its point by word repetition, is by necessity loose and provisional. A phrase is not a whole utterance, and there is no ready-made vocabulary for describing the intrinsic genres of particular utterances. We have no linguistic tools by means of which we could say, *"This* is the intrinsic genre of the meaning, and *that* is the meaning in its particularity." The necessity of an intrinsic genre is a structural necessity in communication and can only be grasped as such; nevertheless, the way that it functions can be made clear. Furthermore, a demonstration of the fact that there are fewer intrinsic genres than there are particular meanings would reveal the distinction between genre and meaning and lay the foundation for a precise and stable definition of an intrinsic genre.

One basis for the distinction between genres and particular meanings can be sought in a consideration that necessitated the genre concept in the first place—the temporal character of speaking and understanding. Because words follow one another sequentially, and because the words that will come later are not present to consciousness along with the words experienced here and now, the speaker or listener must have an anticipated sense of the whole by virtue of which the presently experienced words are understood in their capacity as parts functioning in a whole.[9] The necessity of this anticipated sense of the whole is in no way obviated by suggesting that a speaker can rehearse what he says before he speaks or that an interpreter can experience the whole of a word sequence before he starts to understand the functions of the words. To make this suggestion is merely to delay the inevitable conclusion, for how can a speaker rehearse words that will be spoken in a

9. In the German hermeneutical tradition this is called *Vorverständnis.*

sequence unless he rehearses them in a sequence? And how can he do that unless he entertains a system of expectations, by virtue of which he knows that *this* word may be said now because it belongs to the type of phrase or sentence or series of sentences which he expects to continue and complete later? Similarly, from the side of the interpreter, how can he understand the function of the word he experiences now unless he anticipates the type of phrase or sentence or series of sentences in which the word belongs? It does not help to say that his understanding withholds itself until he has completed the phrase, sentence, or series of sentences, for he cannot know what these are until he has understood the functions of the words, and these he cannot understand unless he has anticipated or guessed the type of whole in which they are occurring.

Now the temporality of speech, to which I have been alluding, is an essential condition for distinguishing an intrinsic genre from the meaning that it governs. This can be illustrated conveniently by taking an extreme example, the first lines of *Paradise Lost:*

> Of Man's first disobedience and the fruit
> Of that forbidden tree, whose mortal taste
> Brought death into the World and all our woe,
> With loss of Eden, till one greater Man
> Restore us and regain the blissful seat,
> Sing heavenly Muse, that, on the secret top
> Of Oreb or of Sinai, didst inspire
> That shepherd, who first taught the chosen seed
> In the beginning how the heavens and earth
> Rose out of chaos.

To understand those lines an immense amount of relevant knowledge is required, but the one overarching conception which determines not only the meaning and function of that long sentence, but also just what knowledge *is* relevant to its understanding is the conception, *Paradise Lost.* No one, no matter how learned and sensitive to poetry, could possibly understand those lines if he did not rightly understand the kind of poem this is, by which I certainly do not mean "a Christian-humanist epic in blank verse" nor any other manageable compound name. To understand those lines it is necessary to grasp, in a way more specific than any label could be, the particular type of "Christian-humanist epic" this is. On the other hand, it would not be warranted to say that those lines could be understood only by someone who had read every word of *Paradise Lost*. It is possible for a reader to know precisely what kind of whole these lines introduce long before he comes to the last word of the last book. Furthermore, and this is the crucial point, it would be possible to understand those lines perfectly even if the thousands of verses which follow them were not precisely the verses that appear in Milton's second edition.

To take an example, Milton might not have included near the beginning of Book III the famous, beautiful lines on his blindness:

> Thus with the year
> Seasons return; but not to me returns
> Day, or the sweet approach of even or morn,
> Or sight of vernal bloom, or summer's rose,
> Or flocks, or herds, or human face divine;
> But cloud instead and ever-during dark
> Surrounds me, from the cheerful ways of men
> Cut off, and, for the book of knowledge fair,
> Presented with a universal blank
> Of Nature's works to me expunged and rased,
> And wisdom at one entrance quite shut out.

Can anyone doubt that the exclusion of these lines would impoverish the poem and, in ways both obvious and subtle, alter its meaning? Yet would their exclusion—and here I must rely on the reader's common sense rather than on any theory he holds about meaning—in any way hinder an accurate understanding of the first lines of the poem? Indeed, need we reach out for such an extreme example? Suppose in those first lines

Milton had dictated "happy seat" instead of "blissful seat." A careful reader will recognize that this would subtly change the sense of that phrase, but would he hold that it changes the sense of the preceding phrases? Surely it does not. Of course, the substitution would alter the meaning of the sentence as a whole, but it would not alter the meaning of most components in the sentence nor would it change at all the type of sentence that it is. I am not suggesting that such relatively minor alterations can *always* be made without changing the intrinsic genre of an utterance, but I am insisting that this example illustrates the difference between an intrinsic genre and the particular meaning it governs.

What the example shows—and anyone can easily invent other examples for himself—is that we can understand the earlier parts of an utterance before we reach the end and, furthermore, that we can understand them in their *determinacy* as meanings functioning in a particular way. (Again, I must stress that determinacy does not necessarily mean either precision or clarity, but simply self-identity.) If that were not so, we could not rightly understand "Of man's first disobedience" until we had made sure that Milton had said "blissful seat" rather than "happy seat." Now the only way we can understand how an early part of an utterance functions in a whole before we have completed the whole is by means of a generic conception that is narrow enough to determine the meaning of the earlier part. This generic conception, while it may be very narrow indeed, has a degree of tolerance by virtue of which the later words of the utterance could be varied within limits without altering the determinate meanings of the earlier words.[10]

10. The term "words" is, however, merely a convenient approximation, since I by no means want to suggest that individual words are discrete, independent semantic units. The primary units of speaking and understanding are larger, sentence-like groupings of words. Cassirer, invoking the authority of von Humboldt, Wundt, and Dittrich calls "the primacy of the sentence over the word" one of the "most secure findings" of linguistics (*Symbolic Forms:* Vol. 1, *Language,* pp. 303–04).

We can now define quite precisely what an intrinsic genre is. *It is that sense of the whole by means of which an interpreter can correctly understand any part in its determinacy.* Since the interpreter can do this before he knows the precise sequence of words in the utterance as a whole, and since more than one sequence of words can fulfill his generic expectations without altering his understanding of the parts he has understood, it follows that this determining sense of the whole is not identical with the particular meaning of the utterance. That particular meaning arises when the generic expectations have been fulfilled in a particular way by a particular sequence of words.

Similarly, the intrinsic genre is as necessary to the speaker as it is to the interpreter. The speaker is able to begin expressing determinate meanings before he finishes his utterance because those meanings (carried by a particular sequence of words) are determined by the kind of meaning he is going to complete in words that have not yet been chosen. The speaker anticipates the kind of thing he will be saying, but his meaning in all its particularity depends on the particular choice of words by which he realizes that type of meaning. Once the speaker has willed "this particular type of meaning" the further determination of his meaning depends entirely upon his subsequent choice of words and patterns falling within the tolerance of the intrinsic genre.

If an intrinsic genre is capable of codetermining any partial meaning, there would seem to be left small *Spielraum* for that useful, catchall term, "the context." Ordinarily we cannot do without the term. If somebody asks, "How do you know the phrase means this rather than that?" we answer, "Because of the context," by which we normally mean a very complex and undifferentiated set of relevant factors, starting with the words that surround the crux and expanding to the entire physical, psychological, social, and historical milieu in which the utterance occurs. We mean the traditions and conventions that the speaker relies on, his attitudes, purposes, kind of vocabulary, relation to his audience, and we may mean a great many other things besides. Thus the word "context" embraces and unifies two quite different realms. It signifies, on the one hand, the givens that accompany the text's meaning and, on the other, the constructions that are part of the text's meaning. For example, the actual signs surrounding a crux constitute a given, but what those signs mean is a construction which we assume to be a given only because it seems less problematical than the crux. Similarly, the situation in which the utterance occurs is a given, whereas such matters as the speaker's attitudes are not given but are construed from the utterance itself. The conventions and traditions which the speaker relies on are not directly given by a milieu. We may know from the milieu what conventions are available to him, but the ones he chooses to rely on are construed by us from his utterance. Furthermore, such aspects of a context as purposes, conventions, and relationship to the audience are not outside the meaning of the utterance but constitutive of it. They are not only aspects which must be construed but also aspects which are intrinsic to meaning.

This is not at all to suggest that "context" is an illegitimate term that should be replaced. My purpose is to show that we use "context" to signify two necessary but distinct functions in interpretation. By "context" we mean a construed notion of the whole meaning narrow enough to determine the meaning of a part, and, at the same time, we use the word to signify those givens in the milieu which will help us to conceive the right notion of the whole. In certain situations certain types of meaning are very likely to occur. In addition to usage traits, therefore, we can have situation traits which help us to guess what type of meaning we confront. But the givens of a situation do not directly determine verbal meanings. They help suggest a probable type of meaning, and it is this type idea which determines the partial meaning which we defend when we invoke the word "context." In other words, the essential component of a context is the intrinsic genre of the utterance. Everything else in the context serves merely as a clue to the intrinsic genre and has in itself no coercive power to codetermine partial meanings. Those external clues may be extremely important, but often (as in some anonymous texts) they are almost entirely absent. To know the intrinsic genre and the word sequence is to know almost everything. But the intrinsic genre is always construed, that is, guessed, and is never in any important sense given.

Since "intrinsic genre" has been defined and distinguished from "context," the preparatory work of this section will be complete when "extrinsic genre" has been defined. Now, an interpreter can use any type idea heuristically to get at the meanings of an utterance. Sometimes, in the course of interpretation, he will find that his original type idea must be discarded or drastically revised, but usually he does not find this necessary. Almost always, he begins with a type idea which is vaguer and broader than the intrinsic idea of the utterance and, in the course of interpretation, merely narrows this idea and makes it more explicit. A preliminary genre idea that is vague and broad is not, however, necessarily extrinsic, but rather, a heuristic tool that has not yet been sharpened to the fine edge necessary for determining all the meanings of the utterance. It would not necessarily be an extrinsic judgment to call *Paradise Lost* a "Christian-humanist epic" since the name serves merely as a preliminary heuristic tool that must be further sharpened before it can discriminate the functions of the partial meanings in their determinacy. A heuristic genre that merely has to be narrowed rather than revised cannot properly be called extrinsic. A genre may properly be called extrinsic only when it is wrongly conceived and used as an intrinsic genre. Thus, any final, generic sense of the whole different from the speaker's would be extrinsic because it would be used to codetermine meanings, of which some would necessarily be incorrect. Similarly, any heuristic type idea which an interpreter applied to a great many different utterances would be extrinsic if it were not narrowed in a different way for different utterances.[11] An extrinsic genre is a wrong guess, an

11. Thus my objection to the dangerous practice of using abstract categories or monolithic "approaches" and "methods" to interpret a

intrinsic genre a correct one. One of the main tasks of interpretation can be summarized as the critical rejection of extrinsic genres in the search for the intrinsic genre of a text.

C. GENRE LOGIC AND THE PROBLEM OF IMPLICATION

It is best to ignore for the moment a great many unresolved problems concerning genres in order to go straight to the crucial issue—the problem of implication. Of course, this problem is not in itself more important than a good many others in hermeneutic theory, but when our central concern is validity we always have to ask whether a particular meaning is or is not implied by an utterance. The correct determination of implications is a crucial element in the task of discriminating a valid from an invalid interpretation. Although disagreements between interpreters are sometimes total, as when one critic asserts that a meaning is ironical and another critic denies it, more often their disagreements center on details of implication, which are, of course, no less important for being details, since the character of the details is codeterminate with the character of the whole. In fact, all interpretive disagreements when they are not merely verbal tend to be fundamental disagreements.[12] At the center of them all is the question, Is this meaning implied or is it not?

In the second chapter I defined an implication as a trait of a type, and in this chapter I have given the name "intrinsic genre" to the type that determines the boundaries of an utterance as a whole. So we may now say that the implications of an utterance are determined by its intrinsic genre. The principle by which we can discover whether an implication belongs to

---

wide variety of texts. The use of such master keys to unlock large numbers of texts often has the effect of fitting the lock to the key rather than vice versa. See Chap. 4, Sec. D and E.

12. For the distinction between "different" and "disparate" interpretations (the former not implying disagreement) see Chap. 4, Sec. A, pp. 128–32.

a meaning turns out to be the concept of intrinsic genre. This general proposition now needs to be developed and illustrated.

This is not the place to discuss the connections between a general theory of verbal implication and the various accounts of implication that have been provided by logicians, though anyone familiar with writings on logic will notice affinities between what I have been saying about verbal implication and certain views of Mill, De Morgan, Bosanquet, and Husserl. Hermeneutic theory owes debts to so many fields that it is not surprising to find it indebted to logic, but verbal implication is at once broader and more limited than the kinds of implication discussed by most logicians, and hermeneutics need not pause very long over elaborate distinctions between varieties of implication, such as "syncategorematic" and "independent" implications or "strict" and "material" implications. Such distinctions are important with respect to a subject matter but rarely with respect to a meaning. For example, it is true that color necessarily implies extension (since it is impossible to perceive a color without perceiving also an area covered by the color), but oddly enough, I can name a color and can be so intent upon its particular quality as a color that I can almost if not totally disregard the idea of extension; certainly I can completely disregard any particular area covered by the color I name. Thus, to insist that color necessarily implies extension leaves out of account all those subtle problems of emphasis in verbal implication which I raised in discussing whether tree necessarily implies roots.

From the standpoint of verbal meaning, then, all implications without distinction are governed by the type-trait model. We know that a given partial meaning is implied by an utterance, because we know that such a meaning belongs in that type of utterance. With due qualifications, and in different terms, this is the point J. S. Mill made about the function of the syllogism.[13] We come to the conclusion that Socrates is mortal

13. J. S. Mill, *A System of Logic, Ratiocinative and Inductive* (London, 1843), Bk. II, Chaps. 2–3.

C. Genre Logic and the Problem of Implication

(that "Socrates" implies "mortality") because Socrates is an instance of a type (man) which past experience has shown to have the trait mortality. Whether the connection between a type and a trait is apodictically necessary or whether it is a habit or an accident or a brute given is, from the standpoint of interpretation, irrelevant. No matter how the connection between the type and the trait arose, all verbal implications are governed by some version of the formula "if the meaning is of *this* type, then it carries *this* implication."

I use the if-then convention of formal logic to point out two interesting aspects of verbal implication as it relates to interpretation. The first is that the correct drawing of implications depends upon a correct guess about the type: "*if* the meaning is of this type," "*if* we have rightly grasped the intrinsic genre." On that "if" everything depends, and there can be no apodictic certainty that our notion is right. But the other half of the proposition also follows: "*then* the meaning carries this implication." From the premised type of meaning, the implication follows with necessity. There is thus a genuine logic of interpretation, which is what Schleiermacher meant when he said that we understand nothing that we do not understand as necessary.[14] The reason for this is simple: if an implication is a trait of a type, it is an aspect that partly defines the type, for if the trait were not there, the type would be a different type; to have the one is to have the other. The uncertainty of interpretation arises because we can never be absolutely certain that we have premised the right type.

The logic of implication is always, therefore, a genre logic, as common sense tells every interpreter. Whether an implication is present depends upon the kind of meaning that is being interpreted. That is why we confidently infer, when a small boy says, "I want to climb a tree," that he does not imply "roots," though he almost certainly does imply "branches." We feel certain of this implication because we are familiar with

14. Fr. D. E. Schleiermacher, *Hermeneutik,* ed. Heinz Kimmerle (Heidelberg, 1959), p. 31.

boys and with the type of activity involved in climbing a tree and, therefore, with the type of meaning uttered by the boy. *Qui non intelliget res non potest ex verbis sensum ellicere.*[15] But, of course, numerous types of meanings are not associated directly with a *res* like tree climbing, but rather with a shared fiction such as unicorn or Leda. Everyone knows that Leda will in most usages imply swan, because a verbal implication, whether or not it has a basis in "reality," always has a basis in a shared type. Unicorn is as much a shared type as tree climbing, and if the type were not shared by the interpreter, he could not draw implications.

These simple examples demonstrate that every shared type of meaning (every intrinsic genre) can be defined as a system of conventions. Something in us rebels, of course, when somebody insists that the meaning "I want to climb a tree" is *nothing but* a system of conventions. We may admit that the words and the syntax of the sentence are conventions, but we will insist that there is nothing merely conventional about tree climbing itself. The word "convention" suggests an arbitrary connection between sign systems and meanings, but there is nothing arbitrary about the implications of hands, and feet, and branches in climbing a tree. Indeed, it has even been argued that it is artificial to speak of conventions with respect to words and syntax, since within a given language group these elements have ceased to be arbitrary at all. But I think these verbal difficulties can be resolved precisely *because* nothing in speaking and interpreting is merely arbitrary, and everything depends on something learned. There is probably no better single word than "convention" to embrace the entire system of usage traits, rules, customs, formal necessities, and proprieties which constitute a type of verbal meaning. It is certainly true that some of these elements may be unalterable while others may be variable, but it is also true that the elements, whether necessary or not, must be shared. That was the point I made about

15. Luther's dictum. See Appendix II, p. 248.

C. Genre Logic and the Problem of Implication

the implication "Pythagorean theorem" in the term "right triangle."[16] The implication is unalterably necessary, but it is not a verbal implication except in certain genres of utterance in which the necessary connection is known and shared. Because the types must be shared in order to carry implications, and because they would not be shared if the interpreter did not know the type, it is genuinely descriptive to call an intrinsic genre a system of conventions.

This emphasis on the conventional character of all genre expectations and inferences leads back to Wittgenstein's metaphor of a game. If the drawing of implications did not vaguely correspond to the moves in a familiar game (the particular game is, of course, the intrinsic genre), then the interpreter would not know what moves to make. He could not know the rules. Yet "rules" is a strong, overly rigid word, as we know from the fact that slight alterations in the system of conventions are possible. A better word might be "proprieties." A genre is less like a game than like a code of social behavior, which provides rules of thumb such as, do not drink a toast to your hostess at a Scandinavian dinner party. That is not a strict rule (since under certain circumstances it would be permissible to drink the toast) but rather a propriety which is, on the whole, socially considerate to observe. The conventions of language are of this broadly social character, since language itself is broadly social and outreaches the rigid, artificially confined rules of a game.

Implications are drawn, then, by observing the proprieties of an intrinsic genre, and it is obvious that these proprieties are two-sided. Given a particular intrinsic genre, both the speaker and the interpreter come under the same constrictions and necessities. It is precisely at this very particularized level that the proponents of "public norms" have their vindication. Their mistake lay not in thinking that there is a supra-individualistic principle which enforces meanings, but in believing

16. See Chap. 2, Sec. G, pp. 64–66.

93

that this principle is somehow automatically given to any "competent reader." It is the speaker who wills the particular intrinsic genre and, having done so, is constrained by its proprieties, but the interpreter can never be completely certain what that genre is and can never completely codify its proprieties in all their complexity. The fundamental criterion for genre proprieties is ultimately the same as that for verbal meaning in general—the criterion of sharability.

It is time to give an illustration of the way implications are determined by the logic of genre proprieties, but it is difficult to find clear examples of such subtle matters! If a text is unproblematical (i.e. "I want to climb a tree"), it cannot serve to illustrate the way in which an alternative generic conception alters the logic of implications, but if a text is problematical, then too many prolegomena are required to defend a particular inference.[17] Fortunately, as I was writing this chapter, a correspondence began to unfold in the letter columns of the *Times Literary Supplement* which saved me the trouble of inventing an artificial illustration. Mr. Hugh MacDiarmid invented one for me by converting into poetry two word sequences that had originally been published as prose by Mr. Glyn Jones and Mr. Hugh Gordon Porteus. Amidst the moral and legal issues that were publicly discussed upon the discovery of Mr. MacDiarmid's genial but unacknowledged transmogrifications, some theoretical issues were raised which go to the heart of all interpretive problems.

What makes this example particularly useful is the agreement by several of the correspondents, including the writer of a leading article on the subject, that the effect of words when they are printed as verse is different from their effect when printed as prose. Of course, prose and verse are enormously broad generic ideas, and in order to interpret either the original

---

17. This difficulty should be kept in mind by those who might wish to find more concrete examples in this theoretical essay. Theory of interpretation can never lead to a method of interpretation. See Chap. 5, Sec. E.

C. Genre Logic and the Problem of Implication

passages or Mr. MacDiarmid's typographical rearrangements, the reader has to make far more particular generic judgments than that. Not all the correspondents agreed, however, that a merely physical rearrangement could change the sound or sense of the words. The following is from a letter published in the *TLS* of 18 February 1965 by Mr. John Sparrow, who has kindly given me permission to quote it, adding that it does not represent his full views on these matters:

> Sir,—This unfortunate business of Mr. MacDiarmid and Dr. Grieve and their transmutations, conscious or unconscious, of the prose of Mr. Glyn Jones and Mr. Hugh Gorden Porteus raises an interesting critical issue. It involves, as Mr. Edwin Morgan points out, the question "Can prose become poetry through typographical rearrangement?" When Dr. Grieve (or Mr. MacDiarmid) turns a passage of prose by Mr. Porteus into the following:
>
>> When a Chinese calligrapher "copies"
>> The work of an old master it is not
>> A forged facsimile but an interpretation
>> As personal within stylistic limits
>> As a Samuel or Landowska performance
>> Of a Bach partita.
>
> is he doing anything more than destroying a decent bit of prose, without producing poetry or verse? Surely not.
> When Mr. MacDiarmid (or Dr. Grieve) performs a similar operation on a rather beautiful prose passage by Mr. Glyn Jones, what happens? The extract (topped up with an opening line and a title, "Perfect") acquires the unity of an independent work of art; but surely it is still not verse, and no more poetry than it was before? Dr. Grieve (or Mr. MacDiarmid) has given it, so to speak, independence and a sort of personality of its own, but what more has he conferred upon it?
> Professor Buthlay (who has committed himself by

warmly praising "Perfect" on the footing that it was entirely the work of Mr. MacDiarmid) naturally does his best for the "transmuters": he suggests that by printing a sequence of words in lines of uneven length, instead of in a solid block, one "adds a dimension" to it; and he describes the dimension as being one of "rhythmical subtlety", saying that it "brings out qualities and relationships of *sound* that enrich the significance of the words." So far as this means anything, it sounds nonsense to me. I do not find that the typographical rearrangement alters the sound of the syllables, nor can I see how any such alteration could change the significance of words except by introducing mental rather than auditory pauses.

Here, for comparison, are the words of Dr. Porteus printed as prose: "When a Chinese calligrapher 'copies' the work of an old master it is not a forged facsimile but an interpretation as personal within stylistic limits as a Samuel or Landowska performance of a Bach partita." Now the rhythm of this prose *is* different from that of the versified transcription, and for precisely the sort of reason given by the editorialist of the *TLS*, 25 February 1965:

Just as pausing for so long at commas is a habit we only learn from experience of hearing people read prose, and pausing for so long at line-breaks is a habit we fall into either from hearing people read verse or by extension of our prose-reading habits, so our tendency to look for an underlying "beat" or rhythm in words arranged in verse form is a convention learnt from experience. It is because there exists this convention that any words arranged in verse form will at once set the trained reader of poetry searching for a rhythm in them—that is to say, seeing if there is not some detectable degree of regularity in the fall of the stresses, and then reading the whole poem with slightly greater emphasis on the natural stresses which coincide with the stresses of the underlying beat.

C. Genre Logic and the Problem of Implication

It is possible to be more specific than this. To know the proprieties of reading most kinds of verse is to anticipate isochronous beats. There will thus be a speeding up or slowing down of the syllables between the beats in order to make them fall more or less at the right place. Since the lines of Mr. Mac-Diarmid's transcription begin with a three-beat pattern, the practiced reader will tend to feel the pattern operating through to the end and will, of course, also tend to pause at the end of the lines:

> When a Chinése callígrapher "cópies"
> The wórk of an old máster it is nót ,
> A fórged facsímile but, an interpretátion
> As pérsonal within stylístic límits,
> As a Sámuel or, Landówska perfórmance
> Of a Bách partíta.

Nobody would read the lines as heavily as my simple marks would suggest, but every practiced reader would tend to slur and speed up "of an old," "but an in . . . ," and so on, because at these points there are more than two syllables between the beats. Similarly, he will slow down at "forged facsimile" because there is only one syllable between the beats. On the other hand, to make merely two contrasts with the rhythms of the prose passage, there will be in the prose distinct pauses after "master" and "personal," but not in the verse.

Much more important, however, are differences of meaning. I would not dare to suggest a definitive interpretation for either the original prose or the poetry, since I have no access to the texts from which they were excerpted, but I am very willing to suggest the kind of differences that generic proprieties could enforce. In prose the passage could be purely a statement about the art of Chinese calligraphy, whereas in poetry the concentrating and symbolizing conventions of the genre lead us to expect wider implications, so that the Chinese calligrapher could imply not only Chinese calligraphy but all tradition-bound art. If we assume for the moment that my hypothetical interpretation is correct, we confront an interesting illustration of the reason that a given word sequence can represent more than one meaning. It can do so because almost any word sequence can be subsumed by more than one intrinsic genre and therefore can carry different implications. The *TLS* controversy illustrated this universal fact in a very clear and simple way. In fact, every disagreement about an interpretation is usually a disagreement about genre, and the typographical transformations of Mr. MacDiarmid raise not merely "an interesting critical issue," but the central issue in most problems of interpretation. They indicate, though very roughly, that genre conventions are essential to all determinations, including phonetic ones, and are particularly essential to the drawing of implications.

However, in the interpretation of speech, the drawing of implications has a dimension which is not usually hinted at in the models of logical inference. We know that in a particular universe of discourse "Socrates" implies "mortality," but how do we know the importance of that implication? Is it more important than "wisdom" or "teacher"? In logic a set of implications is usually spoken of as though it were a merely additive array that could be described by enumeration. This additive conception of submeanings is the underlying mistake in the idea that the most correct interpretation is the most inclusive one, for we know that a correct interpretation can be very sketchy, while an incorrect one can give a very full enumeration of meanings which are indeed implied. A sketchy interpretation can be correct by virtue of the fact that it rightly grasps the principle not only for drawing implications but also for relating them to one another, while a very full interpretation can be incorrect because it gives a false account of those relationships. The logic of verbal implications is therefore incomplete until it describes the principle not only for including and excluding implications, but also for structuring them. The relative importance of an implication is as crucial to meaning as the implication itself.

C. Genre Logic and the Problem of Implication

To speak of a complex verbal meaning as having a structure is, as many have pointed out, to speak inexactly, because "structure" is a spatial term whereas verbal meaning is temporal. One answer to this criticism has been that temporal relationships can be described only in spatial terms and vice versa. I need not pause to consider this interesting problem of description, since there is one conception common to both spatial and temporal relationships—the idea of relative emphasis. The relative importance of an implication can be defined in terms of emphasis, and emphasis can, in turn, be defined as the relative degree of attention that should be paid to an implication. A different system of emphases gives a different meaning both to a temporal sequence and to a spatial configuration, and obviously when the object of interpretation is a mute text, the problem of getting its emphases right is particularly difficult.

How much emphasis should an implication receive? The straightforward answer is, "Just as much relative emphasis as the author willed it to receive." However, we all know that this answer has to be recast in terms of sharable conventions, since we have no direct access to the author's mind. These conventions of emphasis are, predictably, another aspect of the convention system embraced by a particular genre, for what makes one implication more important than another is its function in the meaning as a whole, and obviously not every implication serves functions which are equally crucial. But this argument seems to drive us to a circularity, since the problem of determining the relative importance of a function is the same as determining the importance of an implication, which *is* among other things a function. To determine relative emphasis, therefore, we must have reference to something else that makes the function important, and this something lies at the heart of what a genre is. The unifying and controlling idea in any type of utterance, any genre, is the idea of purpose.

The purpose of any utterance is, of course, to communicate meaning, but obviously a great many of the meaning types under which utterances can be subsumed can be further classified in terms of the effects, functions, and goals which they serve. For example, the categories of prayer, command, and technical essay can be subdivided into smaller groups of utterances which have common purposes and functions. Under "command," for example, there are numerous subtypes, such as the military order, the parent's demand, the boss's request, and under each of these a great number of varieties which reach to the intrinsic genre of the utterance. But what permits such subtypes to be subsumed under a larger type concept, such as "prayer" or "command," is not usually a particular vocabulary or sentence pattern (these will vary immensely), but a particular kind of purpose.

The notion that purpose is the most important unifying and discriminating principle in genres was long ago suggested by Aristotle and echoed by Boeckh:

> The conversation, the letter, and so on are genres of speech and embrace within themselves a further large number of genres which may be distinguished according to their purposes. Naturally, these genres are far more special than the highest classes of speech—poetry and prose. But it is entirely irrelevant whether or not a genre happens to be represented by only one individual; the same purpose under different circumstances could just as well be realized by many individuals.[18]

Boeckh is here reaching out toward the notion of intrinsic genre, and it is extremely interesting that he, like Aristotle, should define it in terms of purpose. This is a notion that may well be considered for a moment.

By the term *Zweck* ("purpose") Boeckh must mean something other than an external goal by means of which an utter-

18. August Boeckh, *Encyclopädie und Methodologie der philologischen Wissenschaften,* ed. E. Bratuscheck (2d ed. Leipzig, 1886), p. 141.

ance serves something beyond itself. Since he is sympathetic to the view derived from Kant that verbal art is in one sense purposeless, that it does not necessarily subserve anything else, he is clearly not suggesting that all generic purposes are external purposes. Presumably he means something like an Aristotelian final cause, and he would be relatively hospitable to some of the ideas of R. S. Crane and the Chicago critics. His *Zweck* must be an entelechy, a goal-seeking force that animates a particular kind of utterance. If we conceive such purposiveness as being limited to the particular purposes of an intrinsic genre, then we have a direct connection between the idea of genre and the controlling principle in meaning—the idea of will—in this case, a particularized genre will that is not arbitrary but channeled within social forms and unified by an idea. The genre purpose must be in some sense an *idea,* a notion of the type of meaning to be communicated; otherwise there would be nothing to guide the author's will. On the other hand, there must also exist the motive force of will, since without its goal-seeking the idea could not be realized through the temporal activity of speaking. The author has an idea of what he wants to convey—not an abstract concept, of course, but an idea equivalent to what we called an intrinsic genre. In the course of realizing this idea, he wills the meanings which subserve it. It is by virtue of this purposive willing that implications have degrees of emphasis or importance with respect to one another.[19]

This rather abstract description may be incarnated in a very simple example—the use of phonetic stresses in actual speech. (It is well to remember Saussure's admonition that writing is a

19. My description departs from that of Aristotle and the neo-Aristotelians by its insistence on the entirely metaphorical character of an entelechy when that concept is applied to a form of speech. A verbal genre has no entelechy or will of its own. It is not a living thing with a soul or vital principle. It is mute inert matter that is given "soul" or "will" by speakers and interpreters. In other words, the purpose of a genre is the communicable purpose of a particular speaker, nothing more nor less. See Chap. 4, Sec. D.

lately developed surrogate of actual speech.[20]) These phonetic stresses follow different conventions in different languages, but their function is the same everywhere. They serve to indicate the relative importance of submeanings and thus the intrinsic genre of the utterance. Everybody is familiar with the immense semantic effect of transposing emphases in a sentence like "I am going to town tomorrow." If we put a strong stress in turn on each of the words, we will get a different sense. Everyone is aware of this fact, but neither logicians nor literary theorists have paid enough attention to its importance for the drawing of implications.

Of course, it might be objected that each of the different senses conveyed by transposing the stresses of this random example will also convey a different set of implications, not merely the same ones arranged in different hierarchies. That is indeed true, but each of these different sets of implications will have a unity, and the relative importance of each will be crucial to meaning. This can be easily seen if we regard the words of the illustrative sentence as individual submeanings which embrace everything the sentence means without any further dimension of implications. In each case the submeanings will be the same, and the meaning will be different. If we observe that conventions of phonetic stress are but one sort of clue to emphasis, and that even these conventions vary in their applicability from genre to genre, we will conclude that the weighing of the relative emphasis of implications is as difficult as it is crucial. It is fortunate that this problem is solved for the interpreter (as it is for the speaker) by attending to the "idea" of the utterance, which is to say, its intrinsic genre.

D. THE HISTORICITY OF GENRES

The intrinsic genre that compels the determination of one meaning instead of another does not always leap into the inter-

---

20. *Course in General Linguistics,* pp. 23–37.

preter's mind but frequently emerges only after a narrowing process. The interpreter does not, of course, consciously follow a logical sequence: "this is a command, yet it is not a military command but a covert civilian command stated by my boss in the form of a polite request." The process of narrowing the genre begins at a far later stage if the interpreter is familiar with the genre and immediately recognizes some of its distinctive traits. That is why an experienced scholar is likely to understand an old text more quickly than a beginner, even when the beginner is quite familiar with the *langue* in which the text is written, but it is also why the beginner may on occasion arrive at an understanding that is truer than the practiced scholar's. The narrowing process of trial and error, guess and counterguess that the beginner must go through may in rare, lucky instances save him from an overly hasty typification. His expectations may be more flexible, and he may therefore perceive aspects that an expert could miss. But every expert was once a beginner; every speaker was once a child learning how to speak and interpret; and it is obvious that the heuristic use of genre concepts is central to this learning process.

My account of genres would therefore be very one-sided if I were to stress intrinsic genres at the expense of provisional, heuristic type concepts. Without these broader types new intrinsic genres could not come into existence. I have defined an intrinsic genre as a shared type that constitutes and determines meanings, since the implications of an utterance could not be conveyed if the genre were not a shared type. How, then, can anyone understand a new type of utterance? How can an interpreter know which implications belong and which do not belong if he has never encountered that particular type of meaning before? If somebody has just left the army for his first job in civilian life, and his new boss writes him a note saying, "Can you conveniently go to New York on the 7:30 train?" what is he to make of this? It is obviously not the same kind of communication as "You will proceed to New York on the 7:30 train," which was what his previous boss would have written.

To interpret properly this new kind of text our hypothetical tyro will have to make an imaginative leap and recognize that it belongs to the same broad type as "You will proceed to New York." If he were not capable of this imaginative leap, he could not understand the new utterance. It is clear, then, that broad, heuristic type concepts are just as essential as intrinsic genres. It is by means of them that new intrinsic genres are able to come into existence and are capable of being understood.

It is an interesting phenomenon that these broad type concepts are just as important to the author as they are to the interpreter. The point is not that the author cannot communicate a totally unfamiliar type of meaning, but the less obvious one that he cannot even formulate such a type. Preexisting type conceptions are apparently as necessary to the imagination as they are to the exigencies of communication. This is one of the many penetrating observations that E. H. Gombrich makes in his book, *Art and Illusion*. He quotes approvingly Quintilian's remark, "Which craftsman has not made a vessel of a shape he has never seen?" and comments: "It is an important reminder, but it does not account for the fact that even the shape of the new vessel will somehow belong to the same family of forms as those the craftsman has seen."[21] This tendency of the mind to use old types as the foundation for new ones is, of course, even more pronounced when communication or representation is involved. Not every convention could be changed all at once, even if the craftsman were capable of such divine creativity, because then his creation would be totally incommunicable, radically ambiguous. The point is stated pithily by Gombrich: "Variants can be controlled and checked only against a set of invariants."[22] In the example above, the invariants included a number of identities between army and civilian conventions. In both cases a superior addressed a subordinate. In both cases the subordinate was asked to do something and could expect unpleasantness if

21. E. H. Gombrich, *Art and Illusion* (New York, 1960), p. 25.
22. Ibid., p. 323.

he didn't. The variants were the two different conventions "You will" and "Can you conveniently," but so many other factors were the same that it required a very small leap of imagination to assimilate the one convention to the other.

In every new genre this process of assimilation is at work. No one would ever invent or understand a new type of meaning unless he were capable of perceiving analogies and making novel subsumptions under previously known types. Every creation of a new type involves the same leap of imagination that flashed in Picasso when he turned a toy car into the head of a baboon. To make such an analogy is not merely to equate two known types—baboon and car—but to create a new one— the car-baboon. It is, in other words, the process of metaphor. Literary critics have long told us that a metaphor is not reducible to its components and is something genuinely new. Every new verbal type is in this sense a metaphor that required an imaginative leap. The growth of new genres is founded on this quantum principle that governs all learning and thinking: by an imaginative leap the unknown is assimilated to the known, and something genuinely new is realized. This can happen in two ways: two old types can be *amalgamated,* as in the car-baboon, or an existing type can be *extended,* as in the case of our demobbed tyro confronting a civilian command. Both processes depend on metaphor—that is, on the making of a new identification never conceived before.

To understand how this process of metaphorical assimilation produces something new we can consider the puzzle that confronts a speaker who has to respond verbally to a new type of situation that cannot be automatically subsumed under previous types of usage. He faces the same problem on a broader level that users of a language must solve when they have to name an object, like a railroad or a laser, that has just come into existence. One simple example that comes to mind is the question that arose with the invention of the telephone. What were the first users of the telephone to say when they picked up the receiver? A social anthropologist could amuse himself by drawing inferences from the various solutions to this problem that evolved in different countries. When the Americans say "hello" they mean, no doubt, essentially what the Italians mean when they say "pronto"—namely, that they have picked up the receiver and are ready to listen. But "hello," unlike "pronto," was a salutation, and to say "hello" in this new situation was to assimilate the telephone response to a salutation. Once that metaphorical leap had been made, however, the new usage ceased to be a salutation at all. A new genre had been created.

That was a simple example of forming a new genre by extending an existing one. Many new genres are formed by using both metaphorical extensions like "hello" and metaphorical amalgamations like the car-baboon. When an author evolves a new literary genre, for example, he usually employs both techniques. He not only extends existing conventions but combines old convention systems in a new way. The description of this process is the task of "influence" studies, and the danger inherent in such descriptions is that they tend to reduce the new genre to the preexisting conventions out of which it was formed. This is equivalent to identifying a metaphor with its elements instead of recognizing that every metaphor is a leap *ins Unbetretene*. In retrospect it is clear, for example, that Byron borrowed conventions from Pulci and Frere as well as from Homer and Virgil to compose *Don Juan*. When Byron said, "My poem's epic" he was relying on the reader's knowledge of traditional epic conventions, and he was also relying on traditional episodes as a schema for his own imagination. The storm at sea in *Don Juan* is there because sea storms belong in epics, and the Haidee episode is there because idyllic romances come after sea storms. Older genre conventions both guided Byron's invention and nourished it, but it is obvious that the genre idea of *Don Juan* is Byron's alone and is a new kind that had never existed before. One reason Byron felt obliged to lard the poem with so many explicit explanations of what he was up to was that his readers needed signposts which

D. *The Historicity of Genres*

he did not have to provide in the somewhat more traditional genre of *Childe Harold.*

To describe the way new genres come into being is of considerable importance both to interpretation and to genre theory. Schleiermacher, with his customary penetration, long ago pointed out that an interpreter must take into consideration whether the genre is new or whether it is well developed, since in a new genre, repetitions and tautologies may not indicate emphasis but may simply arise from the author's attempt to secure a meaning that might otherwise be missed or wrongly understood.[23] Because essential elements of all genres are historical and culture-bound, it is not surprising that the best discussions of the genre concept are to be found not in Aristotle or his modern disciples but in those scholars who have tried to compose histories of traditional genres—scholars like Gunther Müller, Karl Viëtor, and Wolfgang Kayser, who have recognized the powerfully historical character of their subject matter. Even so, they too have sometimes fallen into Aristotelian hypostatizing in assuming that a traditional genre like the "ode" is somehow a species concept which defines the members subsumed under it. "How is it possible," asks Viëtor, "to write a genre history if one cannot first establish the norms that define the genre?" These norms are, he concludes, das *Gattungshafte* and consist in three things: "the particular stance, and the particular inner and outer forms. In their particular unity, these three make up 'the' genre."[24] In such statements Viëtor gives the impression that he believes in the definitive power of broad genre concepts. Gunther Müller, on the other hand, more accurately observed that "there is no such thing as 'the' genre, which necessitates and moulds, but only different *gattungshafte Strukturen* whose mutual relationships must be studied."[25] Yet Müller nevertheless rejects the nominalistic implications of

23. Schleiermacher, *Hermeneutik,* p. 106.
24. Karl Viëtor, *Geist und Form* (Bern, 1952), pp. 305, 300.
25. Gunther Müller, "Bemerkungen zur Gattungspoetik," *Philosophischer Anzeiger, 3* (1928), 146.

this remark. Genre to him is something real, and it is to be found in history, even though what it is in a given case cannot be precisely defined.

These writers seem so close to a satisfactory solution of their problem that we could say they had solved it without knowing it. Müller in his comment on *gattungshafte Strukturen* came very close, and it was only his fascination with verbal difficulties that handicapped him: "The dilemma of all genre history is that we apparently cannot decide what belongs to a genre without knowing what is *gattungshaft,* and we cannot know what is *gattungshaft* without knowing that this or that belongs to a genre."[26] This is, of course, the hermeneutic circle again, but it is not directly relevant to defining the *Seinsweise* of a genre. At the level of history there is no real entity such as a genre if by that word we mean a type concept that can adequately define and subsume all the individuals that are called by the same generic name, such as ode, sonnet, command, prayer, or epic. Obviously such a broad type concept can validly represent some abstractedly identical traits among all the individuals it subsumes, but it is certainly not a species concept which sufficiently defines those individuals. That much Müller and Viëtor perceived. What they failed to state is that the reality of these larger genre concepts exists entirely in the function they actually served in history. *Don Juan* is an "epic" only because this word represents to us, as it did to Byron, *some* of the conventions under which he wrote. The term certainly does not define or subsume his poem.

But if that is so, why did Byron say, "My poem's epic"? Putting aside the touch of irony in the statement (Byron really meant what he said), we find here the real mode of existence of the broader genre concepts. These concepts are broad type ideas that serve speakers in the way that pictorial schemata serve painters. Except in very traditional and formulaic utterances, they are metaphorical assimilations by which a speaker

26. Ibid., p. 136.

and his audience can orient themselves to something new. If traditional genres really were species concepts that constrained a speaker and an interpreter, then new types obviously could not arise. It is no more adequately descriptive to call a poem an epic than it is to call a play a tragicomedy.[27] These words may often stand for convention systems within which texts were written, and the term "tragicomedy" may aptly describe the type idea under which certain dramatists actually wrote. However, the theorist, like the historian, has to distinguish between a type idea that genuinely subsumes a work and a type idea which is actually nothing but a provisional schema. Byron could reasonably call his work an epic since he really did use conventions common to other works identified by that name, but the interpreter or the historian has done very little when *he* calls *Don Juan* an epic. His use of such a term should be as metaphorical and provisional as it was for Byron. The larger genre concepts represent something real only to the extent that they represent norms and conventions that were actually brought into play. Used in this way, the terms are valid even if they are not adequately definitive.

If this view of the traditional genre concepts appears to be highly nominalistic, the reader has misunderstood the purpose of my analysis, which is not to throw aside the traditional concepts but, on the contrary, to show their validity. Some of the traditional types are guiding conceptions that have actually been used by writers and hence are not arbitrary classifications set up by the interpreter. To be able to speak or understand speech, a person must have recourse to a genre idea, and if the utterance is not a mere formula, he usually must have recourse to a genre that is broader than the intrinsic genre. The genre "command" names a type of use that a speaker has learned from previous uses, and he knows that what he says must have significant elements in common with those past uses. But since some of his usages may be new, the type idea he relies

27. A further discussion of broad type ideas such as epic, tragedy, satire, poetry, and literature will be found in the next section.

on subsumes the intrinsic genre only metaphorically. His command may be no more the same as other commands than a car is the same as a baboon. Thus, the larger genre "command" is at best a partial and provisional classification, though it is a necessary one. The real relationship of an intrinsic genre to broader genre ideas is a historical relationship.

The model for this relationship is not, however, a simple genealogical chart. The parents of the intrinsic genre are sometimes very numerous, and they may have widely different provenances. Furthermore, the description of these antecedents does not define the genre, any more than the description of its elements defines the meaning of a metaphor. The best way to define a genre—if one decides that he wants to—is to describe the common elements in a narrow group of texts which have direct historical relationships. Such descriptions can sometimes be very useful propaedeutic tools, but they become less useful to interpretation as their scope becomes broader and more abstract.[28]

The only broad genre concept, then, which is by nature illegitimate is the one which pretends to be a species concept that somehow defines and equates the members it subsumes.

28. We need not, of course, evaluate genre descriptions or the criterion of their usefulness to interpretation; we might be interested in discovering recurrent patterns of mind, and so on. But these patterns can be discovered only *after* interpretation, since we need to be sure that the defining characteristics are really present in the texts. Because such conclusions about recurrent patterns are subsequent to interpretation, their heuristic and descriptive power is not primarily in interpretation itself, but in other domains such as psychology and anthropology. The patterns abstracted from interpreted texts cannot legitimately be reimposed upon the texts as a deeper and higher meaning. (I am thinking here particularly of Northrop Frye's influential system.) Such a reimposed pattern could be nothing but a selective, abstract meaning whose importance belongs to some theory about man. To find the essence of a text by such procedures of abstraction is like finding the essence of a random set of objects (flag poles, billiard cues, pencils) in their being oblong. The distortion is complete when we choose one such *object*—say a phallus—as the primal ground or essence of the others.

E. *Variety of Genres and Unity of Principles*

This is the great danger, for example, in Northrop Frye's classification of literary genres. Classifications are useful, sometimes indispensable conceptual tools in controlling a subject matter, and for purposes of classification it matters very little whether we use Roman numerals, the weeks of the year, or the phases of the moon. The one thing that does matter is the degree of reliance we place in the definitive character of these arbitrary schemata. If we believe they are constitutive rather than arbitrary and heuristic, then we have made a serious mistake and have also set up a barrier to valid interpretation.

E. VARIETY OF GENRES AND UNITY OF PRINCIPLES

The preceding sections on the nature and necessity of genre concepts have brought my argument to a stage where it is possible to draw some general conclusions about the theory and practice of interpretation. It has gradually become clear that the division of speech into *langue* and *parole* forms a conceptual model that does not adequately describe the relationship between the whole array of linguistic types and the highly variable particularities of individual speech acts. Between the enormously broad system of types and possibilities that constitute a language, and the individual speech acts that have made it and continue to make it, there are mediating type concepts which govern particular utterances as meaningful wholes. It is difficult to say whether these necessary concepts, which I have called intrinsic genres, belong more to *langue* or to *parole,* and it would be incorrect to subsume them under either category. It is more important to recognize that they play a definitive role in interpretation, for if they govern both speaking and understanding, it follows that they should, on a more self-conscious and methodological level, govern the categories and procedures of interpretation as a discipline. This is the conclusion I want to emphasize and develop in this final section on genres, particularly since it is a conclusion that bears directly on the concerns of the following chapters.

Hermeneutic theory has always recognized that there may be different kinds of textual interpretation corresponding to different kinds of texts. The most venerable distinction has been that between *hermeneutica sacra* and *hermeneutica profana,* which is, of course, the distinction that Schleiermacher worked so energetically to overcome, though without success, as may be inferred from the continuing tradition of sacred hermeneutics. At the beginning of his famous *Encyclopädie,* Boeckh, who was Schleiermacher's most faithful disciple, states bluntly: "Since the principles under which understanding must occur, and the functions of understanding are everywhere the same, there can be no specific differences in hermeneutic theory corresponding to different objects of interpretation. The distinction between *hermeneutica sacra* and *profana* is therefore thoroughly untenable."[29] However, Emilio Betti, the most eminent recent theorist in what may broadly be called the tradition of Schleiermacher, has insisted on the practical necessity of distinguishing between types of interpretation. He perceives three main types: re-cognitive, presentational, and normative, corresponding respectively to historical and literary texts, dramatic and musical texts, and legal and sacred texts.[30] Hans-Georg Gadamer, on the other hand, rejects any distinction between the understanding, the presentation, and the application of a text's meaning. In his view, all types of interpretation are subsumed under the idea of application.[31]

Within the context of this continuing theoretical debate may be placed a great deal of recent literary theory. (The battle cry "back to the text" was not in itself either a program or a theory.) The most inclusive programmatic idea put forward in the admirable theoretical compendium by Wellek and Warren is the idea that literary interpretation must be intrinsic.

29. *Encyclopädie,* p. 80.
30. *Teoria generale, 1,* 343–57.
31. *Wahrheit und Methode: Grundzüge einer philosophischen Hermeneutik* (Tübingen, 1960), pp. 280 ff.

E. *Variety of Genres and Unity of Principles*

They insist that the study of literature ought to be literary, just as the study and interpretation of philosophical texts ought to be philosophical. Behind this programmatic idea is a notion of validity: the literary study of literature is not simply an appropriate mode of interpretation; it is the only really valid mode. To treat a literary text as though it were a document in history or biography is to misrepresent its nature, and such a misrepresentation constitutes a perversion of its meaning. All valid interpretation is thus intrinsic interpretation: whatever one may do with a literary text *after* it has been understood on its own terms achieves validity only because that preliminary task has been performed. This argument, which is mutatis mutandis my own view, has obvious relevance to the question whether there exist different types of interpretation corresponding to different types of texts.

One result of the preceding discussion of the genre concept has been to suggest that the distinction between types of interpretation is not really antithetical to the idea that "the functions of understanding are everywhere the same." If understanding is always governed by the genre conventions of an utterance, it follows that different types of texts do indeed require different types of interpretation. But, on the other hand, the underlying hermeneutical principle is always and everywhere the same: valid interpretation is always governed by a valid inference about genre. Thus, while the same methods and categories are not universally applicable to all texts, the proper categories are nevertheless always determined by a universal principle—namely, their appropriateness to the intrinsic genre of a text. This cursory resolution of an old debate now requires further elaboration, and it will also require a rejection of some of the assumptions under which the debate has been conducted.

The first assumption to be rejected is the notion that the larger classifications of texts represent an adequate foundation for defining different types of interpretation. On this point I side strongly with Schleiermacher and Boeckh and shall take as an example the interpretation of philosophical texts. Do these, taken as a whole, constitute a single genre that can be adequately described with a single set of categories and canons of interpretation? Suppose we say that all philosophical texts must be interpreted philosophically. Does that mean we should always ask whether the text is true? If so, do we always apply the same criterion of truth? Does truth always imply consistency and absence of contradiction? Perhaps so, if by truth we mean coherence, but suppose we are told that truth is a bacchanalian revel in which not one member is sober, as a famous philosopher once said. Or suppose we are told that truth means correspondence to a reality which is not necessarily coherent. Would we understand such texts if we assumed that truth is equivalent to coherence? Suppose we are told that all philosophy is ultimately concerned with Being. Would we have to throw out some of our texts and call them by a different name, or would we twist and contort the ones we ordinarily call philosophical to show that they really are ultimately concerned with Being? Philosophical texts, we could say alternatively, are always attempts to clarify concepts, not attempts to transcend conceptual thinking. Out go Kierkegaard and Bergson. Of course, we are constantly being told by philosophers what philosophy is. But that "is" usually means "ought," since any generalization about philosophical texts can be dismantled in the way I dismantled the statement that "all philosophical texts aim at truth."

Yet one generalization does hold: all philosophical texts are called philosophical texts. This tautology is not totally empty. We call a text philosophical because it bears resemblances to some, though not to all, texts going by that name. The broad genre is a loose family group. Many of the resemblances borne by members of the group have arisen by historical assimilation, while others are due entirely to the exigencies of thought and reality. The members are grouped together as a class for conceptual convenience, but there is no single specific difference common to them all. Nevertheless, it is appropriate to group them in this way because they form a more or less continuous series in which any two neighbors may closely resemble each

114

other yet not at all resemble the members at the other end of the series. Under the heading "philosophical texts," we could put at one end the *Principia Mathematica* and at the other Pope's *Essay on Man*.

However, this arrangement of the members in the series would still represent a somewhat arbitrary procedure. It would be impossible to make a definitive arrangement, because it would be impossible to formulate a linear series that takes into account all the significant traits that the various members might have in common. Does *De Rerum Natura* stand closer to Pope's *Essay on Man* or to Schelling's *Ideen zu Einer Philosophie der Natur?* Obviously, our answer will depend upon the traits we consider. Nevertheless, the model of a linear series is serviceable—quite as serviceable as the broad family which we call "philosophical texts." The conceptual model of a series suggests the important truth that there are no clear and firm boundaries between the larger genre classifications. Everyone recognizes this fact. But since it is a fact, what can we properly mean when we speak of the philosophical interpretation of philosophy or the literary interpretation of literature?

I suggest we cannot properly mean that there is one particular set of categories and canons appropriate for each of the families of texts that we happen to call literary, philosophical, legal, or sacred. To be more blunt, there is no such thing as the philosophical interpretation of philosophy or the literary interpretation of literature, but there emphatically is such a thing as the intrinsic interpretation of a text. Of course, certain categories and canons of interpretation can properly be applied to reasonably large groups of texts. Aristotle, for example, attempted to formulate them for one tradition in Greek drama. Yet these groups of texts are smaller than is usually assumed. Take, for example, Viëtor's useful generalization about the sonnet:

> Enforced abundance is the distinctive characteristic of the sonnet—pregnant expression of strong feeling with reflective profundity. This oneness of spirit and feeling,

thought and sensitiveness are also essential characteristics of other lyrical genres—the ode, for example. But in the sonnet this abundance is characteristically more concentrated, more constrained and definite in its relationships of tension and resolution than anywhere else. The tendency towards a sententious close can be easily explained from this. This dialectical tension is therefore constitutive of the genre.[32]

This is very illuminating and provides an interpreter with some useful conceptual categories for interpreting a great many sonnets. But surely it does not hold for all sonnets—certainly not for all of the frequently relaxed and comic sonnets of Belli. Similarly, what W. H. Auden says about the logic of the detective story and what Thomas M. Greene has described as the norms of epic are highly useful typifications that provide conceptual wedges into a great many individual texts.[33] But such typifications are not, as Viëtor claims, constitutive. To think of them in that way is to misapply a very valuable heuristic tool.

If special categories and canons cannot be formulated that are invariably adequate to limited genre concepts like the sonnet and the detective story, how much less likely is it that one set of canons, categories, and procedures can be adequate to larger families like lyric poetry, or still larger ones like literature and sacred scripture. Why is it that concepts such as the image, the persona, the intellectual space, tension, irony, and even that useful catchall "style" have not really proved to be so universally applicable to literature as it was once hoped? One answer might be that there is nothing wrong with these literary categories, only with their inappropriate or tactless use. That answer seems just and suggests another: these categories have been used inappropriately because they are not everywhere

32. *Geist und Form,* p. 298.
33. W. H. Auden, "The Guilty Vicarage," in *The Dyer's Hand* (New York, 1962); and Thomas M. Greene, *The Descent from Heaven* (New Haven, 1963), Chap. 1.

equally appropriate; a dozen others might be found that served the purpose just as well and in some cases better. I shall have more to say on this subject in the next chapter, but this is the place to make the point that the applicability of an interpretive category is as closely tied to the proprieties of a genre as are the usage traits of the genre itself. As in the problem of implication, the key element is proper emphasis. To misrepresent the purposes and emphases of a text by applying single-mindedly a favored category is hardly better than to misunderstand it, and the two mistakes usually go together. To misconstrue the purposes and emphases of a text is to misunderstand it.

Does this equation of intrinsic interpretation with the particular norms of an intrinsic genre lead to a chaotic atomism? If we did not have broad genre concepts and equally tolerant interpretive categories, how could we talk about texts at all? These are the obvious objections to my very particularized description of intrinsic interpretation, and they are valid. We must use these broad and rough tools if we are to interpret, but every self-critical interpreter knows that his commentary does not adequately describe and that his tools are essentially heuristic. To remind him of this is not to adopt an atomistic view but to arouse a proper skepticism with regard to favored words and habits of mind.

One very practical value of the genre concept, therefore, is its power to arouse this healthy skepticism. Suppose a literary student were asked to compare the following similar passages:

1. There would seem to be two methods by which these extra-triangular regions might be fixed in a less arbitrary way. We might agree to fix them as being as large as possible. Or we might fix them as being as small as possible.

2. There seem to be two methods by which we can fix these regions outside the triangle in a less arbitrary way. We might agree to make them as large as possible. Or, we might make them as small as possible.

Any clever undergraduate majoring in literature could do a creditable job of analyzing the differences between the passages. He would point out that the first passage is written in a more textbookish style. "There would seem to be" is more formal and at the same time more tentative than "There seem to be." The subjunctive in the first phrase indicates a carefully uncommitted and distantly objective attitude, while the indicative case in the second phrase suggests greater decisiveness and definiteness. This contrast is more striking when we compare "extra-triangular regions" with "regions outside the triangle"; the first is an abstract, technical-sounding phrase which coincides with the tone of distant impersonality, while the second is more straightforward and concrete. This contrast between the passages is definitively confirmed by the tendency of the first author to use the passive voice, and the second the active. On the other hand, the first author may have the advantage of precision in the last two sentences, since "fix them as being" is more precisely descriptive of the hypothetical exercise involved than the more direct and concrete "make them." Still, this precision and care are misplaced, since the hypothetical character of the operation is clear from "we could agree."

Our undergraduate could no doubt continue for at least another paragraph, and many on reading his analysis would, I think, find it largely convincing. Ultimately it would probably show that the tone and style of the second passage is to be preferred to the first; that the second implies greater decision, clarity, and commitment, while the first implies a meaning that is more coldly impersonal; that the imagery, persona, and style of the two passages are different. Our undergraduate would be shocked, and so might many of his teachers, if someone were to say that the meaning of the first passage is identical with the meaning of the second.

Now the first passage is quoted from *Scientific Explanation* by R. B. Braithwaite;[34] the second is my own. Braithwaite is

---

34. Harper Torchback ed., New York, 1960, p. 66.

generally a clear and forceful writer, and on the page preceding the quoted passage he writes: "Outside this triangle the figures may be of any size or shape you wish, provided only that no two of them overlap one another"—a sentence that has all the virtues allotted to the second example. Braithwaite does not seem to care very much whether he says "extra-triangular" or "outside this triangle" or whether he uses the passive or the active voice. How can this be so? Has he changed his imagery, persona, and style from one page to the next? Is it not more reasonable to suppose that he is writing in a genre whose purposes and conventions permit "extra-triangular" to mean exactly the same thing as "outside the triangle" and allow an arbitrary interchange between active and passive voice? We might answer that there must have been some reason for Braithwaite's choice of words and syntactical patterns in each instance, and that this reason cannot be irrelevant to his meaning. But suppose his reasons were a desire for euphony and a desire simply to vary his mode of expression. Are these reasons necessarily relevant to his meaning? Might they not simply be symptomatic implications that have nothing to do with his meaning? That could certainly be the case if the conventions of his genre did not embrace subtle stylistic norms but were entirely subservient to the purpose of conveying concepts that are independent of *any* particular symbolic formulation. Anyone might believe this, I think, if he were to glance a little further down the page from which our example was taken, where he would find the sentence: "This will enable us to derive the formulae $\lambda \leftrightarrow ((\gamma \upsilon a) \upsilon \beta')$, $\mu \leftrightarrow (a \upsilon \beta)$, $\nu \leftrightarrow (\beta \upsilon \gamma)$. If our quoted passage was leading up to that, why should the substitution of an active for a passive voice make any difference to the purpose and meaning of the passage?

Let me quickly say that there are limits to the possibilities of synonymity even in the genre in which Braithwaite is writing. I think, for example, that this genre is so close to and borrows so many conventions from less technical types of exposition that Braithwaite cannot overlook the convention which requires the end of a sentence to be more emphatic than its middle.

I was very careful in rewriting his passage to preserve his usage in this matter. Furthermore, I would be very reluctant to claim dogmatically that I had perfectly succeeded in reproducing the original. I would claim, rather, that the two meanings *could be* perfectly synonymous in the particular genre in which Braithwaite was writing. My point is that the undergraduate's stylistic analysis would be not only inappropriate but misleading. It would be bound to overstate the differences between the passages, would distort the system of emphases proper to the genre, and would therefore be bound to produce a misinterpretation. The clever undergraduate was, bluntly, wrong, and there was no way he could avoid being wrong so long as he so single-mindedly practiced one sort of stylistic analysis. He was using inappropriate categories because he did not pay attention to the variability of genre conventions and purposes.

One could say, of course, that his mistake lay in applying literary categories to a nonliterary text, but this conclusion would simplify and distort the point I am making. I am, after all, denying that there are such things as literary categories universally applicable to all literary texts. I do not reject only the idea that literary analysis can be applied to all texts, but also the idea that it can be applied automatically to the texts that we call literary. If we use analytical devices that get the purposes and emphases of a genre subtly or grossly wrong, then it doesn't matter a bit that we call both the device and the genre "literary." That doesn't make our interpretation intrinsic, and it certainly does not make it valid.

The crucial importance of genre proprieties in interpretation was summed up in an oblique way by Robert Frost in his famous definition, "Poetry is what gets lost in translation." The theoretical interest of the remark lies in its implication that the things that count most in a great deal of poetry are word associations that are endemic to a particular language, plus the rhythmical and phonetic aspects of those words. Neither aspect could possibly be perfectly translated. Yet can any reader doubt that Braithwaite's book could be perfectly translated? If he does doubt this, I suspect him of being a literary critic with a deeply rooted belief in "the heresy of paraphrase." That heresy does apply to lyric poetry, because what we call lyric poetry is by purpose and convention language-bound. I have no doubt that most of the texts which we call literary are to some degree language-bound, but it is a mistake to believe that they are all equally so. Is it not probable that on this criterion something like a continuous series stretches from Keats to Braithwaite, a series that certainly does not depend on normal genre classifications like poetry and prose, lyric poem and novel? Many poems are less language-bound and thus more fully translatable than Joyce's two novels, *Ulysses* and *Finnegans Wake*. The degree to which unique meanings are bound to unique expressions depends not on these broad genre distinctions, but on the intrinsic genre of a text—the particular norms and conventions under which it was composed. Most heresies, fallacies, canons, and methods are to be looked upon with a cold and skeptical eye when they pretend to offer rules for interpreting all texts or even a large number of them.

Yet one principle does remain universally applicable: valid interpretation depends on a valid inference about the proprieties of the intrinsic genre. The final question that now remains to be asked in this chapter is, "How does this generalization coincide with our earlier identification of understanding with the re-cognition of an author's meaning?" I have already suggested that the author and the interpreter are both constrained by genre proprieties, and that the author's meaning is determined by his willing of a particular intrinsic genre, but more must be said on this point—particularly with reference to those genres which Emilio Betti has called "normative." In the second chapter, where my main concern was meaning rather than interpretation, I identified implications with willed types that can be shared. What I have subsequently called an intrinsic genre is a larger, complex type conception that governs all these individual willed types as a whole. The genre concept turned out to be the principle for determining whether a particular meaning was willed—whether it belonged. Yet certain texts such as the Constitution of the United States and the Bible do seem to require that meaning go beyond anything that a human and historical author could possibly have willed. The same kind of problem often arises when scholars interpret literary texts. Shakespeare could not have known anything of Freudian psychology, yet many can perceive that *Hamlet* does have Freudian implications. Is there a difference, as Betti has suggested, between the legal and the scriptural example, on the one hand, and the example of Shakespeare, on the other? Is it proper to go beyond the author's meaning in construing laws but not in construing the plays of Shakespeare?

It will be useful to examine the example of *Hamlet* first. Of course, it would be most unwise to settle the theoretical issue on the basis of a particular interpretation of *Hamlet*. What is needed is a hypothetical instance that will clarify the nature of the problem. Let us suppose, therefore, that Shakespeare *did* want to suggest Hamlet's sense of repugnance at the idea of his mother's sexual relationship with the murderer of his father, but *did not* mean to suggest that Hamlet entertained an unconscious wish to sleep with his mother. Although Freud has argued that every (nonfictional) male tends to have such a wish whether he knows it or not, we have nevertheless supposed that Shakespeare's Hamlet neither knew this nor dimly and unconsciously meant this. He could possibly have done so, of course, but that is not our present supposition. What, then, are we to make of the fact that a Freudian interpretation is not only possible but to many readers convincing? They can point out that in the light of new psychological knowledge the situations and the utterances within the play do have Freudian implications, and that nothing can change this objective fact. It is part of the meaning of the play whether Shakespeare or anyone else before Freud knew it or not.

Here we have, I think, a clear-cut problem that is capable of a definitive solution. We have posited that Shakespeare did not mean that Hamlet wished to sleep with his mother. We confront an interpretation which states that Hamlet did wish to sleep with his mother. If we assert, as I have done, that only a re-cognitive interpretation is a valid interpretation, then we must, on the basis of our assumed premise about the play, say that the Freudian interpretation is invalid. It does not correspond to the author's meaning; it is an implication that cannot be subsumed under the type of meaning that Shakespeare (under our arbitrary supposition) willed. It is irrelevant that the play permits such an interpretation. The variability of possible implications is the very fact that requires a theory of interpretation and validity.

Is the case different with the Constitution and the Bible? Does the identification of valid interpretation with re-cognitive interpretation do justice to texts which would lose their function if their meaning were limited to what the author knew and consciously or unconsciously intended? Must these texts be put in a special category, and if so, does that nullify the claim that the underlying principles of interpretation are the same everywhere? This kind of question caused Gadamer to insist that all textual interpretation must go beyond the author, must mean more than he or any individual interpreter could know or understand. For Gadamer, all texts are like the Constitution and the Bible.[35]

By this time a percipient reader will have guessed what my answer will be—namely, that for some genres of texts the author submits to the convention that his willed implications must go far beyond what he explicitly knows. This is to some degree

---

35. *Wahrheit und Methode,* pp. 280 ff. My criticism of Gadamer's conception and my reasons for rejecting the analogy of interpretations with legal "pragmatism" or "activism" will be found in Appendix II. The inadequacy of identifying textual meaning with "tradition" or some other changing norm is seen first of all in the total impracticality of such a norm on the level of scholarly interpretation. Certainly, in scriptural questions, changes in interpretation can be institutionalized at any moment by an authoritative pronouncement about the "consensus ecclesiae." Similarly, in legal questions, changed interpretations can be institutionalized by a pronouncement from the highest court. But in the domain of learning such pronouncements cannot carry authority. No one, for example, would hold that a law means "what the judges say a law means" if there were not a supreme tribunal to decide what, after all, the judges say. There could never be such arbitrary tribunals in the domain of knowledge and scholarship.

an aspect of most texts, as I pointed out in Chapter 2: the principle for including or excluding implications is not what the author is aware of, but whether or not the implications belong to the *type* of meaning that he wills. In the example of *Hamlet,* we rejected the implication that Hamlet wished to sleep with his mother because we posited that such an implication did not belong to the type of meaning Shakespeare willed. We did not reject it because Shakespeare failed to think of such an implication or because he could not have stated the implication in distinctly Freudian terms. These grounds are properly judged irrelevant. We rejected the implication because it was not, on our premises, the kind of trait that belonged to the type of character Shakespeare imagined. In both cases, the principle for including or excluding implications is to ask whether they are embraced by the author's will to mean "all traits belonging to this particular type."

Now the Constitution is a document that belongs to the broad genre called "laws." As an example of the kind of convention system under which such texts are composed we could give the following very simple example. Suppose, in drawing up a civil code, I write: "It shall be an offense for any automobile, bicycle, or any other wheeled vehicle, using the public road, not to come to a complete stop at a facing red light." Suppose, then, some years after the law has been enacted, there comes into use a new type of vehicle which moves on a stream of compressed air and is completely without wheels. Does the law apply to such a vehicle? Did my meaning embrace this unknown and unforeseen state of affairs? If, as a judge, I had to decide on the validity of this interpretation, I would certainly say, "Yes, the meaning is implied, and this new type of vehicle is embraced by the law." I would support my decision in this way: when the law stated "any other wheeled vehicle using the public road" the type that was willed was "any vehicle," the adjective "wheeled" being an unfortunate overspecification traceable to the fact that when the law was written all the vehicles using the public road were "wheeled." It can be reasonably inferred, therefore, that "all wheeled vehicles" embraces the meaning "all vehicles serving the function of wheeled vehicles within the purpose and intent of the law." No doubt, in my written opinion, I might recommend that the law be amended and made unambiguous, but I would have no reasonable doubt about my interpretation. I know that, since no law can predict all the future instances which will belong to the type, the conventions of lawmaking and law interpreting must include the notion of analogy. The idea of a law contains the idea of mutatis mutandis, and this generic convention was part of the meaning that I willed.[36] The compressed-air vehicle was implied in my meaning, even though I had never conceived of a compressed-air vehicle. It belonged to the willed type.

It may seem that this case has been treated differently from the Freudian interpretation of *Hamlet,* but I would quickly answer that the two examples have not in principle been treated differently at all. In the case of *Hamlet,* a judge could not properly infer Oedipal implications that were embraced "within the purpose and intent of the play," whereas he could properly make such an inference in the case of the law. In both examples the normative criterion was the author's willed meaning, and we observed that in some genres this willed meaning deliberately embraces analogous and unforeseeable implications. The will to extend implications into the unknowable future is explicitly mentioned in many laws and usually belongs to the convention system of a law whether it is mentioned or not. Of course, such an extension into the unknown is also a convention in many serious literary works where the range of willed implications is immensely broad, and it is reasonable to assume that Shakespeare intended his play to embrace the widest possible range of implications about human nature. Thus, the Freudian argument *could* be valid. (There is, as I shall suggest in the next chapter, nothing fundamentally unsound in casting an interpretation in terms that would be

36. The legal distinction between modes of construing criminal and civil laws is a purely practical and humanitarian distinction which is irrelevant to the logic of interpretation.

strange and foreign to the original author.) The mistake would not be in using Freudian terminology, but in discovering Oedipal implications that do not belong to the type of meaning Shakespeare willed. He may have willed very broad implications, but he did not necessarily will all possible ones—any more than our quoted law willed the implication "pedestrians" in the phrase "wheeled vehicles."

The principle of subsuming implications under the author's willed type is a genuinely universal principle and extends also to the interpretation of sacred scripture. But I prefer to let anyone who is at home there to make the extensions for himself. That is easily done, I think, if we remember that the requirements of validity are everywhere the same even though the requirements of interpretation vary greatly with different intrinsic genres. Validity requires a norm—a meaning that is stable and determinate no matter how broad its range of implication and application. A stable and determinate meaning requires an author's determining will, and it is sometimes important, therefore, to decide which author is the one being interpreted when we confront texts that have been spoken and respoken.[37] All valid interpretation of every sort is founded on the re-cognition of what an author meant.

---

37. The "sensus plenior," a conception in scriptural interpretation under which the text's meaning goes beyond anything the human author could have consciously intended, is, of course, a totally unnecessary entity. The human author's willed meaning can always go beyond what he consciously intended so long as it remains within his willed type, and if the meaning is conceived of as going beyond even that, then we must have recourse to a divine Author speaking through the human one. In that case it is His willed type we are trying to interpret, and the human author is irrelevant. We must not confuse his text with God's. In either instance the notion of a sense beyond the author's is illegitimate. The same point holds, of course, for inspiration in poetry: either we are interpreting the poet's text or that of the muse who possesses him, one or the other. The fact that two different minds can intend quite different meanings by the same word sequence should not by now be surprising. Nothing is gained by conflating and confusing different "texts" as though they were somehow the same simply because they both use the same word sequence.

4.

UNDERSTANDING, INTERPRETATION, AND CRITICISM

> *One could never be a rhapsode if one did not*
> *comprehend the utterances of the poet, for the*
> *rhapsode must become an interpreter of the poet's*
> *thought to those who listen, and to do this well is*
> *quite impossible unless one knows just what the*
> *poet means.*
>
> *Plato*

A. THE BABEL OF INTERPRETATIONS

The analyses and arguments of the preceding chapters have paid scant attention to the practical exigencies of textual commentary. Those chapters were concerned broadly with the conditions that make valid interpretation possible and with the unchanging theoretical principles that underlie the interpretation of all verbal texts. I have tried to show that the immense universe of verbal meaning stretching from casual conversation to epic poetry is uniformly governed by the social principle of linguistic genres and by the individual principle of authorial will. Both principles are formally necessary to the determination of verbal meaning and to its correct interpretation. In the course of these analyses, I have more than once touched on the distinction between meaning and significance and have suggested that this distinction has very great importance for practical criticism. Here my aim will be to examine some of the corollaries of that distinction in their application to the practice of criticism and ultimately to show that valid interpretation is a feasible enterprise, despite the apparent lawlessness of textual commentary from the heyday of Alexandria to the present.

Chapter 4: Understanding, Interpretation, and Criticism

How can a consensus be reached with regard to a text's meaning when every known interpretation of every text has always been different in some respect from every other interpretation of the text? The standard answer to this question is that every interpretation is partial. No single interpretation can possibly exhaust the meanings of a text. Therefore, to the extent that different interpretations bring into relief different aspects of textual meaning, the diversity of interpretations should be welcomed; they all contribute to understanding. The more interpretations one knows, the fuller will be one's understanding.

I am not suggesting that this answer is inadequate in every respect. In fact, I shall try to describe more precisely how different interpretations can and do support one another and how they can deepen our understanding. The answer is inadequate only insofar as it fails to account for the distinction between compatible and incompatible interpretations. The answer seems to assume that all "plausible" or "respectable" interpretations are compatible merely because they are all capable of being confirmed by the text. However, not all plausible interpretations are compatible. An interpretation of *Hamlet* which views the hero as a dilatory intellectual is not compatible with one that views him as a forceful man of action thwarted by circumstances. Both interpretations are plausible, and perhaps both are incorrect, but they are not compatible. Nor would their incompatibility be removed by concluding that both traits are present in Hamlet's character. That compromise would represent a third interpretation distinct from and incompatible with each of the other two.[1] Interpretive disagreements do exist, and they are not always partial or trivial disagreements.

But the fact that all interpretations are different warrants neither the sanguine belief that all plausible interpretations are helpful and compatible nor the hopeless proposition that all

---

1. See Appendix I, pp. 227–30.

128

interpretations are personal, temporal, and incommensurable. The apparent babel of interpretations leads to tender-mindedness or despair only if we fail to discriminate between the kinds of differences which interpretations exhibit. All interpretations are indeed different in some respect or other, but not all different interpretations are disparate or incompatible. For example, two interpretations could be different in a vast number of ways—the subjects they treat, the vocabulary in which they are written, the purposes they are designed to serve—yet might nevertheless refer to an identical construction of meaning. On the other hand, two interpretations might be highly similar in vocabulary and purpose but might nevertheless refer to two quite different constructions of meaning. Only the second kind of difference ought properly to be at issue, and in that case we should speak not of different but of disparate interpretations.

This distinction between the meaning of an interpretation and the construction of meaning to which the interpretation refers is one of the most venerable in hermeneutic theory. Ernesti called it the distinction between the art of understanding and the art of explaining—the *subtilitas intelligendi* and the *subtilitas explicandi*.[2] In normal usage both of these functions are embraced flaccidly by the single term "interpretation," but clarity would be served if we limited that word to the *subtilitas explicandi*—the explanation of meaning—and delimited the *subtilitas intelligendi* by the term "understanding."

It is obvious that understanding is prior to and different from interpretation. Anyone who has written a commentary on a text has been aware that he could adopt a number of quite different strategies to convey his understanding and, furthermore, that the strategy he does adopt depends upon his audience and his purposes quite as much as it depends upon his understanding of the text. On the other hand, every reader of interpretations has noticed that he accepts some of them and

2. J. A. Ernesti, *Institutio Interpretis Novi Testamenti* (Leipzig, 1761), Chap. 1, Sec. 4. Referred to by Schleiermacher in *Hermeneutik*, p. 31.

rejects others and, furthermore, that even when he finds himself in agreement with an interpretation its effect upon him is not always simply to confirm his original conception. Sometimes, it is true, an interpretation merely "deepens" his understanding, but sometimes it may genuinely "alter" his understanding. These two functions illustrate very well the distinction between different and disparate interpretations. When a commentary deepens our understanding of a text, we do not experience any sense of conflict with our previous ideas. The new commentary does indeed lay out implications we had not thought of explicitly, but it does not alter our controlling conception of the text's meaning. We find ourselves in agreement from the beginning, and we admire the subtlety with which the interpreter brings out implications we had missed or had only dimly perceived. But this "deepening" effect, instead of changing our original understanding, emphatically confirms it and makes us more certain of its rightness. The unnoticed implications laid out by the interpreter belong to the type of meaning we had already construed. On the other hand, when we read a commentary that alters our understanding, we are convinced by an argument (covert or open) that shows our original construction to be wrong in some respect. Instead of being comforted by a further confirmation, we are compelled to change, qualify, adjust our original view. The two functions of "deepening" and "altering" are quite distinct and correspond to the two ways in which interpretations differ. A very brief and elliptical commentary might be in complete agreement with a long and "inclusive" one, since both could refer to precisely the same controlling conception of meaning. In that case the interpretations would be different but not disparate.

In the final chapter I shall consider the problem of discriminating between disparate interpretations, and also the corollary problem of deciding which of them is most likely to be right. However, here it is more important to emphasize the fact that two different interpretations are not necessarily disparate, for all interpretations are different, and if no two of them could be identified, then there could be no discipline of interpretation. Of course, any two interpretations will always be concerned with different sorts and ranges of implications, but they will not necessarily differ in their conception of the implications they treat in common or in the importance they allot to those implications with respect to the controlling purposes and emphases of the text. Two interpretations that differ in this way can refer to an absolutely identical meaning. How is this possible? Is it not imprecise to overlook the subtle variations in meaning suggested by subtle variations in written commentaries? Is it not the case that meaning can never break away completely from the categories that an interpreter happens to use?

I have already suggested that the art of interpreting and the art of understanding are separate functions, too often confused. Two interpreters might, after all, use different strategies and categories to convey the same conception of meaning, but the exigencies of written commentary do not account for all the differences among interpretations. Some of these differences are owing to the fact that interpreters notice and emphasize different aspects of meaning—even on the level of understanding. In such a case is it possible or reasonable to assert that their interpretations refer to the same construction of meaning? Even if their interpretations were broadly compatible, is it not farfetched to assert that they are ultimately identical? What they say is always different, but is it not also true that what they *see* is always different? Is not the babel of interpretations still, after all, a babel?

These questions touch on the same group of problems that had to be faced in dealing with the reproducibility of meaning and with the psychologistic conception of meaning. Certainly, it can be reasonably presumed that two interpreters always notice slightly different aspects of meaning even on the level of understanding, but the different aspects might nevertheless be traits belonging to the same type. Similarly, the different meanings which different readers of a text might notice can refer to precisely the same type—which is to say, to the same meaning. This principle is constantly being exemplified in visual experience. When two observers look at a building from different standpoints, they each see quite different aspects of the building, yet, remarkably enough, both observers see the same whole building. They may not even be looking at the same sides, yet each of them imagines (vaguely or explicitly) the unseen sides—otherwise, they would not conceive the object as a building. Thus, while the explicit components of vision are in each case different, what those components refer to may be absolutely identical. A similar phenomenon occurs when one interpreter notices or emphasizes traits that are different from those noticed by another. The explicit components of meaning are different, yet the reference is to a whole meaning, not a partial one, and this object of reference may be the same for both interpreters. That is why a brief and elliptical comment on a text can be in complete agreement with a detailed exegesis. Their mutual compatibility is not based on their incompleteness or partiality, but quite the contrary on the identity of the whole meaning to which they refer.

The intentionality of understanding and interpretation, which I have just been describing, and which I discuss at greater length in Appendix III, is the foundation for the discipline of interpretation as a field of knowledge. Of course, the main purpose of textual commentary is often not to make the meaning of a text understood by others, but rather to indicate its value, to judge its importance, to describe its bearings on present or past situations, to exploit it in support of an argument, or to use it as a source of biographical and historical knowledge. These legitimate concerns of textual commentary, and many similar ones, belong to the domain of criticism. Clarity requires that this function—that of criticism —should be distinguished from interpretation. In ordinary speech it is convenient to lump these several functions—understanding, interpretation, judgment, and criticism—under the term "criticism," and certainly, in practice, these functions are so entangled and codependent that a separation could seem artificial. But the same might be said of many codependent aspects of reality—light and heat, form and content, color and extension. The fact that the functions of criticism are entangled together does not necessitate an imitative confusion of thought. Understanding, interpretation, judgment, and criticism are distinct functions with distinct requirements and aims. That they are always copresent in any written commentary and that they always influence one another are facts that must be reckoned with in this chapter.

B. UNDERSTANDING, INTERPRETATION, AND HISTORY

Understanding speech—either spoken or written—is within the capacity of anyone who can himself speak or write. Because of the inherent double-sidedness of speech, the act of speaking implies in itself a projected or imagined act of understanding. Indeed, one central idea in my discussion of genres was that the genre conception which controls speaking closely parallels the genre conception which controls understanding. A great deal has been written about the theory and practice of understanding, especially in the German tradition, where the word *Verstehen* has long since taken on the grandeur of an institutional slogan and still carries the emotional overtones and the conceptual vagueness that such slogans generally acquire.[3] Certainly the psychology of understanding is an intensely fascinating subject that has been fruitfully studied both by linguists and psychologists, but it is not a subject that has a central place in this book: from the standpoint of interpretation as a discipline, the psychological process of understanding is neither a theoretical nor a practical problem. Everybody who thinks he understands an utterance certainly does understand some meaning or other. The appropriate subject for this dis-

3. See, for example, the historical account in J. Wach, *Das Verstehen* (3 vols. Tübingen, 1926–33).

133

cussion, therefore, is not how to understand but how to judge and criticize what one does understand. The problem is to decide whether one's understanding is probably correct. This is ultimately the problem of validation, which is the subject of my final chapter. In this section I shall discuss some of the more direct consequences of the simple (and generally ignored) fact that understanding is not an immediate given but is always a construction from physical signs.

The definitive proof that understanding requires an active construction of meaning and is not simply given by the text is the obvious fact that no one can understand an utterance who does not know the language in which it is composed. This would seem to be trivial, but trivial truths can imply far from trivial conclusions. It implies, first of all, that understanding is autonomous, that it occurs entirely within the terms and proprieties of the text's own language and the shared realities which that language embraces. To understand an utterance it is, in fact, not just desirable but absolutely unavoidable that we understand it in its own terms. We could not possibly recast a text's meanings in different terms unless we had already understood the text in its own. Every speaker and every interpreter must have mastered the convention systems and the shared meaning associations presupposed by a linguistic utterance.

The mastery of these necessary conventions (required for any construction of meaning from linguistic signs) may be called the philological presuppositions of all understanding. Here the word "philological" is to be taken in the older, broader sense which comprises the whole range of shared realities and conventions—concrete and social, as well as linguistic—which are required in order to construe meaning. Verbal meaning can be construed only on the basis of its own presuppositions, which are not given from some other realm but must be learned and guessed at—a process that is entirely intrinsic to a particular social and linguistic system. The obvious fact that we cannot understand a Greek text when we happen to know only English remains true at the most subtle levels of understanding.

B. Understanding, Interpretation, and History

One cannot understand meaning without guessing or learning the prerequisites to construing meaning, and since all understanding is "silent"—that is, cast only in its own terms and not in foreign categories—it follows that all skeptical historicism is founded on a misconception of the nature of understanding.

That is the most important consequence of the "trivial" point that one has to know the language of a text in order to understand it. The skeptical historicist infers too much from the fact that present-day experiences, categories, and modes of thought are not the same as those of the past. He concludes that we can only understand a text in *our* own terms, but this is a contradictory statement since verbal meaning has to be construed in *its* own terms if it is to be construed at all. Of course, the convention systems under which a text was composed may not in fact be those which we assume when we construe the text, but this has no bearing on the theoretical issue, since no one denies that misunderstanding is not only possible but sometimes, perhaps, unavoidable. The skeptical historicist goes further than this. He argues—to return to our previous analogy —that a native speaker of English has to understand a Greek text in English rather than in Greek. He converts the plausible idea that the mastery of unfamiliar meanings is arduous and uncertain into the idea that we always have to impose our own alien conventions and associations. But this is simply not true. If we do not construe a text in what we rightly or wrongly assume to be its own terms then we do not construe it at all. We do not understand anything that we could subsequently recast in our own terms.[4]

Understanding is silent, interpretation extremely garrulous.

4. See Appendix II, pp. 252–54. The perspectivism of the radical historicist is not radical enough by half. He forgets that meaning itself is perspective-bound and that, in order to understand verbal meaning from any era including his own, the interpreter has to submit to a double perspective. He preserves his own standpoint and, at the same time, imaginatively realizes the standpoint of the speaker. This is a characteristic of all verbal intercourse.

Interpretation—the *subtilitas explicandi*—rarely exists in pure form, except in paraphrase or translation. Just as understanding is a *construction* of meaning (not of significance, which I discuss later on), so interpretation is an *explanation* of meaning. However, most commentaries that we call interpretations are concerned with significance as well as meaning. They constantly draw analogies and point out relationships which not only help us to understand meaning but also lead us to perceive values and relevancies. But while interpretations are almost always mixed with criticism, they nevertheless always refer to meaning as well, and if the meaning referred to is wrong, the interpretation is wrong too—no matter how valuable it may be in other respects.

If we isolate for a moment the interpretive function of commentaries as distinct from their critical function, we will observe that the art of explaining nearly always involves the task of discussing meaning in terms that are not native to the original text. Of course, this is not constantly true: many good interpreters quote frequently from the original, and one of the best interpretive devices is simply to read a text aloud to an audience. But all interpretations at some point have recourse to categories and conceptions that are not native to the original. A translation or paraphrase tries to render the meaning in new terms; an explanation tries to point to the meaning in new terms. That is why interpretation, like translation, is an art, for the interpreter has to find means of conveying to the uninitiated, in terms familiar to them, those presuppositions and meanings which are equivalent to those in the original meaning. However, different modes of interpretation can, as I have already shown, refer to the very same construction of the original meaning.

The fact that different interpretations can be in agreement throws into perspective the old nostrum that every age must reinterpret the great works of the past. This is a comforting truth to each new generation of critics who earn their bread by reinterpreting, but it is a truth of very limited application. To

B. Understanding, Interpretation, and History

the extent that textual commentary functions as interpretation in the strict sense, and not as criticism, the old nostrum simply means that every age requires a different vocabulary and strategy of interpretation.[5] Indeed, each different sort of audience requires a different strategy of interpretation, as all teachers and lecturers are aware. The historicity of all interpretations is an undoubted fact, because the historical givens with which an interpreter must reckon—the language and the concerns of his audience—vary from age to age. However, this by no means implies that the meaning of the text varies from age to age, or that anybody, who has done whatever is required to understand that meaning, understands a different meaning from his predecessors of an earlier age. No doubt Coleridge understood *Hamlet* rather differently from Professor Kittredge. That fact is reflected in their disparate interpretations, but it would be quite wrong to conclude that this disparity was caused merely by the fact that they lived in different periods. It would do both Coleridge and Kittredge an injustice to argue that the times necessitated their manner of understanding, or even that their positions could not be reversed. Both of them would have agreed that at least one of them must be wrong. On the other hand, even if they had entertained the same conception of *Hamlet,* they could not have *written* about the play in the same way. Their purposes, their times, and their audiences were different and so, therefore, were their styles of exposition, their emphases, and their categories. However, the historicity of interpretation is quite distinct from the timelessness of understanding.

5. What is primarily meant by the nostrum is that each new critic or age finds new sorts of significance, new strands of relevance to particular cultural or intellectual contexts. Usually, therefore, it is more descriptive to say that each age must *recriticize* the works of the past in order to keep them alive and ourselves alive to them. As critics we should remind ourselves that we are not perceiving a new work or a new meaning, but a new significance of the work which often could not exist except in our own cultural milieu. That phenomenon in itself proves the relational character of significance.

Chapter 4: Understanding, Interpretation, and Criticism

All serious students of texts from the past—texts of any genre—are historians. It is not surprising that literary scholars should be particularly sensitive to the formative influence of historical givens and should observe that critics of the past have not only interpreted differently but have understood differently from critics in the present. And it may indeed be true that a larger proportion of readers could correctly understand Donne in 1930 than in 1730, and this may have been entirely due to the intellectual atmosphere of the times. But these far from surprising possibilities do not have the theoretical importance that is usually attached to them. Not all readers of the same era tend to understand a text in the same way—as we know from our present-day experience. Furthermore, the emphases and categories which characterized the interpretations of a particular time are not the same as the emphases and categories of its understanding. All understanding is necessarily and by nature intrinsic, all interpretation necessarily transient and historical.

A colleague once pointed out to me that Simone Weil could not have written so brilliantly on the way *The Iliad* discloses the role of brute force in human life if she had not passed through the horrors of Nazism, and, furthermore, that her emphasis on this aspect of *The Iliad* would not have struck a responsive chord in her readers if they had not also witnessed those times. In this observation we can see how closely connected in practice are understanding, interpretation, and criticism, and how necessary it is to distinguish them in theory. Surely Simone Weil's emphasis on the role of force in *The Iliad* brilliantly exploited the experiences she shared with her audience, and probably she did not overemphasize the role of force within Homer's imagination. The element of *criticism* in her commentary was her implication that Homer was right— human life is like that, and we, in this age, know it. The element of *interpretation* in her commentary was her laying out in an ordered way Homer's implications about the role of force in life. But we do not respond to her interpretation just because we live in a violent age; we agree with it because we too have read *The Iliad* and have perceived that same meaning—even if we have not perceived it so explicitly. I cannot imagine any competent reader of any past age who did not implicitly grasp this meaning in *The Iliad,* though I can certainly imagine a time when readers did not feel this meaning to be a comment on life worthy of a special monograph.

If an interpreter exercises tact, he can emphasize any matter or theme he likes without suggesting a false emphasis. A single qualifying comment from time to time, a passing modest disclaimer, or an acknowledgment of the place his theme has in the meaning of the whole will suffice to avoid giving a false impression. It does not matter what one says about a text so long as one understands it and conveys that understanding to a reader. There are no correct "methods" of interpretation, no uniquely appropriate categories. One does what is necessary to convey an understanding to a particular audience. There are many ways of catching a possum. In his function as an interpreter, the critic's first job is to discover which possum he should catch.

C. JUDGMENT AND CRITICISM

The limitation of verbal meaning to what an author meant and the definition of understanding as the construction of that meaning does not, as I have shown, constitute a narrow and purist notion of meaning. Both meaning and understanding embrace a world that can surpass the mental cosmos of any too-limited interpreter and tax his imagination to the utmost. Furthermore, the definition places no rigid limit on the number of implications verbal meaning might have, though at some point the drawing of further, similar implications becomes trivial. My purpose in defining understanding and meaning is not to suggest that the task of understanding is easily managed but to show that it is a determinate task that can be distinguished from other tasks. In particular, I have earnestly desired to clear up the confusion between meaning and significance in order to diminish the skepticism to which that confusion has, I think, generously contributed.

Earlier, I defined significance as any perceived relationship between construed verbal meaning and something else. In practice we are always relating our understanding to something else —to ourselves, to our relevant knowledge, to the author's personality, to other, similar works. Usually we cannot even understand a text without perceiving such relationships, for we cannot artificially isolate the act of construing verbal meaning from all those other acts, perceptions, associations, and judgments which accompany that act and which are instrumental in leading us to perform it. Nevertheless, we certainly can isolate or at least emphasize a particular goal for our activity. We can decide at a given moment that we are mainly interested in construing what the author meant rather than in relating that meaning to something else; we can devote our attention to that meaning and can use all our related knowledge entirely in the service of that goal. On the other hand, we could assume that we have already rightly understood what the author meant and could devote our attention entirely to placing that meaning in some context or relationship. Normally we adopt neither sort of goal exclusively. Sometimes the relationships we perceive are used heuristically in the service of construing meaning; sometimes they themselves are the objects of attention. Almost all commentaries about texts discuss these relationships both for their own sake and for the sake of inducing an understanding of the text's meaning. All textual commentary is a mixture of interpretation and criticism, though usually a choice has been made as to which goal is to receive the main emphasis.

We cannot, therefore, say in advance whether a particular sort of statement is interpretive or critical. To say that *The Waste Land* is an allusive poem is certainly to perceive a relationship between the poem and a wider class or attribute system, but this perceived relationship might be used entirely in the service of orienting another person to Eliot's meaning, not in calling his attention to the similarities or dissimilarities of Eliot's poem to other works or in pointing to some other kind of relationship. On the other hand, the statement could simply assume an understanding of Eliot's poem on the reader's part and could point entirely to some other dimension in which the allusiveness of *The Waste Land* illustrated the mood of the late teens and early twenties, Eliot's intellectual snobbery, the originality of the poem's idiom, or anything else that could be conceived. In the first case the statement would be directed primarily toward a perception of the work's meaning; in the second it would be directed primarily toward a perception of its significance with respect to some context or other. Yet the indication of significance assumes that a prior construction of meaning has been made, and the indication of meaning exploits a relationship, which is to say, a significance. The two functions and goals are distinct, though they are never separate in textual commentary.

The distinction between interpretation and criticism, meaning and significance, points to a phenomenon that is not limited to textual commentary. It represents a universal distinction that applies to all fields of study and all subject matters. In the field of biography, for example, interpretation corresponds to the understanding of a man's life as it was lived and experienced, while criticism corresponds to the placing of that life in a larger system of relationships. It is one thing to trace the life of the Duke of Marlborough and another thing to discuss the significance of his life with respect to European political history in the seventeenth and eighteenth centuries, or to such exemplary moral values as prudence and patience, or to the development of constitutional monarchy. Biography would be a poor thing without such criticism, but everyone would agree that there is a difference between a man's life on the one hand, and its significance within various historical, moral, and social contexts, on the other. Similarly, if one's subject matter is a still wider domain such as the English party system in the seventeenth century, it is one thing to describe that system, another to relate it to later developments in English politics. One's subject matter can be as large or as small as he likes, but the distinction between understanding the subject matter and placing it in some context or relationship will always be a viable one that will help him to keep in mind just what his subject matter is and just what aspects of its significance he wishes to lay bare.

That is why my rigid separation of meaning and significance with respect to textual commentary is less artificial than it might at first appear. I must remind the reader once more that I am using these words very strictly in order to bring into relief those aspects of textual commentary which function in the service of a common discipline and can lead to shared knowledge. The term "understanding" is generally used to embrace not only the perception of an author's meaning, but also the perception of how that meaning fits into his world or our own. This use is legitimate, because "understanding" implies knowledge, and the perception of significance belongs as much to genuine knowledge as does the perception of verbal meaning. But one great difference justifies a stricter definition for the purpose of analysis: when we construe another's meaning we are not free agents. So long as the meaning of his utterance is our object, we are completely subservient to his will, because the meaning of his utterance is the meaning he wills to convey. Once we have construed his meaning, however, we are quite independent of his will. We do not have to accept any longer the values and assumptions he entertained. We can relate his meaning to anything we want and value it as we please.[6] On the other hand, so long as our object is knowledge, we are still

6. Even in this case, however, we cannot completely relinquish the author's perspective (i.e. his values and categories) since his meaning is permanently bound to (i.e. constituted by) his perspective. We must continue to entertain his viewpoint even when we find it false or inadequate, since we cannot construe or continue to possess his meaning except from his perspective. Valid criticism necessarily entails this double perspective.

not completely free. We emancipate ourselves from the author only to be enslaved (if we are honest and percipient) by whatever reality it is to which we have chosen to relate his work. However, this is a new kind of subservience and ought to be given a different name. By "understanding," therefore, I mean a perception or construction of the author's verbal meaning, nothing more, nothing less. The significance of that meaning, its relation to ourselves, to history, to the author's personality, even to the author's other works can be something equally objective and is frequently even more important. What shall we call that function by which we perceive significance?

The obvious choice is "judgment": one understands meaning; one judges significance. In the first instance, one submits to another—literally, one stands under him. In the second, one acts independently—by one's own authority—like a judge. However, there is one difficulty. In common usage "judgment" implies an act of evaluation, of weighing, and significance, while it embraces value judgments, includes descriptive judgments as well. But sanction for this broader use of the term comes from logic, where a judgment is the binding together of any two relata—a "subject" and a "predicate"—by some kind of copula which defines the relationship. The act of judging is the construing of this relationship, whether it be that between a meaning and criteria of value or between a meaning and anything else imaginable.

The patient reader must be prepared for one final terminological refinement. Instead of following the standard practice of calling all essays about texts by the name "criticism," I have sometimes found it convenient to use the more neutral term "commentary" and to reserve the term "criticism" for commentary that is primarily about significance. This parallels my use of the term "interpretation" to name commentary that is primarily about meaning. I have already suggested that interpretation and criticism are both present in all textual commentary and that the two functions can be distinguished only by deciding which goal is preeminent, but I think it important to remind ourselves of these different goals, if only to make clear that significance is distinct from criticism in precisely the same way that meaning is distinct from interpretation. Criticism is not identical with significance, but rather refers to it, talks about it, describes it. By analogy with my previous analysis, two pieces of criticism can refer to the same significance even though the commentaries are quite different. This reemphasizes the point that significance is in a given instance just as determinate and real as meaning and is very often more important. Criticism is, by its nature, more valuable than interpretation alone, particularly when it is criticism which embraces interpretation. Moreover, significance is just as much an object of knowledge as meaning is. Value relationships as well as other relationships can be accurately perceived and conveyed. Perhaps the most important function of criticism as distinguished from interpretation is to show that a work is valuable or valueless in some respect. But in what respect? Is there one, most valid type of criticism? Is there such a thing as "intrinsic criticism"? This is a subject to which I shall largely devote the next section.

D. INTRINSIC CRITICISM

Since criticism is that field of endeavor which describes the relationships of texts to larger contexts of reality and value, it would seem that the phrase "intrinsic criticism" (a shibboleth of modern critical theory) is either a contradiction in terms or a pointless redundancy. For criticism is always intrinsic to the particular subject matter within which some aspect of the text has been placed and is always extrinsic to textual meaning itself, insofar as the critic directs his attention to concepts and criteria which lie outside that meaning. There is therefore a puzzle in the idea of intrinsic criticism. A literary (i.e. intrinsic) criticism of literature, a philosophical criticism of philosophy— what does this kind of notion amount to? In considering this currently important problem, my focus will be on literary criticism, but for the most part the analysis ought to hold good when "religious" or "philosophical" or "scientific" or "historical" or "conversational" is substituted for "literary."

As everyone knows, the recent preoccupation of scholars with a literary consideration of literature is partly the outcome of a reaction against nineteenth-century positivism and its concern for brute facts and causal patterns. Modern students of literature have objected justly that the analogy of literary science with natural science is as unworkable as it is uninformative. Literature is a subject matter peculiar to itself, requiring its own intrinsic concepts and methods; to treat it in terms of alien concepts is to neglect two central and paramount aspects —meaning and value. Nowadays there are few critics in Europe or America who do not share these objections to naïve forms of positivism.

On the other hand, the renewed impulse to discuss what a text means rather than how, when, or where it was caused is the continuation of a tradition that is far more venerable than the positivism against which modern scholars reacted. Close commentary, particularly on religious texts, goes back farther than any recorded interpretations to an ancient tradition of teaching and oral exegesis. Consequently, the interpretive side of the new movement was not what was new in it, for the primary aim of close commentary has always been interpretation, not criticism. Of course, the establishment of the word "criticism" as an all-embracing term for commentary (as René Wellek tells us) does go back to the seventeenth and eighteenth centuries and has remained the dominant term in England and America.[7] But Emil Staiger, in his version of the new sort of intrinsic literary commentary, prefers the term "interpretation," a word that is very often more descriptive of modern practice.[8] The phrase "intrinsic interpretation," however, is

7. René Wellek, "The Term and Concept of Literary Criticism," in *Concepts of Criticism,* ed. S. Nichols, Jr. (New Haven, 1963).
8. Staiger, *Die Kunst der Interpretation,* pp. 9–33.

obviously a redundancy. All interpretation is necessarily intrinsic because the exclusive object of interpretation is understanding, which, as I have demonstrated, is by nature intrinsic.[9] But the modern movement has aimed not just at a literary interpretation of literature, but a literary criticism of literature, and intrinsic criticism is another matter altogether.

A great deal of effort has gone into the formulation of special terms that are peculiarly appropriate for discussing special kinds of texts, and this effort has been for the most part highly fruitful. As I argued in the previous chapter, however, the language of commentary can never have an absolute validity or appropriateness and is to be valued entirely by its practical effectiveness in pointing to meaning and significance. No one vocabulary is more intrinsic than another for all purposes and audiences; when scholars use a common vocabulary it is because such shared terms are serviceable for a field of study, not because the terms themselves have an absolute and unalterable status. Furthermore, the principal function of a special vocabulary is the delineation of a special field of interest, and the effect of such a vocabulary is therefore to focus attention on a particular subject matter that is wider than the text itself—such as rhetoric, or psychology, or some favored conception of the "nature of literature." In short, the use of a special vocabulary does not in itself make criticism intrinsic. The idea of intrinsic criticism is fundamentally an idea about a special, preferred context within which literary texts ought to be considered.

When the call went forth for a literary study of literature, it was understood, I think, that this special, preferred context ought not to be history, biography, morality, or society, but the realm of literature itself. The relationships to be discussed were those that subsisted between a literary text and others belonging to the same broad genre, or to the same literary "tradition," or simply to literature in general. Eliot defined one

9. See above pp. 134–35.

version of this special, preferred context when he spoke of the "simultaneous order" of all literary texts. In one form or another (and there have been many forms), this is the implicit conception under which a great amount of modern academic criticism has been carried out. The conception has been a generously tolerant one, permitting the critic to conceive his context as the discipline of rhetoric, the domain of art in general, a particular literary tradition selected or created by himself, a period of literature, a genre of literature, or as the literary or imaginative world of a man or a period. In other words, the literary context can be as broad and as variable as one could wish, provided only that its components are taken primarily from the world of literature—that is, from literary texts—and not from external nonliterary dimensions of reality, such as psychology, economics, technology, or sociology—unless these domains have been assimilated to literature itself. While this conception has by no means governed all criticism (the obvious exceptions are Freudian and Marxist varieties), it has remained dominant and has won the loyalty of most scholar-critics.

The right of such a conception to a preferred or special status can in one respect be granted without hesitation. The discussion of literary texts within the context of literature is a form of criticism that is by nature closely allied to interpretation. If the broader context is literature, it follows that whatever is discovered about the nature of literature can be directly helpful in understanding the nature of a particular text that belongs to literature—just as botany can be more directly helpful in understanding the nature of a tree than physics or meteorology. In broad terms, it is fair to say that the subject matter of the modern movement has been literature itself— its nature, its special characteristics, its dominant and recurring patterns. Because of its emphasis on verbal analysis, this modern literary study of literature has been of great importance in forwarding the discipline of interpretation and, for that reason alone, has been of immense value. Nevertheless, the broad context of literature in general is obviously not always the most helpful context for interpretation. Botany is more directly useful in understanding a tree than is physics, but even more useful than botany is its special branch called forestry, and within forestry it is still more directly useful to know all about the peculiarities of the particular kind of tree one wants to understand. In other words, to place literary texts within the general context of literature may be highly useful, but it is not automatically a specially privileged mode of proceeding. Furthermore, the special value of a particular kind of criticism is not in any case to be found in its value to interpretation, since the object of criticism is not the object of interpretation at all. Hence, the claim that literature is the proper context for criticizing literary texts has to derive its sanction elsewhere. For if it is interpretation and not criticism which justifies the literary study of literature, then self-consciously literary criticism becomes a handmaiden of no greater instrumental value than any other subject matter (like philology or history) which subserves interpretation. What then is the special justification for a literary criticism of literature?

I know of two answers that have been given by modern theorists. First, the only proper way to evaluate a literary work is to judge it as literature and not as some other thing. Second, literature is a specially privileged subject matter which tells us more about man in his depth and breadth than any other discipline. This second justification will have force for anyone who devotes his energies to the study of literature, but it is not an argument about the special appropriateness of literature as the context for criticizing literary works. It is an argument about the value of one branch of humane studies, and a somewhat provincial argument at that—one which a historian or a philosopher would not find specially compelling. It converts, really, the study of literature into a branch of philosophical anthropology. At least two important theorists —Emil Staiger and Northrop Frye—embrace this consequence with enthusiasm, and he would be dull of spirit who did not to some extent share their enthusiasm for so important and exciting a subject. But the viewpoint is provincial to the extent that it excludes nonliterary phenomena from philosophical anthropology. The literary critic has his contribution to make to that broad field, but he has no valid reason other than convenience for limiting his context entirely to literature. The only really compelling justification for an exclusively literary criticism of literature is the first argument: that the proper way to evaluate a literary work is to judge it as literature and not as something else. This is the single crucial and viable issue in the programmatic ideal of a literary criticism of literature.

To understand a poem as a poem is an aim that has every right to be considered privileged, since that is the only understanding of a poem that can possibly exist. Until the nature and purposes of a text have been grasped, its meaning will remain inaccessible, because its meaning is precisely something willed, something purposed. If I *understand* a poem as a newspaper headline (assuming that it is not a newspaper headline poem), then I have simply misunderstood it. Moreover, it might seem particularly silly to *evaluate* a poem as a newspaper headline (or—a thing Robert Graves once did to "The Solitary Reaper" —as a cablegram), since the criteria would be completely irrelevant to the author's aims and purposes.[10] Thus it would seem that the only proper way to evaluate a poem is as a poem and not as some irrelevant kind of instrumental value within a nonliterary context.

Up to this point most critics are in agreement; beyond this point there is confusion and controversy. While the problems raised are extremely complex, the basic reason for this confusion and controversy is quite simple: agreement has never been reached as to what a poem is and what its implicit aims and purposes are. While there may be some small measure of

10. See Robert Graves, "Wordsworth by Cable," *The New Republic, 137* (Sept. 9, 1957), 10–13: SOLITARY HIGHLAND LASS REAPING BINDING GRAIN STOP MELANCHOLY SONG OVERFLOWS PROFOUND VALE.

agreement about which poems are good "as poems," there is far less agreement about what makes them good, that is, about the special criteria they have managed to fulfill. Furthermore, this disagreement is bound to continue because the assumptions on which the controversy is usually conducted are mistaken. It is, for example, a mistake to assume that poetry is a special substance whose essential attributes can be found throughout all those texts that we call poetry. These essential attributes have never been (and never will be) defined in a way that compels general acceptance. I have argued in the previous chapter that poetry is not a substance but a vague grouping of intrinsic genres whose members do not share any single, universal attribute or set of attributes which distinguishes them from nonpoetry. The same can be said of literature or of any other broad grouping of texts. In other words, the judging of a particular poem as a poem is an inherently impossible task, a misconceived task disguised by a verbal repetition. It is proper to judge something according to its nature, but such rough, serviceable notions as "literature" and "poetry" do not have any nature beyond a very complex and variable system of family resemblances.

My Wittgensteinian skepticism with respect to the judgment of literature as literature or poems as poems would not seem to apply to the genre criticism associated with neo-Aristotelian theory, which acknowledges that no single standard or set of standards is appropriate to all forms of literature or poetry. According to this theory, the proper norms are to be determined from the genre to which the particular text belongs: the proper way to judge a lyric poem is not as a poem but as a lyric poem. Yet, does the broad genre called lyric poetry have a status that is different in principle from the still broader genres called "poetry" and "literature"? Is there an implicit purpose or norm shared by all lyric poems as distinguished from other genres? Are not the boundary edges just as fuzzy in this case as they were in the others? Suppose we defined a lyric poem rigorously as any poem shorter than two hundred lines. Would this admittedly unambiguous definition serve as the basis for determining norms implicit to all poems of the class? And if we formulated other definitions which did imply intrinsic norms, would these obtain for all texts that we call lyric poems? I firmly doubt it, because groupings like lyric poems or even narrower groupings like elegies, odes, and effusions are not species ideas at all, but vague categories with fuzzy edges that have been developed by historical accretion and conceptual convenience.

My objections to these generalized conceptions of so-called intrinsic evaluation can be stated in another way. It is not merely an error of description to say that all texts of a certain broad class share the same broad aims and implicit norms; it is also an error of conception. A text that is subsumed under a particular category should not be thought to partake of the peculiar nature of that category, to be helplessly trapped in it, and to lack a will of its own. Under this conception, if I write a novel, then what I write must partake of the nature and the implicit aims of a novel. But what if my aims are, either from ignorance or genius or perversity, different from those implicit generic aims? Would any of the following criticisms of my novel be intrinsic? "It is a bad novel because it doesn't do what a novel should do." "It is bad because it doesn't succeed in being a novel." "It is bad because, whatever it might be called, its aims are of little or no value." Obviously, all of these criticisms might be both useful and valid, but none of them can properly be called intrinsic. The aims and norms of a text are determined not by the category we happen to place it in, but by the aims and norms which the author entertained and, under the broadest conception of communicability, managed to convey.

Genuinely intrinsic judgment is founded entirely on the author's aims and norms and is nowadays too frequently underrated as an important form of judgment. If I write a book in which one of my aims is clarity, and if because of stylistic and conceptual ineptitude I do not succeed in making my ideas clear, then it is a highly valuable form of criticism for me as an author and for my readers if someone points out where and how I have succeeded or failed in my aim. On the other hand, extrinsic criticism is usually of equal or greater importance. I might not have aimed at clarity at all, and yet, perhaps, I should have done so—not because my *kind* of book intrinsically ought to be clear (no entelechy beyond my own will applies to an intrinsic genre which has been determined by my communicable will), but because I should have written another kind of book. The kind I chose to write is, for some reason or other and in some respect or other, not a very valuable undertaking. Both forms of evaluation are important and valid, but no trick of thought can convert the second form into intrinsic evaluation.

If I write lyric poetry in which some of my aims are to achieve a perfect phenomenology of perception, a total indifference to emotion, and a deliberate breaking away from the so-called connotative dimension of individual words, I might very well fail because the form I chose might not allow me to fulfill aims so much at variance with the usual aims of texts written in that form. Yet suppose I managed, by singleness of purpose and by sheer quantity of production, to educate my readers to my new convention system. Suppose I produced three volumes of the following sort of thing:

> Outside, external and beyond the window
> And above, below, and on the window
> Was the sight of light, of dark, of the park
> Of the hill and the sky—through and on the window,
> Beyond and in the window.

If a critic then said, "This is not really poetry because poetry aims at the evocation of emotion and exploits the connotative values of words," would his statement be a fiat or a description? If it is a description, it is not in itself an evaluation; if it is a fiat, it is not intrinsic criticism.

D. Intrinsic Criticism

Let me give another example. In an appendix to this book
I have adversely criticized H.-G. Gadamer's treatise on interpretation because his conception cannot provide any satisfactory norm of validity. In making this objection I was perfectly aware that Gadamer was not much interested in the
problem of validity, that he was concerned with quite another
sort of problem, namely, how the historicity of understanding
affects the conduct of interpretation. Therefore my criticism
is extrinsic—particularly since I deny some of the basic assumptions on which his inquiry was conducted. But does that
in itself make my criticism invalid? Simply in order to understand Gadamer's book I had to see what he was up to, and I
could see that he fulfilled his purpose impressively. However,
as a critic, do I not have a right (perhaps a duty) to judge his
purpose by extrinsic criteria, particularly if I believe that purpose to be misguided or deleterious in some respect? If I had
limited myself to intrinsic criticism, I would not have undertaken the essay at all, since it would have been for the most
part singularly uninteresting to me and my readers. Intrinsic
criticism is not always useless, and it is certainly an aid to
sympathetic understanding, but it is frequently the least interesting form of judgment. Certainly it is not of much use when
we want to know whether one text is more valuable in some
respect than another.

Furthermore, intrinsic criticism is rather difficult to practice,
since a silly aim cannot always be distinguished from a technical ineptitude. If somebody wants to write a vague and un-
clear essay it is useless to criticize his stylistic competence: it is
much more to the point to criticize his attitudes, values, and
lack of common sense—all very extrinsic criteria. The anti-
intentionalists are surely right when they insist than an author's
aim is not to be taken for his accomplishment, his wish for
his deed, since the whole point of intrinsic criticism is to contrast the wish with the deed, not to confuse the two. Despite
its difficulties, pitfalls, and frequent dullness, intrinsic criticism
is not a trivial undertaking, particularly in the classroom

where it is an aid to understanding, and in journalism where the critic can be of direct service to an author and his readers. However, what we usually want to know about the value of a text is not how well it does what it aimed to do, but whether that aim is worth fulfilling, whether the text is worth reading, and why.

I do not wish to suggest that the literary criticism of literature is a totally misguided undertaking or to assert that broad genre criteria are totally irrelevant to judicial criticism. Such extreme nominalism would be mistaken because the relationship between a broad genre and an intrinsic genre is rarely a purely arbitrary subsumption. Usually the implicit aims that characterize most of the texts subsumed under "poetry," "lyric poetry," "elegy," and the like also characterize the particular text or texts we are criticizing. That is why we chose to subsume our texts under those categories in the first place. Furthermore, as my farfetched poetic example suggested, the demands of communicability never allow an author to stray too easily from the habitual aims of his form. The evaluation of a particular text in relation to the implicit aims and criteria of a broad genre is frequently a genuinely intrinsic evaluation.

After making this qualification, namely, that the literary evaluation of literature may be intrinsic in a given case, there is still another important objection to be made against the assumptions of the modern program. This objection, which has been heard more and more often in recent years, is that the literary criticism of literature has often been conducted under a too narrowly formalistic or aesthetic conception of "literary." One justification for this aesthetic conception is that the degree of emphasis laid on craft and formal excellence is usually much greater among literary than nonliterary texts, and it would be a failure both of criticism and of understanding to neglect such aims in texts where they are paramount. But although formal excellence is a goal of most "literary" or "imaginative" texts, it is certainly not an aim that distinguishes these texts from all others, nor is it even the primary aim of all "literary" texts. Literary aims are variable, and they are changing with the growth of new genres. The only kind of text for which aesthetic criteria would be both intrinsic and sufficient are texts which have only aesthetic aims. In general, it is fair to say that much so-called intrinsic criticism has been intrinsic within too narrow a compass. One of my purposes in the next section will be to suggest that both intrinsic and extrinsic criticism have a right to a broader scope than they are sometimes allowed in scholarly criticism, and that both are compatible with the discipline of interpretation as a common enterprise.

E. CRITICAL FREEDOM AND INTERPRETIVE CONSTRAINT

Undeniably the ideal of intrinsic criticism has redirected scholarly activity toward a welcome and productive emphasis on interpretation. My observations in the preceding section were prompted in part by a desire for clarification and in part by a concern about the constructing influence which the ideal of intrinsic criticism has often exerted in the academies, where many scholars share the conviction that certain categories and contexts of commentary are improper because they are "unliterary." This constricting influence has extended not only to modes and manners of interpretation but even to criteria of evaluation. Recently, it is true, some critics have begun to rebel against the inhibitions imposed by a "literary study of literature" and have entered a plea for less formalistic, more socially oriented categories and criteria in literary criticism.[11] But socially oriented criticism is not necessarily superior or broader than formalistic criticism. Phenomenological criticism is not better or more profound than psychological criticism or Marxist criticism. In this section my purpose is to defend the

11. See, for instance, Walter Sutton's approving account of some recent pleas in *Modern American Criticism* (Englewood Cliffs, N.J., 1963), pp. 268–90.

right of literary criticism (or any other criticism based on a broad generic idea) to be as "literary" or "unliterary" as it pleases and still to qualify as objective knowledge and objective valuation. At the same time, I shall attempt to define the constraints upon critical freedom whenever criticism pretends to be valid in some respect. I shall argue that the discipline of interpretation is the foundation of all valid criticism.

The perception that understanding precedes judgment was undoubtedly one of the insights that fostered the intrinsic movement, and it is certainly the case that some modes of criticism are more helpful to understanding than others. It is only reasonable that a literary scholar should prefer a context like literary history or rhetoric to a context that is less directly helpful to interpretation, like philosophy or economic history; he knows that in his role as the preserver and reviver of a heritage, his first task is interpretation. But there are now a great many workers in the field of literary scholarship, and some of them can well afford to cultivate outlying acres that have small yield for interpretation. Subject matters other than stylistics or intellectual history or literary history have their own interest and use, and within those other contexts literary texts can have great significance. Furthermore, it is not less literary to investigate the bearings of pulp romances on social attitudes than it is to investigate the bearings of *Paradise Lost* on religious thought in the seventeenth century. Intellectual history as a subject matter is no more or less literary than sociology or than rhetoric—taken as a subject matter. For someone interested in the way literary works reflect the development of natural science, the history of science is as reasonable a subject matter as the history of styles. Literary works are sufficiently varied and the aims and interests of men sufficiently diverse to make any a priori limitation of the modes of criticism unwise and futile.

In particular circumstances, however, it is reasonable to say that some subject matters are inappropriate because they are pointless. *Paradise Lost* could be discussed in relation to the history of mathematics, but inappropriately, since the poem is not significant in that context. On the other hand, can we say in advance that no literary text could have an important bearing on mathematics? Wordsworth's poetry had a surprising importance in the development of inductive logic—if J. S. Mill rightly analyzed the influences upon him. Why should we reject the consideration of such relationships just because they tell us rather little about Wordsworth's poetry? The critic's interest is not always chiefly or exclusively in interpretation, and it is therefore impossible to predict what kind of subject matter will always be appropriate to his purposes in considering literary texts. The appropriateness or fruitfulness of a context depends entirely upon the *critic's* aims and upon the nature of the texts he considers.

On the other hand, the public evaluation of texts seems to require a narrower conception of appropriateness. Those who would grant the critic the right to examine a text within any context he chooses might not so willingly grant him the right to evaluate it on any criteria he chooses. Such a conclusion would seem to invite an arbitrary subjectivism which is already too prevalent in public criticism. But subjectivism is not avoided by following a particular method or adopting a particular vocabulary and set of criteria. The most firmly established method can disguise the purest solipsism, and the more tough-minded or "objective" the method appears to be, the more effective will be the disguise. Objectivity in criticism as elsewhere depends less on the approach or criteria a critic uses than on his awareness of the assumptions and biases that deflect his judgments. The requirements of self-critical thinking are the same regardless of a critic's subject matter and criteria of value. Nevertheless, there does seem to be a distinction between appropriateness of context and appropriateness of value judgment. It is at least conceivable that *Paradise Lost* with its compendious lore might have some significance for the history of mathematics in the seventeenth century. But would the historian of mathematics, assuming that he is a sensible man, evaluate *Paradise Lost* on the criterion of its usefulness to the history of mathematics? If he did so, he would *not* be a sensible man. How, then, are we to define this felt distinction between the appropriateness of context and the appropriateness of value criteria?

In the preceding section I argued that all subject matters broader than the text are extrinsic to textual meaning even when they have a heuristic function in disclosing that meaning. Similarly, I argued that all value criteria are extrinsic which do not correspond precisely to the purposes the author aimed to fulfill. Most evaluative criticism is quite properly extrinsic, since not only the author's purposes but also the value of those purposes are proper subjects for evaluative criticism. The critic is no more obliged to accept the author's values as absolute than he is to accept the author's intention as being his accomplishment. How then, are we to distinguish the kind of criticism which values *Paradise Lost* as a poem, and the kind which values it for its importance in the history of mathematics? Both can be forms of extrinsic criticism, yet clearly one is far more appropriate than the other.

What precisely is the difference between appropriate and inappropriate extrinsic evaluation? It is no doubt an extrinsic criticism of *Paradise Lost* to object that Milton makes God speak like a school divine, since that is the way Milton, for his own purposes, wanted God to speak. Of course, Pope's objection could conceivably be a form of intrinsic criticism if Milton had intended a different effect, or if the effect he did intend conflicted with his own larger purposes, since it is a form of intrinsic criticism to expose conflicting intentions in a literary work. But assuming for the nonce that Pope's criticism is extrinsic and that Milton achieved precisely what he wanted to achieve without any inconsistency of purpose, many critics would still feel that Pope's objection is apt, and I am certainly one of them.

Why should this sort of extrinsic criticism be judged more appropriate than that of the historian who objects that *Paradise*

Lost is not a very good source of mathematical lore? The answer is far less easy than it might at first appear. Instinctively we would reply that Pope's comment is appropriate to the kind of work Milton wrote, while the historian's is not. Yet the historian's judgment is objective and valid. If it is also silly, that is presumably because no one would expect *Paradise Lost* to be a source of mathematical information. Appropriate judgments would seem to be based on criteria that we could reasonably expect a work of a certain kind to fulfill. But the kind of work Milton wrote does fulfill (as we have assumed) Milton's purposes. If Pope demands different purposes, he is judging like our putative historian. Why, then, is his comment more appropriate? A kind of work in which God were made to speak less theologically (or even in which he spoke not at all) might be very similar in all other respects to *Paradise Lost* as it stands, but it would not be precisely the same kind of work.

It would seem, then, that appropriate extrinsic criticism is always close to intrinsic criticism in one respect: the critic may disagree with the author's purposes and hierarchy of purposes, with his taste and methods, but always takes those purposes into consideration. That is to say, he judges with respect to *some* of the purposes and values entertained by the author and does not simply ignore the conventions, aims, and systems of expectation under which the work was composed. Appropriate extrinsic criticism differs from intrinsic criticism primarily in weighting the author's values and aims differently from the author. Such criticism is extrinsic because the critic's hierarchy of aims and values is different from the author's, but it is appropriate because many of the critic's criteria are the same as the author's even though they are weighted or valued differently. Pope, for instance, implied that dramatic effectiveness and the evocation of awe should have been more important aims in Milton's portrayal of God than rational theological justification. Certainly Milton did aim at dramatic effectiveness and the evocation of awe in Book III, but he valued theological justification more than Pope. While critic and author are in disagreement over relative values, they do at least have a common foundation for their disagreement.

Nevertheless, critical freedom is and ought to be unlimited. An inappropriate evaluation can be just as true and objective as an appropriate one. And the range of appropriate evaluation is itself immense. All extrinsic criticism implies a hierarchy of criteria different from the author's, and so long as critics are not gods, their hierarchies of interest and approval cannot make absolute claims. The truth and objectivity of value judgments exist only in their relationship to a particular hierarchy of criteria. Judgments have no truth or objectivity outside such a context. Although the critic is free to judge on any criteria he likes, his valuations do not attain to objective knowledge until he has established what his criteria are—until he knows what he is doing and why. Of course, if he simply states preferences without grounding them (as most of us do when we are not composing public criticism), then he is not committing an immoral act, but merely expressing personal taste and perhaps performing a useful service in doing so, particularly if he introduces his audience to values they would otherwise miss.

Most prescriptive theories of criticism attempt to limit critical freedom, or at the very least they recommend a program that is designed for a particular cultural situation. New fads and fashions in criticism arise when the old ones seem worn out and boring or when their one-sidedness arouses opposition and reaction. In a book of this sort, which is more concerned with the laying out of principles than with the formulation of a new program, it would be a mistake to advocate a particular kind of evaluative criticism. However, it is not out of place to state my own preferences and my reasons for having them, since I do not want to give the impression that my defense of critical freedom is an invitation to critical irresponsibility. True, the most inappropriate evaluation can be objective, and the most subjective evaluation can be useful. Even an evaluation based on a misinterpretation can be both useful and informative if we read the critic imaginatively, as if his interpretation were ac-

curate: if the work really were as he imagined it to be, then
what he says would be valid as well as interesting in its own
right. This is certainly the way we should read critics whose
ideas command interest and respect even when they misunderstand their authors. However, my own preference is for judicial
criticism which is based upon valid interpretation and which is
also appropriate in the sense I have defined.

Judicial criticism should be appropriate because it is almost
always an adjunct to interpretation, and vice versa. Nothing
could be more antithetical to the purposes of interpretation
than to pronounce value judgments having little or no relevance to the author's purposes. To disagree with those purposes, to suggest that others would be preferable, to show that
the purposes could be better fulfilled in some other way—all
these judgments take cognizance of the author's aims, which
is to say, his meanings. It is equally appropriate to judge how
well those aims are achieved and how worthy they are. But to
disagree with purposes the author did not entertain or to praise
him for meanings he did not mean is to invite misunderstanding. Inappropriate judicial criticism conflicts with valid interpretation, and I rank valid interpretation as the scholar-critic's
highest and first duty. Others would argue that relevance is
more important than validity. But false relevance—relevance
founded upon a false and self-created image rather than upon
the actual meanings and aims of another person—is a form of
solipsism, and since most solipsistic judicial criticism also
parades as interpretation it compounds disreputable philosophy with unwitting deception.

Inappropriate judicial criticism commits another sin, one of
omission. By seeking values irrelevant to the author's aims, it
not only induces misinterpretations but fails to enhance the
peculiar and unique values that a work potentially has for the
critic's audience. This particular failing is endemic to all critical
monism—that lazy habit of mind which persistently applies
the same approach and the same criteria to all texts. Such
monism is generally based upon some prior definition of good

161

literature: good literature is always original or ironic or vision-
ary or compact or sincere or impersonal or what have you. Any
such universal criterion is bound to be inappropriate to some
works and appropriate to others and will inevitably induce
misinterpretation and blindness to those peculiar qualities
which more appropriate criteria would bring to light. That is
why new programs, methods, and approaches in criticism may
be regarded with suspicion; they have always been and always
will be impermanent. No method or approach in descriptive
or judicial criticism can be appropriate to any large number of
heterogeneous texts—even when the texts are given a single
generic name, such as "literature" or "tragedy" or "the such
and such tradition."

While I firmly believe that inappropriate judicial criticism is
often harmful to the purposes of interpretation, that it frequently ignores the unique values of unique works, and that it
is frequently quite pointless, I must concede any judicial critic
his right to search for generalities, to plump for a favored
system of values, and to ignore local values when these do not
suit his purposes. I must also concede the descriptive critic his
right to ignore local details when his principal concern is with
a subject matter that is far wider than a particular text. What
cannot be ignored or escaped is the quite central fact that
almost all judicial and descriptive criticism is predicated on
understanding. This is true even when interpretation is not a
principal aim. A meaning has to be construed before anything
can be said about its wider relationships or values. If an account of these relationships and values is to be valid, the prior
construction of meaning (at least that aspect of meaning which
is referred to) must be valid. From the standpoint of knowledge, valid criticism is dependent on valid interpretation.

It follows that every critic has a stake in the discipline of
interpretation whether he is actively engaged in textual study
or depends for his understanding on the researches and interpretations of others. In what respect is interpretation really a
discipline? This is equivalent to asking, Is there really a pos-

E. Critical Freedom and Interpretive Constraint

sibility of showing that an interpretation is valid? Can knowledge of a text's meaning be established objectively like other forms of knowledge? Can an interpretation be validated in a way that will compel assent from all or from most qualified observers? Finally, is interpretation really a discipline, or is it just a playground for the jousting of opinions, fancies, and private preferences, where the stake is not knowledge but the so-called higher humane values? This book has concerned itself hitherto with establishing that interpretation does at least have a determinate object of knowledge—the author's verbal meaning—and it has shown that such knowledge is in principle attainable. Validation is the process which shows that in a particular case such knowledge has probably been achieved. Without validation no interpretation could be shown to be more probable than another, and no interpreter could hope to achieve knowledge in any objective sense. The practical and theoretical exigencies of validation, knotty as they are, must finally be faced.

5.

PROBLEMS AND PRINCIPLES
OF VALIDATION

*The only proper attitude is to look upon a successful
interpretation, a correct understanding, as a
triumph against odds.*

I. A. Richards

A. THE SELF-CONFIRMABILITY OF INTERPRETATIONS

The activity of interpretation can lay claim to intellectual respectability only if its results can lay claim to validity. On the
other hand, its claims need to be moderated to suit the
peculiarities and difficulties attending the interpretive enterprise. Aristotle made the appropriate remark on this point in
his *Ethics,* where he observed that no conclusion should ar-
rogate to itself a greater certainty or precision than its subject
matter warrants. In this section I shall describe a fundamental
difficulty of interpretation which hinders any neat formulation
of correct methodology and must sober any self-convinced interpreter of a text. The fact that certainty is always unattain-
able is a limitation which interpretation shares with many other
disciplines. The special problem of interpretation is that it
very often *appears* to be necessary and inevitable when in fact
it never is. This appearance of inevitability is a phantasm raised
by the circularity of the interpretive process.

The belief that written language carries its own indubitable
force has a lineage as ancient as the primitive belief in the
magical properties of words. But a nearer source for the
endemic (and now epidemic) belief in the semantic autonomy

164

of language is the fact that interpretation very often induces a profound sense of conviction. The interpreter is convinced that the meanings he understands are inevitable, and this timeworn experience (quite aside from any of our peculiarly modern proclivities) has always lent credibility to the idea that meanings are directly given by words. When an interpreter maintains his unruffled certainty in the face of contrary opinions, we may assume that he has been trapped in the hermeneutic circle and has fallen victim to the self-confirmability of interpretations.

There lurks a partial, but nonetheless helpful, analogy to the self-confirmability of interpretations in the process of deciphering totally unknown sign systems. The memory of Ventris' achievement in this field is still fresh, yet for all its compelling brilliance, Ventris' decipherment of Linear B was not at first universally accepted. Some scholars very justly objected that such a decipherment had the property of confirming itself because its internal consistency was guaranteed in advance. The decoded elements had been used to construct the very system which gave rise to the decoded elements. The text unfailingly confirmed the theory because there was nothing in the text which was not sponsored by the theory in the first place: from a mute array of inscrutable signs the only meanings to be gleaned were those which were sponsored by the theory they purported to confirm. Ventris was able to meet this objection convincingly only after his decipherment had been further confirmed by newly discovered texts that had played no part in the construction of his hypothesis.

The circularity of such a decipherment, while only partially analogous to the circularity of interpretation, does serve to remind us that a mute sign system must be construed before it furnishes confirmation of an interpretation. Furthermore, the manner in which the signs are construed is partly predetermined by the interpretation itself. When interpreters construe texts differently, the data they use to support their constructions are to some degree sponsored by those constructions. So we confront a very slippery sort of entity when we read a text.

The word patterns and stylistic effects which support one interpretation can become different patterns and effects under a disparate interpretation. The same text can sponsor quite different data (though some of the data will remain constant), and each set of data will very powerfully support the interpretive theory which sponsored it in the first place.

I have given one convenient example of this incestuous relationship in my comment on Donne's "Valediction Forbidding Mourning." The words of the text take on a consistent pattern of meanings when we suppose that they are spoken by a dying man but a quite different pattern under a different hypothesis. The disagreements of experts may be harder to resolve than this, but they usually follow the same pattern. Every interpreter labors under the handicap of an inevitable circularity: all his internal evidence tends to support his hypothesis because much of it was constituted by his hypothesis. This is another description of the relationship between an intrinsic genre and the implications which it generates. An interpretive hypothesis —that is, a guess about genre—tends to be a self-confirming hypothesis.

Thus, the distressing unwillingness of many interpreters to relinquish their sense of certainty is the result not of native closed-mindedness but of imprisonment in a hermeneutic circle. Literary and biblical interpreters are not by nature more willful and un-self-critical than other men. On the contrary, they very often listen patiently to contrary opinions, and after careful consideration, they often decide that the contrary hypotheses "do not correspond to the text." And of course they are right. The meanings they reject could not possibly arise except on the basis of a quite alien conception of the text. It is very difficult to dislodge or relinquish one's own genre idea, since that idea seems so totally adequate to the text. After all, since the text is largely constituted by the hypothesis, how could the hypothesis fail to seem inevitable and certain?

This circular entrapment is not, unfortunately, merely a psychological difficulty. The problem of correctly judging be-

A. The Self-Confirmability of Interpretations

tween interpretations is not solved simply by the interpreter's determination to entertain alternative hypotheses about his text—though that is the necessary precondition for objective judgment. The interpreter faces the much more difficult problem of comparing hypotheses which are in some respects incommensurable: when a text is construed under different generic conceptions, some of the data generated by one conception will be different from those generated by the other.

This tendency of interpretations to be self-contained and incommensurable is, I believe, the principal handicap that will always plague the discipline of interpretation. Interpretations have a propensity Pope observed in eighteenth-century watches —none goes just alike, yet each interpreter believes his own. Paradoxically this very proliferation of opinions accounts for unwarranted optimism on the one side and equally unwarranted cynicism on the other. The optimist assumes that so many convinced and competent readers cannot be wrong, and he therefore views their divergences not as representing genuine disagreements but as reflecting different aspects and potentialities of the text. In criticizing this conception, I have already observed that different interpretations can indeed be reconciled, not because they are complementary but because they sometimes take different paths toward the same generic meaning.[1] However, I also observed that sometimes the generic meanings implied by interpretations *are* disparate. To dream that all expert interpretations are ultimately members of one happy family is to abandon critical thinking altogether.

The optimist does, in one respect, push closer to the truth than the invincible cynic who disbelieves all interpretations equally. His willingness to adjust and reconcile in order to demonstrate the "area of agreement" shared by different interpretations at least avoids the futility of controversy over merely verbal issues and dispels merely apparent disagreement where no substantial divergency exists. But the optimist also glosses

1. See Chap. 4, Sec. A.

over disagreement where it does exist and thereby avoids the responsibility of rational choice. The cynic, on the other hand, quite rightly perceives that disagreements are sometimes final and irreconcilable. He observes that one interpreter rarely if ever persuades another, because each feels as convinced of his own view as does the cynic himself. He therefore concludes that the interpreter's sense of conviction cannot be objectively based but must arise from the peculiar constitution of the interpreter himself—his historicity, psychology, personality, and so on. Ultimately, the critic's choice of a reading must be ascribed to his personal preference. The cynic naturally prefers his own competent reading to that of another, yet he open-mindedly recognizes the right of another to be just as blithely closed-minded as himself. Secretly he may consider other views to be silly or tasteless, but since he has no objective grounds for rejecting them, he equally tolerates all interpretive views which do not conflict with known facts. On a practical level it is thus sometimes difficult to distinguish such a tough-minded cynic from his optimistic counterpart, since both of them preserve an identical tolerance to a wide variety of readings. Both represent the same abject intellectual surrender, the same abandonment of responsibility.

In contrast to such intellectual withdrawal there persists among many interpreters a continuing faith in the possibilities of self-critical and rational thought. Indeed, every written interpretation with which I am familiar is implicitly or explicitly an argument that attempts to convince a reader. The use of quotations, for example, aims not only to illustrate an interpretive theory but also to support it—which is to say, validate it. Validation is practiced by the most unsystematic and arbitrary of interpreters, and the principles of validation are put into practice even by those who are most scornful of self-critical habits of mind. Furthermore, the attempt to win adherents to an interpretive theory by means of validation is generally an implicit attempt to convince readers that other theories should be rejected or modified.

My purpose in this chapter will be to describe the fundamental principles that govern the validation of interpretations and lead to objectively grounded discriminations between conflicting interpretations—despite the circularities and complexities which bedevil the interpretive enterprise. As in the previous parts of this book, my aim is to clarify concepts and encourage a degree of methodological self-consciousness, not to offer some novel panacea. The principles of validation are constantly being put into practice, very often with a high degree of sophistication and self-critical integrity. Native wit and devotion to knowledge have always been capable of reaching valid conclusions, but they must sometimes be defended against the incursions of skeptical theories which sponsor cynicism and opportunism. Of course, it is far more important to keep in view all the concrete evidence relevant to a particular interpretive problem than to follow elaborate principles of validation. But a sense of confidence that such principles do exist can have a certain practical efficaciousness. One of my practical aims in this chapter is to show that such confidence is not misplaced.

B. THE SURVIVAL OF THE FITTEST

Although the use of quotations is a universal technique of validation, it is not, of course, an adequate technique by itself. On the contrary, the circularity of the interpretive process makes quotation alone a totally inadequate means of validation. Quotation is the first, primitive stage of the process, serving to demonstrate merely that a particular interpretive hypothesis is legitimate and could therefore be correct. Validation has the more ambitious goal of showing not only that an interpretation is legitimate but that its likelihood of being correct is greater than or equal to that of any other known hypothesis about the text. The aim of validation is to give objective sanction to a particular interpretive hypothesis and thereby to provide the only possible foundation for a consensus omnium with regard to the text. That consensus would not, of course, endorse any particular written interpretation, but rather the whole meaning to which several interpretations might refer—a particular intrinsic genre capable of governing implications, rather than a particular selection of implications. Such selections always vary and can do so without changing in any respect the whole, generic meaning of the text.

The exigencies of validation should not be confused with the exigencies of understanding. It is perfectly true that the complex process of construing a text always involves interpretive guesses as well as the testing of those guesses against the text and against any relevant information the interpreter might know. Thus the very process of construing a text involves validations of a sort. But the process and psychology of understanding are not reducible to a systematic structure (despite the many attempts to do so), because there is no way of compelling a right guess by means of rules and principles. Every interpretation begins and ends as a guess, and no one has ever devised a method for making intelligent guesses. The systematic side of interpretation begins where the process of understanding ends. Understanding achieves a construction of meaning; the job of validation is to evaluate the disparate constructions which understanding has brought forward. Validation is therefore the fundamental task of interpretation as a discipline, since wherever agreement already exists there is little practical need for validation.

Such a consensus may, of course, be quite temporary, since the wit of man is always devising new guesses, and his curiosity is always discovering new relevant information. A validation is achieved only with respect to known hypotheses and known facts: as soon as new relevant facts and/or guesses appear, the old conclusions may have to be abandoned in favor of new ones. In order to avoid giving the false impression that there is anything permanent about an interpretive validation or the consensus it aims to achieve, I now prefer the term "validation" to the more definitive-sounding word "verification." To verify is to show that a conclusion is true; to validate is to show that a conclusion is probably true on the basis of what is known.[2] From the nature of the case, the goal of interpretation as a discipline must be the modest one of achieving validations so defined. But it also follows from the nature of the case that interpretation is implicitly a progressive discipline. Its new conclusions, based on greater knowledge, are more probable than the previous conclusions it has rejected.

With respect to the discipline of interpretation, the demonstration that a reading is valid implies, therefore, a great deal more than individual interpreters generally provide. A validation has to show not merely that an interpretation is plausible, but that it is the most plausible one available. Life is too short and boredom too imminent to demand that every interpreter lay out all the considerations which have led to such a decision, but when interpretive disagreements do occur, genuine knowledge is possible only if someone takes the responsibility of adjudicating the issue in the light of all that is known. That few such adjudications exist merely argues strongly that many more should be undertaken. An interpreter is usually deceiving himself if he believes he has anything better to do. Certainly the task of such adjudication is frequently part of an editor's function and is recognized as such by some editors, though far too many of them find ways of escaping their responsibility in this matter.[3]

2. In transcendental philosophy "validation" (*Geltungsprüfung*) applies to a poiori certitude whereas "verification" means empirical verification. I am assuming, however, most readers feel as I do, that in everyday usage a "valid" conclusion implies one that has been reached by acceptable reasoning, although it may not be certainly true. A "verified" conclusion, on the other hand, strongly suggests direct confirmation and certainty. For this reason I have abandoned my earlier use of "verification" (Appendix I) in favor of the less definitive-sounding term.

3. Textual choices frequently depend upon interpretations, just as interpretations depend upon texts. The aim of the textual editor is to determine what the author wrote or intended to write, and no purely

To emerge successfully from the rigors of an adjudication, the victorious hypothesis must have been compared with every disparate hypothesis severally or with hypotheses that had already emerged victorious over other competitors. Such a process is inevitable because the determinations must be made by individual comparisons. An interpretation stands or falls as a whole. As soon as the judge begins to pick and choose elements from several hypotheses, he simply introduces new, eclectic hypotheses, which must in turn stand or fall as wholes. Belief in the possibilities of mere eclecticism is based on a failure to understand that every interpretation necessarily refers to a whole meaning. It is possible that details of exegesis can be brilliantly right while the tendency of the whole is wrong, but the rightness of such details merely confirms the notion that disparate interpretations can have some implications in common. The judge's primary function is not to relish brilliant details of inference but to decide on the most valid principles for generating them. This principle of holism would be applicable even if the text at issue were a small crux within a larger text.

Sometimes the arguments for two interpretive hypotheses are so strong and our knowledge so limited that a definite decision is impossible. The aim of validation, therefore, is not necessarily to denominate an individual victor, but rather to reach an objective conclusion about relative probabilities. In comparing two interpretations it is always possible to reach a firm conclusion, but it may be simply that the two hypotheses are, on the basis of what is known, equally probable, and that no definite choice can be made. One may conclude that interpretation A is more probable than B, that it is less probable, or that neither of these conclusions is warranted. This third sort of decision is just as firm and objective as the other two, and it is just as much a decision. Thus, one function of validation

----

mechanical system which ignores interpretation could ever reliably reach such a determination.

can be to show that two or more disparate interpretations are equally valid and thereby to spur further research, since two disparate interpretations cannot both be correct.[4]

This distinction between the present validity of an interpretation (which can be determined) and its ultimate correctness (which can never be) is not, however, an implicit admission that correct interpretation is impossible. Correctness is precisely the goal of interpretation and may in fact be achieved, even though it can never be known to be achieved. We can have the truth without being certain that we have it, and, in the absence of certainty, we can nevertheless have knowledge—knowledge of the probable. We can reach and agree upon the most probable conclusions in the light of what is known. The objectivity of such knowledge about texts has been and will continue to be disputed so long as criticism is marred by its predilection for advocacy without any corresponding predilection for adjudication, but such knowledge is nevertheless objective and founded on well-established principles. The nature of those principles will be the subject of the following two sections.

C. THE LOGIC OF VALIDATION: PRINCIPLES OF PROBABILITY

It is a distinct misfortune that influential writers on probability theory should have been so predominantly oriented to mathematics and the natural sciences, for the logic of uncertainty

---

4. I remind the reader that by the term "disparate interpretation" I refer to different constructions (i.e. different understandings), not merely different interpretations. In defending the objectivity of an adjudication despite the fact that it can be superseded in the future, I am following the conception of J. M. Keynes to whom I am much indebted. Keynes pointed out (in *A Treatise on Probability*) that the rejection of a probability judgment in the light of new evidence does not change the objectivity or the *validity* of the earlier judgment. Its validity was entirely a function of the evidence on which it was predicated.

is fundamental to all the humane sciences as well. It is a further misfortune that probability theory in the eyes of the uninitiated is a game whose rules are entirely arithmetical and statistical. But the majority of probability judgments that we draw in everyday life are not reducible to definite numerical quantities. We are content to judge that an event is probable, highly probable, or almost certain, without allotting any numerical values to these judgments. On the basis of this observation, J. M. Keynes concluded that probabilities can be qualitative rather than quantitative.[5] His notion has been vigorously and justly attacked, but even if it is true that probability judgments are at bottom quantitative, it is also true that the quantities involved may be vague concepts like "more," "less," "very," and "slightly."[6] This lack of numerical precision in no way impairs the truth of such judgments. A man can easily and correctly judge that one pile of sand is larger than another without being able to estimate the precise number of grains in each pile or even the relative proportion of one pile to another. Furthermore, under some circumstances, there might not exist any possibility of making his judgment numerically more precise. That is often the case both in ordinary life and in the humane sciences. It is a fallacy to equate the numerical precision of a probability judgment with its correctness. Indeed, under some conditions, "more" and "less" are the most descriptive and accurate judgments that can be drawn.

Since probability judgments are the staple of the historical sciences and underlie the activity of interpretation at every point, from the construing of a text to the validation of a particular construction, it is of some use in an essay on fundamental principles to describe briefly the general foundation of probability judgments as they apply to interpretation. The

5. J. M. Keynes, *A Treatise on Probability* (Torchback ed. New York, 1962), pp. 34–37.
6. Even these vague concepts involve estimates of relative frequency. See the convincing arguments of Hans Reichenbach, *Experience and Prediction* (Chicago, 1938), pp. 301–404.

C. The Logic of Validation: Principles of Probability

basic fact about any probability judgment is its uncertainty. It refers to a reality that is partly unknown and which may (as in the case of interpretation) never be known with certainty. Forgetfulness of this basic, defining characteristic of probability judgments has led some theorists astray into the fallacious notion that probability judgments bear a necessary relation to the unknown reality and that their correctness may be evaluated according to the subsequent experience of that reality. As Keynes rightly observed, probability judgments bear a necessary relationship only to the evidence on which they are based.[7] Because the reality referred to is partly unknown, it follows that a probability judgment may be perfectly correct in relation to the known evidence, yet incorrect as a statement about the unknown reality. This inevitable and consistent paradox of all probability judgments derives from the simple fact that no matter how hard we may think about a reality that is inaccessible to direct experience, we cannot know what it is until we do experience it. If we could directly experience it, there would be no point in guessing about it, but if we merely guess about it, our guess could be wrong. Probability judgments are informed guesses. They contain no magical potency capable of converting an inaccessible unknown into something known. They are a rational means of reaching conclusions in the absence of directly experienced certitude.

From the fact that a probability judgment reaches conclusions about something inaccessible to experience (whether that something be in the past or the future), it follows that the judgment must somehow assimilate its unknown object to that which is known. This is the central purpose of a probability judgment, and everything that goes into the judgment subserves this purpose. The unknown must somehow (even if gropingly and wrongly) be assimilated to the known, otherwise there would be no rational access at all to the unknown—not even of a tentative nature. This purpose and requirement in all

7. Keynes, pp. 3–9.

probability judgments determines the fundamental axiom and assumption that must underlie all such judgments whether they be made in the service of statistical sciences or everyday life: namely, that all members of the same class will tend to act in the same way. If we cannot subsume the unknown under some kind of known class, then we cannot make a probability judgment, for we have no way of assimilating the unknown to the known. The basic and necessary assumption of all probability judgments is the uniformity of the class.

This assumption is far from arbitrary and can be easily defended. The idea of a class in itself entails an idea of uniformity at some level, for we subsume different individuals under the same class only because we observe that those individuals are the same in some respects. The respects in which they are the same become the defining characteristics of the class. Class uniformity at some level is a corollary to the very idea of a class. This point has application to probability judgments by virtue of the fact that the unknown to which they refer is never entirely unknown. If nothing were known about it, we would have no object at all, but simply a pure blank about which nothing and anything could be predicated. These known aspects of the object permit us to place it in a class possessing some of the same traits. The more we know about the object, the narrower and more reliable we can make the class. Then, on the basis of what we know about other individuals belonging to the same class, we make a guess that the unknown traits of any such object will be the same as the corresponding traits of most individuals in the class—more often than not. This is the structure of every probability judgment. It is a frequency judgment based on our past experience of other individuals that we conceive to belong to the very same class as the unknown.

Before examining some of the implications of this structure for interpretation, I should pause to take note of the immediately relevant problem that is said to trouble all historical science: namely, that its objects of knowledge are not regular and uniform, as in the determined natural order, but individual and unique, as befits the human realm of freedom. This distinction has been one of the main grounds for asserting that the principles of critical thought in the two branches of knowledge are radically different. But insofar as this radical separation applies to the necessary use of probability judgments in both branches of knowledge, the theory of two distinct cultures does not hold. It is simply not true that the objects of knowledge in the cultural sciences are thoroughly unique. If that were so, they could not be objects of knowledge. Dilthey's motto, *Individuum est ineffabile,* has as its corollary, *Individuum non est intelligibile.*[8] This maxim must hold, at any rate, for the knowledge about individuals that we gain through probability judgments. The unknown traits of human beings, human actions, and human meanings are completely inaccessible unless we manage to judge that they belong to a class in which such traits are thus and so more often than not. If we assume that the unknown traits are radically unique, we cannot subsume individuals under a class and cannot make an informed guess about their traits.

That probability judgments inhere in all aspects of textual interpretation is easily demonstrated. First of all, we notice that the construction of meaning from a text embraces elements already construed and accepted for the moment as being known, and other elements acknowledged to be unknown which are the objects of our construing. The obvious example of this is the construing of a crux by an appeal to a known context. But the example of a crux does not represent merely a special case. The object of our construing is always for the nonce a question mark, that is, a crux, and the basis for our choice of a particular sort of meaning is always our appeal to what we assume we already know about the text. On the basis of that assumption, we infer that these words coming in this place in a text of this sort probably mean thus and so. On the one side we have the context and the sequence of words; on the other we

8. The phrase goes back to a letter from Goethe to Lavater, September 1780. Before that, it had been an untraced scholastic maxim.

have the meanings which we judge the words to represent in this case. We reach those meanings entirely on the basis of our judgment that such meanings will occur more often in an instance of this sort than will other meanings, and we are able to make that inference because we have concluded that the instance *is* of this sort (i.e. class) rather than another sort. If we could not subsume the unknown meanings under a class on the basis of what we already know, then we could not make such an inference. The exigencies of probability judgments here have a direct kinship with the type-trait judgments which I described earlier in this essay. The kinship is not accidental. The type-trait model which is required to determine implications is a special application of the class-instance structure in all judgments of probability.[9]

There is another point of identity between probability judgments in general and the particular variety of them which we use in understanding a text. I pointed out that in order to determine the meaning of a word sequence it is necessary to narrow the supposed genre of the text to such a degree that the meanings are no longer doubtful. I called this very narrow and particularized conception of the text as a whole its (posited) intrinsic genre. Now this process of narrowing the genre is a version of the principle, well known in probability theory, of narrowing the class. The principle arises because there are two questions at issue in any probability judgment: first, what, probably, are the unknown traits of the object, and second, how probable is it that our judgment is true? This double question is always at issue, and our answer to the second part of it determines whether we say that our conclusion itself is probable, highly probable, or almost certain. The degree of reliance that we place on a probability judgment depends on this secondary decision about its likelihood of being true. The likelihood will increase the more we know about our object and the more

9. The principal difference is that the type-trait model implies wholeness of the type while the notion of class does not. See Chap. 2, Sec. D, pp. 49–50.

narrowly, by consequence, we can define the class to which it belongs. If we narrow the class so that our object becomes almost identical with other known objects (the more of them the better), then we can be less and less doubtful about the remaining unknown traits of our object.

I have already given one familiar example of the way doubtfulness is diminished as the class is narrowed in alluding to the likelihood that a woman will live longer than a man of the same age. Such a judgment, though true, is very doubtful in individual cases; if one could narrow the class to which the man and woman respectively belong (as insurance companies try to do), then one might completely reverse the judgment and decide that this particular man will probably live longer than this particular woman. Similarly, one might quite correctly judge that any medieval narrative poem is likely to be allegorical (since this is true more often than not), but a particular medieval narrative poem might belong, by virtue of certain traits, to a class whose members are nonallegorical more often than not. Anything we can do to narrow the class, such as determining authorship, date, tradition, and so on, will decrease the doubtfulness of our probability judgment—that is, increase its likelihood of being true.

Three criteria are decisive in determining the reliability of our guess about an unknown trait—the narrowness of the class, the number of members in it, and the frequency of the trait among those members. Though the copiousness of instances must obviously diminish as the class narrows, we nevertheless achieve increased reliability by narrowing the class. This is true even when the narrower class has merely two members, one being known and the other being the unknown object under scrutiny. This follows from the fundamental assumption of probability judgments, namely, the uniformity of the class. For a class is narrowed and its members made more uniform by increasing the number of class traits. When more and more of these traits are identical, the unknown traits of our object will have more and more likelihood of being identical with the known traits of the subclass. When we narrow the class, we decrease the instances, but at the same time we increase the defining traits of the class, and that is the chief goal. This process of narrowing the class is the decisive element in validating interpretations, as I shall show in the next section.

D. THE LOGIC OF VALIDATION: INTERPRETIVE EVIDENCE

An interpretive hypothesis is ultimately a probability judgment that is supported by evidence. Normally it is compounded of numerous subhypotheses (i.e. constructions of individual words and phrases) which are also probability judgments supported by evidence. Hence, the objectivity of interpretation as a discipline depends upon our being able to make an objectively grounded choice between two disparate probability judgments on the basis of the common evidence which supports them. Unless firm principles exist which permit such comparative judgments to be drawn, neither interpretation nor any other discipline built upon probability judgments can aspire to objective knowledge. The existence of such principles does not guarantee that men will apply them—any more than the existence of logic can guarantee that men shall think logically—but their existence does guarantee the possibility of objective knowledge, and that is the major thesis which this book undertakes to defend.

Since we can never prove a theory to be true simply by accumulating favorable evidence, the only certain method of choosing between two hypotheses is to prove that one of them is false. In the predictive sciences this can be accomplished by devising an experiment which conforms to the following conditions: if theory A is true, then the result of the experiment must be thus and so. If the result turns out not to be thus and so, theory A in its original form is permanently falsified. Theory B, on the other hand, is still consistent with the new results and must be accepted for the nonce. After such a decisive experiment, it is still not certain that theory B is true, but it is certain that theory A is false, and that is a great step forward. In the historical sciences such a result can seldom be achieved because decisive, falsifying data cannot be generated at will, and if such data had already been known, the two hypotheses would not have been in serious competition. Sometimes, of course, decisive data does by good fortune turn up, but usually neither competing hypothesis can be falsified, and both continue after their separate fashions to account for the evidence. In that case, since the direct path of falsification is closed, we have to make our way through a thicket of probability judgments on the basis of the evidence that we have.

As every interpreter knows, this evidence is usually conflicting. If that were not so, we would not usually be troubled with conflicting hypotheses. Indeed, as I observed earlier, some of the evidence supporting one hypothesis cannot even exist under the other, since some of the "internal evidence" can be generated only by a particular interpretation. Such incommensurable, dependent evidence cannot of course serve any direct function in comparing interpretations, and I shall therefore discuss later the ways in which this handicap can be overcome. But that is not in any case so crucial an issue as the problem of directly conflicting evidence. Normally the interpreter is faced with the dilemma that some independent evidence favors one hypothesis, while other independent evidence favors its rival. This is the normal state of affairs in interpretation.

I bring forward a rather detailed example of such a conflict in Appendix I, where I quote from two disparate interpretations of Wordsworth's "A Slumber Did My Spirit Seal." At issue is the fact that the evidence for a pessimistic and unconsoled tone conflicts with the evidence for a tone of invincible affirmation. In a brief space I have tried to show that one kind of evidence outweighs the other, though my comparison (first published several years ago) is not nearly so detailed as it would have to be in order to carry universal conviction. A really thorough examination, bringing forward evidence which I did not consider, might reverse the verdict or indicate that the evidence does not warrant a clear choice. I do not consider my little illustration to be a thoroughgoing adjudication, but it does illustrate the way interpretive evidence can be and usually is in conflict whenever interpretations are in conflict.

Another example is the conflicting evidence that supports two disparate modes of interpreting Blake's *Songs of Innocence and of Experience.* Again, I have (elsewhere) laid out the conflicting evidence, and in this case I was able to be more thorough than in the case of Wordsworth's poem,[10] but I still cannot claim that my effort is a model of adjudication, since the issue is still in the stage of advocacy. In order to reach a really firm decision between these two hypotheses about Blake, it would be wise to wait for the opposing advocates to bring forward unfavorable evidence which I might have missed. At that point a more reliable adjudication could be made, since the advocates would then presumably have brought forward nearly all the important relevant evidence. For an exemplary discussion of typically conflicting evidence, the reader may wish to consult M. H. Abrams' "Five Types of Lycidas."[11] Such examples remind us that conflicting evidence is the main problem in making an adjudication.

Thus the crucial problem in judging between disparate interpretations is usually the comparative weighing of relevant evidence. We must be able to conclude that the evidence favoring one hypothesis outweighs the conflicting evidence favoring its rival; otherwise we would have no basis for choosing one hypothesis over the other. Furthermore, our judgment about the relative weight of evidence must be objectively founded if we are to claim objectivity for our decision. However, the objectivity of our decision cannot consist (as in the convenient

10. *Innocence and Experience: An Introduction to Blake* (New Haven, 1964).
11. In C. A. Patrides, ed., *"Lycidas": The Tradition and the Poem* (New York, 1961).

D. *The Logic of Validation: Interpretive Evidence*

device of falsification) in finding some means of avoiding a direct judicial comparison. Our decision is publicly compelling only when our probability judgments are sanctioned by objectively defined and generally accepted principles. We need principles for determining the admissibility (i.e. relevance) of evidence and the relative weight of evidence.

Of course, an interpretive hypothesis need not explain all the evidence that comes along the stream of experience. It may be true that the best hypothesis always explains the most evidence, but that evidence must also be the most relevant evidence. Indeed, a less probable hypothesis may sometimes be based on a greater absolute quantity of data than the more probable one. For example, the predictive hypothesis that this woman will live longer than this man is based on an immense accumulation of evidence embracing millions of instances, but, on the other hand, the evidence about the relative life expectancies of healthy men compared to women of the same age having chronic nephritis may be extremely modest—say, a hundred instances. Yet this modest sample may provide evidence that is much more relevant to our actual case than the millions of instances which support the contrary hypothesis. We know very well that one datum does not necessarily bear a significant relationship to another datum, and fortunately we do not have to enter the Alice-in-Wonderland world of "material implication" in which we are compelled to reason: "if New York is a large city, then grass is green." The evidence that we are concerned with in comparing the probability of one hypothesis with that of another is relevant evidence, and our immediate concern must now be to define relevance as applied to interpretive evidence.

Since an interpretive hypothesis is always a probability judgment, it follows that the evidence which is relevant to that judgment must have some function in affecting the probabilities involved. If a fact or observation has no effect upon these probabilities, then, obviously, it is irrelevant to that particular probability judgment. Now a probability judgment is always a guess about the unknown traits of a partly known instance. That guess is made on the strength of the known traits possessed by other instances which belong to the same class as the instance under scrutiny. We infer that an eighteenth-century writer using the word "wit" probably means something general like "intelligent competence" rather than just "clever repartee," because the former is what other eighteenth-century writers mean by "wit" more often than not. In this case our subsuming class is "uses of the word 'wit' in the eighteenth century," and our guess about the meaning of this instance is based on the frequent occurrence of that meaning in other known instances of the class. If we did not know that our text belonged to the eighteenth century, we could not subsume our instance under that class. It follows from this structure of all probability judgments that evidence will be relevant which helps define the subsuming class and which increases the number of instances within the subsuming class. These two criteria of relevance bear directly on the problem of weighing evidence.

In order to decide whether a guess about a trait is probably correct, we need answer only one question: does the trait occur in the subsuming class more often than not? Quite obviously some guesses will be far more reliable than others; that is to say, the probability that the probability judgment will be correct varies a great deal. If, for example, we had fifty instances of the word "wit" in the eighteenth century and found that thirty-five of them used the word in its broad sense, then we would, *in the absence of other, narrowing data,* be obliged to guess that the instance under scrutiny also conveys that broad sense. But while our judgment, on the basis of the known data, would be valid, we could place very little reliance on it and would undoubtedly seek to make our guess more reliable. If, on the other hand, all known instances of "wit" in the eighteenth century conveyed the broad sense, then we could place far more reliance on our guess, since its probability of being correct would have greatly increased. Alternatively, if only twenty-seven of our fifty instances used the broad sense, we would be wise to conclude that the reliability of our guess is so small that the probabilities of the conflicting guesses are about equal and no decision is warranted in the absence of other data. We are forced to conclude that broad subsuming classes like "uses of 'wit' in the eighteenth century" cry out for more particular data when we want to make our guess reliable or weighty.

The supplementary data we need are not simply more instances of "wit" in the eighteenth century; presumably, we already have all the instances available. The kind of evidence we need is information concerning those instances which are more and more like the instance about which we are guessing. If, for example, we ascertain that our text is by a man named Rivers, and if we discover that Rivers apparently always uses "wit" to mean "clever repartee," then, on this further evidence, we would be right to guess that the present use also means "clever repartee," even though this guess is in conflict with the guess made on the basis of all known uses of the word in the eighteenth century. For this new, more delimited evidence is far more relevant to our hypothesis than the previous, general evidence. It serves to define a much narrower subsuming class of instances, and a judgment based on this narrower class is necessarily more weighty and reliable as a probability judgment than one based on a broader class. This necessity follows, as I observed in the previous section, from the basic assumption of probability judgments, namely, the uniformity of the class. By narrowing the class, we have, in effect, created a new class far more relevant to our guess than the previous one, and this narrower subsuming class always has the power to overturn (or to confirm) the evidence and the guess derived from the broader class. The previous frequencies are then no longer functional. The main thing that counts at that point is the relative frequency of our guessed-at trait within the new, narrower class. Here, then, is one principle for weighing conflicting interpretive evidence: the evidence of the narrower class is always the more weighty—no matter what the frequencies are within that class or any broader one that comprises it. The further addition of instances to our narrow class does increase the weight and reliability of our evidence, as does an increase of the relative frequency within it, but for any given accumulation of data the evidence of the narrowest subsuming class is always the weightiest evidence.

This inference was already implicit in comparing the life expectancy of a healthy man with that of a woman of the same age who had chronic nephritis, but that example is remote from interpretive problems and is, in any case, misleading in one respect. We do not make such a judgment simply because we happen to know that there is a direct causal connection between one trait (chronic nephritis) and another trait (nearness of death). Relevance of evidence is not always dependent on our knowing the connection between one trait and another. It is dependent simply on our past observation that one trait within the subsuming class will go with another trait more often than not.

In the domain of interpretation the simplest and clearest examples of the way a narrower, more fully defined class lends weight to evidence may be found in the work of the textual editor. The editor of old manuscripts always has to make probability judgments when choosing among (or even when rejecting) all the variant readings of his manuscripts. His sole aim is to guess correctly the word that the author intended, and in order to make this guess he has to consider an immense amount of evidence, including (as some editors apparently forget) evidence about the most valid interpretation of the passage as a whole. Most conscientious editors recognize that no rules of thumb can lead mechanically to the most probable reading. The genealogy of the manuscripts (if known) sometimes lends weight to a particular variant, but the editor knows that the reliability of any favored manuscript is uneven and that its general probability of being right can be reversed by other evidence—since mistakes of transcription occur even in authors' holographs.

D. *The Logic of Validation: Interpretive Evidence*

A very telling example of the way textual evidence becomes more weighty as the class of instances is narrowed was given to me by the editor of a medieval English homilist. At one point in the text the medieval author had given the pagan god Jupiter two attributes. One of them, according to all the manuscripts, was pejorative, and the second, according to many of them, positive. About this second attribute there was manuscript disagreement as to whether the word should be *þrymlic* (magnificent, splendid, etc.) or *þwyrlic* (perverse, contrary, etc.). Of course, I cannot hope to lay out all the conflicting evidence favoring one or the other of these readings, but I can for the purposes of illustration describe a few crucial pieces of evidence. First, it is in general very likely that a medieval homilist would be hostile to the pagan gods. Second, it is usual that a homilist would not confuse matters by making his judgments only halfheartedly pejorative. Thirdly, the positive word *þrymlic* is unlikely, since the author rarely uses *þrymlic,* whereas he lards his homilies with the pejorative *þwyrlic.* All of this evidence converges to make *þwyrlic* the more probable reading, and if it were all the evidence we had, *þwyrlic* would have to be chosen. But a fourth and single piece of evidence overturns all these mutually supporting class frequencies: a few lines earlier the author has written of another pagan god, Saturn, and the manuscripts show beyond reasonable doubt that he gave Saturn two attributes, one pejorative, the other favorable. This second, solitary instance is similar to the crux in so many respects—author, context, subject matter, point in time, etc.—that it serves to define a very narrow class under which the problematic reading can be subsumed. Obviously, this broad array of identical traits constitutes a class which is far closer to the unknown instance than the broader and more distant class frequencies supporting the double pejorative. This narrow class is not highly reliable, since it consists of only two members. Thus the choice of *þrymlic,* while valid, is still somewhat doubtful. However, it *is* the valid choice, since a judgment based on a narrower class is always capable of reversing a judgment based on a broader one.[12] The evidence of such a class about a particular trait is always weightier than the evidence from a broader class. Any editor with common sense would, on the basis of the evidence given, choose *þrymlic*. (Informed common sense always follows the logic of probability judgments, since that logic is the foundation of common sense.)

This example illustrates how evidence can be weighed according to the narrowness of the subsuming class and, as a corollary, how the task of narrowing the class entails the ferreting out of as much detailed information as possible. Evidence from other works of the same general period is less weighty or reliable than evidence from other works by the same author; evidence from all his works is less weighty than evidence from his works similar to the one at hand; evidence from all similar works by the author is less weighty than evidence taken from his similar works composed at the same period as the text under scrutiny, and so on, mutatis mutandis, for other class-defining traits. Obviously, if there are no exceptions, if a trait always occurs even in the broader class, then it will always occur in the narrower class as well. But when there is inconsistency in the trait's occurrence, and when, therefore, there is conflicting evidence, a decision can be reached whenever one conclusion is based on a subsuming class that includes not only all the defining traits of the class supporting the rival conclusion but also further defining traits of its own.

The resolution of conflicting evidence in interpretation is often less neat than this because sometimes there are pieces of conflicting evidence whose classes are incommensurable. For example, in the case of *þrymlic* vs. *þwyrlic,* we might have been faced with the disconcerting fact that the majority of the

12. This assumes, of course, that no other *kinds* of favorable or unfavorable evidence exist. (That is why I chose a simplified example.) The problem of coordinating and weighing different kinds of evidence is discussed below.

manuscripts give *þwyrlic* (though in fact they do not). If we had learned that for this text the majority reading is usually right, our two results would conflict, and there is no obvious way that we can compare the evidence from majority readings with the evidence from attributes given to pagan gods in this text—at least there is no way of comparing them on the criterion of their relative class narrowness.[13] On the other hand, we might compare the reliability or weight of each judgment on other grounds—for example, by showing that the majority of the manuscripts are correct only about seven times out of ten, whereas the author, when he uses similar examples to make his points, *always* treats them similarly. If we could not make such a decision about reliability, we would have to conclude that the two readings were equally probable—a situation which an honest editor acknowledges in his apparatus.

The comparing of such disparate classes immediately raises the question of mutually incommensurable internal evidence. It is sometimes possible to compare two conflicting interpretations on the basis of internal evidence alone, but this opportunity arises far less often than many interpreters believe. I mention skeptically some possible criteria for making such comparisons in Appendix I—namely, legitimacy, generic appropriateness, correspondence, and coherence. I observe that comparisons on the basis of coherence cannot be conducted simply on the basis of internal evidence, since coherence is a variable concept. The same objection can be made against the criterion of generic appropriateness, since the genre of the text is also a variable concept—a construction or hypothesis rather than a given. Legitimacy (i.e. the possibility that a word could mean what it is construed to mean) is often equally indefinite, since legitimacy cannot be determined by fiat, but

13. One basis for choice in editing is that of the more "difficult" reading. This criterion, too, is based on a class subsumption: copyists will not *usually* convert an expected word to an unexpected one. Obviously this is only one sort of criterion which has different weight in different circumstances and may always be overturned if contrary evidence is weightier.

only by observing whether contemporary readers could construe the word in that way. Whenever expert readers have so construed the word, legitimacy ceases to be a discriminating criterion. In short, it is usually the case that internal evidence can discriminate between hypotheses only on the criterion of correspondence.[14] That is to say, internal evidence by itself might possibly indicate that one hypothesis makes functional more elements of the mute text than a rival hypothesis, and the hypothesis which makes functional the greater number of traits must, in relation to that limited evidence, be judged the more probable hypothesis.

This conclusion follows from the general probability that style and sense, word choice and intended meaning, will support each other. We know that the verbal choices men make have a function in conveying their meaning more often than not. However, it would be a grave mistake to conclude that the correspondence of an interpretation with the greater number of internal traits is necessarily decisive. In the first place, the notion that the intended meaning is the one which makes the most elements functional is not a universal law, but simply a general probability whose weight varies from one kind of text to another and, indeed, from one text to another. In the second place, it is usually impossible, when comparing serious contenders, to reach a really firm conclusion on this issue, since one hypothesis will make functional different traits from the other. For instance, the theory that the Wordsworth poem expresses inconsolable grief makes highly functional the negatives in

> No motion has she now, no force,
> She neither hears nor sees.

The opposing theory that the poem is ultimately affirmative must explain these repeated negatives as mere contrasts with

14. By "correspondence" I mean here the capacity of the interpreted sense to explain or "correspond to" the vocabulary, style, and syntax of the text. This criterion is further discussed below.

the living girl which are not so absolutely negative as the repetitions might indicate. On the other hand, the theory of affirmation makes highly functional the series, "rocks, and stones, and trees," in the last line. The affirmative interpretation can explain why living "trees" should conclude the series, whereas the theory of inconsolability must regard "trees" only as static, inert, and passive objects like the body of the dead girl. Consequently, on one theory "trees" must be explained away, just as on the other theory the negatives must be. Clearly it would not be warranted to conclude that one theory makes functional a greater number of textual traits than the other, for each makes functional different traits. That is the usual pattern when internal evidence is compared on this quantitative criterion.

To discover an example where the criterion of correspondence can lead to a clear choice, we will ordinarily have to look beyond the disparate interpretations of experts, for if a clear choice could be made on these fairly obvious internal grounds, then most experts will have made it before committing themselves to print. One might expect the criterion to be decisive in comparing, say, my students' opinion about Donne's "Valediction Forbidding Mourning," discussed earlier, with the expert opinion that the poem is not spoken by a dying man.[15] As I observed, the students' reading is plausible, coherent, and also legitimate, for there is not a single word in the poem which could not legitimately be understood in Donne's own time as our students understand it: "Mourning" could mean grieving for someone dead; to "go" could mean to die. Moreover, the idea that the souls of the speaker and his beloved continue to live is perfectly consistent with the idea of physical death, while the famous simile of the compass with which the poem ends could reasonably be understood as suggesting a reunion in Heaven.

But this final simile at last begins to diminish the explanatory

15. See pp. 73–74.

power of the students' hypothesis. Donne explicitly calls the soul of his beloved the "fixt foot" of the compass and goes on to say:

> And though it in the center sit,
> Yet when the other far doth rome,
> It leaves, and hearkens after it,
> And grows erect, as that comes home.
> Such wilt thou be to mee, who must
> Like th'other foot, obliquely runne;
> Thy firmness makes my circle just,
> And makes me end, where I begunne.

The standard reading makes functional many more traits of this final simile than does the students' reading. It explains, for example, why the fixed foot never has to move in order that there be a reunion; if the departure of the other foot is understood to be death, it would follow that the fixed foot would also have to depart in order to achieve a reunion. Furthermore, the standard reading reveals a connection between the fixity of the girl (i.e. her faithfulness) and the return of the speaker. Under the students' reading most elements in the simile are not functional, and the simile seems loose and inept. It is quite warranted to say, therefore, that one hypothesis makes functional more traits of the text than the other and is, on the basis of internal evidence alone, the more probable hypothesis.

However, our example worked neatly only because our students were straw men and their reading a sitting duck. This kind of demonstration cannot suffice to validate a single expert reading I know of at the expense of its expert rivals. Not only is it usually difficult to decide that one hypothesis makes functional more textual traits than another, but it is also totally unsatisfactory to leave the matter at that. A validation requires a consideration of all the known relevant data. For example, if Donne had written several poems called "Valediction" and if they were all spoken by dying men, that evidence would make us far less certain of our conclusion in the above case. It so happens, of course, that Donne's other valedictions are not spoken by dying men but, rather, play on the similarities between death and momentary physical absence. That further evidence, as it happens, supports our conclusion reached on the criterion of correspondence. However, in making a validation we cannot rest content with the fact that one single kind of evidence favors one of the hypotheses. We want to know how the hypotheses stand with respect to *all* the relevant evidence that has been brought forward. Internal evidence is, as I have just indicated, the evidence that is least likely to enable a decision on its own grounds. Even in the case of anonymous texts of uncertain date, there always exists relevant evidence beyond such internal evidence, and failure to use it simply makes our guesses unreliable and all attempts at adjudication well-nigh impossible.

Since the very limited and doubtful criterion of correspondence is the only one that applies to internal evidence taken by itself, we need to discover and generate other sorts of evidence that will serve to discriminate between disparate interpretations. To make such discriminations interpreters have recourse to judgments at two distinct levels of comprehensiveness. At the most comprehensive level, they can decide which of two contenders is more likely to be right in its controlling or generic conception of the text. On this level, for example, we can judge that Donne's "Valediction Forbidding Mourning" is more likely to refer to the lover's temporary physical absence than to his death, and we make this judgment partly because we are familiar with a class of poems which Donne calls "valedictions." I made a similar sort of generic probability judgment about "A Slumber Did My Spirit Seal" when I observed that, in the rest of Wordsworth's poetry written at the same period, the connection between the death of a person and the processes of nature ("earth's diurnal course") almost always implies an affirmation of continuing life, a spark that does not die. We know that this may not be true in this instance, but we must accept the fact that such evidence does favor one hypothesis at the generic level.

But such general, large-scale probability judgments are not decisive because there always remains a great deal of small-scale evidence which can support or overturn such a conclusion. This small-scale evidence is sometimes called "internal" since it comprises individual words and phrases of the text, but the appellation is misleading, since "outside" information must necessarily be applied in order to make a probability judgment about these elements *in* the text. For the subunits are made to function as evidence in the following way: we posit what the unit would have to mean under one interpretation and what it would have to mean under the other. Then, *in isolation from other parts of the text,* we ask which of these two subordinate constructions is more likely to be correct. This careful isolation is necessary in order to exclude arguments appealing to the coherence of a subhypothesis with the rest of the text. Such appeals to coherence are useless because, as I have pointed out, they are circular.[16] Each small-scale construction will automatically be coherent with the rest of the text under the controlling conception of the text which sponsored the construction in the first place. Moreover, this manner of isolating details of construction can embrace every comparison that might be made according to the criterion of correspondence. It thus also renders that criterion supererogatory.

For example, we can isolate the opening lines of Donne's "Valediction" and compare my students' construction of the simile with that of the experts. According to the students' view, the fifth and sixth lines, like the initial simile, refer to death:

> As virtuous men passe mildly away,
> And whisper to their soules to goe,
> Whilst some of their sad friends doe say,
> The breath goes now, and some say no:
> So let us melt and make no noise,
> No tears-floods, nor sigh-tempests move.

16. See Chap. 4, Sec. A, as well as Appendix I, pp. 236–38.

D. *The Logic of Validation: Interpretive Evidence*

Now the students' is a possible (i.e. legitimate) construction: "let our parting in death be like the peaceful death of virtuous men." That is the sort of simile a poet might conceivably use; indeed, the romantic poets are fond of similes or metaphors which (in W. K. Wimsatt's terms) fuse tenor and vehicle. However, it is a far less probable interpretation than the standard one, because it does not represent the sort of simile that Donne customarily uses. Donne habitually makes the disparity between tenor and vehicle as striking as possible—as in fact he does (on both interpretations) elsewhere in this very poem. Obviously, this probability judgment is not based on merely internal evidence. It is based on the evidence that Donne's similes are of a certain character far more often than not, and we have gleaned this evidence from as many instances as we could find.

Similarly, the disparate interpretations of Wordsworth's poem compel two different constructions of the line, "She seemed a thing that could not feel." In the disconsolate interpretation, the word "thing" is regarded as a deeply ironic foreshadowing of the time when the girl would become a thing. Indeed, the interpretation compels that construction, since it is predicated on a jolting contrast between the living girl and the dead girl. Unless the word "thing" is used as ironic foreshadowing, it tends to negate rather than enforce this opposition. Yet, under the more affirmative reading the word "thing" is in no way pejorative or ironic but tends to reinforce the idea of continuing sameness in life and death. Which of these two constructions of "thing" is the more probable? If we consider the normal usage of Wordsworth's time, we will conclude that the first is more probable. If we consider Wordsworth's habitual use of the word in poems contemporary with this one, we will conclude that the second is more probable. Quite obviously this second conclusion, based on the narrower class, is the valid judgment.

But neither our conclusion about the word "thing" nor our conclusion about Donne's first simile could be decisive by itself. Each is a single small-scale judgment which has to be considered along with other small-scale judgments and large-scale ones as well. Each of our small-scale judgments concerns the probability of a subhypothesis which has been compelled by a particular large-scale hypothesis. We judge the relative probabilities of disparate individual implications generated by disparate conceptions of the whole. Our purpose in making these small-scale judgments is always primarily to determine which large-scale interpretation is victorious more often than not, for each result of comparing the probabilities of two sub-hypotheses is subsequently to be regarded as a piece of evidence favoring one or the other generic interpretations. When one of the larger interpretive hypotheses is victorious more often than the other, we say that it "explains" more evidence and is therefore more probable. This is often what interpreters mean when they say that an interpretation corresponds better to the text or explains the text better. As I have shown, such a description is quite inaccurate and misleading; both interpretations correspond to the text equally well, and both serve to explain everything in the text. What is really meant is that the explanations or subhypotheses implied by one interpretation turn out, on the basis of all relevant evidence, to be usually the more probable explanations. When the verdict of these small-scale judgments supports a large-scale interpretation which is also more probable on other grounds (as was the case with Donne's poem), then we can consider our choice to be highly reliable. However, when there is conflict between these two levels, we have to decide whether the cumulative small-scale probabilities are weighty enough (by their individual weight and their consistency) to overturn the large-scale probability. Usually this will be the case, but when it is not, we may have to reach the opposite decision or conclude that both hypotheses are equally probable.

My reason for refusing either to defend or reject my previously published opinion about Wordsworth's poem is that many readers privately raised points which I had not explicitly considered. To review them all would in this context be digressive and inconclusive, but my experience does raise a highly

D. The Logic of Validation: Interpretive Evidence

pertinent issue with regard to the adjudication of disparate interpretations. The really crucial necessity in reaching reliable conclusions is to accumulate numerous disparate subhypotheses like those I have just brought forward in illustration. Precisely such subhypotheses were brought forward by some of my dissenting readers. This illustrates the principal virtue of the advocacy system in interpretation as in law. The advocates have the task of bringing forward evidence favorable to their side and unfavorable to their opponents. In doing so, they may bring to light evidence which a judge might not have thought to consider. But without a judge all those relevant pieces of evidence float uselessly. Advocates are needed to discover subhypotheses capable of sustaining decisions, as well as other sorts of evidence capable of favoring an interpretation. However, unless advocates sometimes serve as judges, none of this activity will actually contribute to knowledge.

I can now sum up the principles governing decisions about the weight and relevance of interpretive evidence. To make a reliable adjudication, all relevant evidence, "internal" and "external," should be considered. The admissibility of evidence is determined by the criterion of relevance. Evidence must be accepted as relevant whenever it helps to define a class under which the object of interpretation (a word or a whole text) can be subsumed, or whenever it adds to the instances belonging to such a class. The relative weight or reliability of a judgment based on such evidence is determined by the relative narrowness of the class, the copiousness of instances within the class, and the relative frequency of the trait among these instances. A judgment based on a narrower class is always more weighty or reliable than one based on a broader class—no matter how meager the narrower class may be. When we have conflicting evidence from two disparate subsuming classes, we should try first to form a third, narrower class by combining the defining traits of the classes. When this is impossible, and the judgments based on the two classes are in conflict, we must decide which judgment is the more probable by comparing the copiousness of the subsuming classes and the relative frequency of the predominant trait within the classes. However, such comparisons are often unreliable and insecure.

The application of these principles in judging between interpretations occurs at two levels. On the generic level, we consider the relative likelihood (apart from consideration of "internal" evidence) that the text will be of one sort rather than another. This generic guess should be conducted separately, in isolation from many of the internal traits which support it, because those traits are to some extent constituted by the generic guess itself. The evidence which goes into this guess is thus partly "external"—date, authorship, milieu, and so on—but it is necessarily founded on such indubitable "internal" traits as vocabulary, form, and title. On the other hand, we can also make small-scale probability judgments about the disparate constructions of details that have been sponsored by the disparate generic hypotheses. The evidence which goes into these judgments is likewise both internal and external, as I have shown. Usually an effort to apply these principles will result in the conclusion that the more probable generic guess is the one often favored by subsidiary probability judgments. When this happy result fails to occur, the tendency of the subsidiary judgments is usually the more reliable evidence, since it embraces several judgments based on fairly narrow classes. If, in such a conflict, however, these judgments fail to tend heavily in one direction, then no clear decision is warranted. In the course of making any of these probability judgments, the interpreter's chief concern is to narrow the class; that is to say, his chief concern is to find out as much as he can about his text and all matters related to it. That everyone has always known this conclusion is another illustration of the fact that the logic of uncertainty is the logic of common sense.

E. METHODS, CANONS, RULES, AND PRINCIPLES

The theoretical grounding of a discipline would seem to have as its ultimate object the formulation of firmly reliable methods which, when followed, will lead to valid results. The theory of interpretation, on this view, should lead to a methodology of interpretation. This ideal floated from time to time before the fertile mind of Schleiermacher and guided his attempts to formulate reliable canons of interpretation. It was taken up with greater confidence and system by Boeckh, who used the word *Methodologie* in the title of his treatise. However, canons of interpretation had been in existence long before Schleiermacher wrote—in the *hermeneutica sacra* of biblical scholars, in the methodological asides of the Pergamene and Alexandrian schools, and most fully in the long tradition of legal interpretation, several of whose rules still attest their provenance in medieval law: *noscitur a sociis; ejusdem generis; reddendo singula singulis*. In literature this practical tradition persists very powerfully in the many handbooks which provide the undergraduate with methods of interpreting literary texts by telling him the questions he should ask and the categories he should apply.

The most noteworthy feature of this tradition is the variety of the interpretive rules it has brought forth. The rules do not always contradict one another, but they do proliferate in the most diverse directions. Obviously, the literary scholar needs different canons from the legal or biblical scholar, and even within these broad domains the canons required for one sort of text will be different from those required for another. The legal scholar is not interested in canons which determine whether a text is allegorical, but, for that matter, the literary scholar may not, in a given case, require such a canon either. The scholar who confronts an interpolated text may find useful Schleiermacher's canon that "a sentence which is uninterruptedly governed by the same subject or predicate as the discourse itself is to be regarded as having a direct connection with it," but if the text is not interpolated, this canon is of course quite pointless.[17] It would, on the other hand, be not only pointless

17. *Hermeneutik,* p. 100.

but misleading to apply to all texts the legal canon that "the word 'and' may be read 'or' and vice versa."[18] Anyone who pores over the practical rules of interpretation quickly observes that their range of application is always limited. No one has ever brought forward a concrete and practical canon of interpretation which applies to all texts, and it is my firm belief that practical canons are not consistently applicable even to the small range of texts for which they were formulated.

The most considerable attempt to formulate really general canons universally applicable to all texts was that of Schleiermacher, but his efforts betray some very contradictory impulses which indicate how uncomfortable he sometimes felt with his project of formulating a method of interpretation. With his eye constantly on the problems of interpreting the New Testament, he found himself generating canons about "the main topic" and "the subordinate topic" that were obviously more specialized than he originally intended. Even some of his most deliberately general canons, the most general ones that have ever been formulated, do not have truly universal application. His first and firmest canon, for example, is as follows: "Erster Kanon. Alles was noch einer näheren Bestimmung bedarf in einer gegebenen Rede, darf nur aus dem dem Verfasser und seinem ursprünglichen Publikum gemeinsamen Sprachgebiet bestimmt werden."[19] I translate it as follows: "Everything in a given text which requires fuller explanation must be explained and determined exclusively from the linguistic domain common to the author and his original public." This is obvious enough, since the *verbal* meaning of an author can only be a meaning which his audience could possibly share. That sharability is implied by the phrase "common linguistic domain" and the purpose of the canon to exclude private meanings and anachronisms. However, that laudable purpose fails to embrace those texts which deliber-

18. F. J. McCaffrey, *Statutory Construction: A Statement of the General Rules of Statutory Construction* (New York, 1953), p. 52.
19. *Hermeneutik,* p. 90.

ately strive to extend their application into the future—such as legal texts. It is true that the "determinations" (*Bestimmungen*) of a legal text have to be deduced first from that common linguistic domain of which Schleiermacher speaks, but they must not be limited to that domain, since they are also meant to apply to objects and situations which did not exist when the law was formulated and which thus could not be comprehended or comprehensible within that original linguistic domain.

Does it stand any better with the second canon? "Zweiter Kanon. Der Sinn eines jeden Wortes an einer gegebenen Stelle muss bestimmt werden nach seinem Zusammensein mit denen die es umgeben."[20] My translation is: "The meaning of any word in a given passage must be determined according to its coexistence with the words that surround it." This "rule" is of course a description of what every interpreter has always done, whether he knew the rule or not, since in order to construe a word at all he has to construe its function, and that cannot be done in isolation from the larger sense which the word conveys in alliance with the surrounding words. Undoubtedly, therefore, this canon has real generality, but it is perfectly useless as a practical rule. It tells everyone to do what everyone has always done and will continue to do without the rule, but, more important, it has no capacity to enforce practical decisions. Every word *is* always construed in connection with its neighbors, and when there are alternative constructions, the senses of the surrounding words will vary accordingly. The context is not a fixed given, but something that can be just as variable as the word at issue. Thus, one could just as well set down as a corollary canon that "the sense of a word must determine the senses of the surrounding words." Both elements are variable and codependent, as Schleiermacher himself often implied in his doctrine of part and whole. Indeed, the real worth in Schleiermacher's epoch-making writings on hermeneutics is

20. Ibid., p. 95.

to be found not in his canons, but in his intelligent, lengthy, and digressive qualifications of them.

It may be set down as a general rule of interpretation that there are no interpretive rules which are at once general and practical. A truly general rule will fail, as in the example above, to guide us in a specific case, and a practical rule—that is, a specific and concrete one—cannot be truly general: it may or may not lead to the valid conclusion. Much of Schleiermacher's energy went into qualifying both his own rules and the traditional ones he inherited. He wisely said, for example, "The old rule—do not seek beyond the text when sufficient clues of explanation are present in it—is of very very limited application."[21] Similarly, he said of canons dealing with verbal repetitions: "The maxim—take as much as possible as being tautological—is just as false as—take as much as possible as being emphatic."[22] We find precisely the same qualifications in the traditional canons of legal interpretation. "We ought not to deviate from the common use of the language, *unless* we have very strong reasons for it"; "Where a word has a fixed technical meaning, it is to be taken in that sense, *unless* the context or other evidence of meaning indicates a contrary legislative intent"; "Where the same language is used in different parts of the statute . . . it is to receive the same construction . . . *unless* the general meaning and intention of the act require a different construction"; and so on.[23] Every practical

21. Ibid., p. 103.
22. Ibid., p. 105.
23. See, for example, the various rules of construction by Vattel, Domat, and Lieber in Theodore Sedgwick, *A Treatise on the Rules Which Govern the Interpretation and Application of Statutory and Constitutional Law* (New York, 1857), pp. 266–90. Despite his formidable title Sedgwick is sanely skeptical with regard to his subject: "Nor do I believe it easy to prescribe any system of rules of interpretation for cases of ambiguity in written language that will really avail to guide the mind in the decision of doubt. . . . It would seem as vain to attempt to frame positive and fixed rules of interpretation as to endeavor, in the same way, to define the mode by which the mind shall draw conclusions from testimony" (p. 228).

rule of interpretation has an implicit "unless" after it, which means, of course, that it is not really a rule.

What then is the status of the many traditional canons and maxims of interpretation, and what is their purpose? Clearly, they are provisional guides, or rules of thumb. In the absence of compelling indications to the contrary we follow them because they hold true more often than not. In other words, the practical canons of interpretation are preliminary probability judgments based on past experience. More often than not a legal text will mean the same thing when it uses the same words —and there are very plausible reasons why this should be so. However, since all practical interpretive canons are merely preliminary probability judgments, two consequences follow with regard to their intelligent application. First, the canon is more reliable the narrower its intended range of application. Practical canons that apply to a very strictly limited class of texts will be more reliable for those texts than canons which lay claim to broader application. Second, since any interpretive canon can be overturned by subsuming the text under a still narrower class in which the canon fails to hold or holds by such a small majority that it becomes doubtful, it follows that interpretive canons are often relatively useless baggage. When they are general, they cannot compel decisions, and even when they are narrowly practical, they can be overturned. The important point about a rule of thumb is that it is not a rule.

The notion that a reliable methodology of interpretation can be built upon a set of canons is thus a mirage. Precooked maxims carry less authority than informed probability judgments about particular cases, and verbal constructions cannot possibly be governed by *any* methods. No possible set of rules or rites of preparation can generate or compel an insight into what an author means. The act of understanding is at first a genial (or a mistaken) guess, and there are no methods for making guesses, no rules for generating insights. The methodical activity of interpretation commences when we begin to test and criticize our guesses. These two sides of the interpretive

Chapter 5: Problems and Principles of Validation

process, the hypothetical and the critical, are not of course neatly separated when we are pondering a text, for we are constantly testing our guesses both large and small as we gradually build up a coherent structure of meaning. We want to be sure that we are getting the matter right, and we are constantly asking ourselves whether a guess is probable in the light of what we know about the text so far. But the fact that these two activities require and accompany one another in the process of understanding should not lead us to confuse the whimsical lawlessness of guessing with the ultimately methodical character of testing. Both processes are necessary in interpretation, but only one of them is governed by logical principles. The legal phrase "canons of construction" is thus a typical misnomer which reflects a long-standing confusion of the two processes. There can be no canons of *construction,* but only canons which help us to choose between alternative meanings that have already been construed from the text.

Schleiermacher, despite his flirtation with canons of construction, stated this distinction imprecisely but vividly:

> For the whole enterprise of interpretation there are from the start two functions—the divinatory and the comparative—which reflect back on one another and should not be isolated from one another. The divinatory is the function by which one as it were transforms himself into the author, seeking directly what is individual. The comparative function regards what is to be understood first as something general, and then finds out what is unique by comparing it with other things subsumed under the same general idea. The former is the female force in human knowledge, the latter the male.[24]

What Schleiermacher calls the "divinatory function" is the productive guess or hypothesis for which no rules can be

24. *Hermeneutik,* p. 109.

formulated but without which the process of interpretation cannot even begin. The critical, masculine function, on the other hand, cannot bring forth, but it can judge and test. Schleiermacher calls it "comparative" partly because he has recognized that interpretive guesses are always tested by making comparisons, i.e. by subsuming the object of interpretation under a class of similar instances. He thus recognized implicitly the comparative nature of probability judgments, and though he rightly insisted that the divinatory and comparative functions go together, he failed to notice that one function is always prior to the other, that female intuition brings forth the ideas which the comparative male judgment then tests and either accepts or rejects.

Despite his metaphorical imprecision Schleiermacher is worth quoting for another reason. He suggests that the female divinatory function and the male comparative function are the two principal forces not only in interpretation but in human knowledge generally. The implications of that insight stretch beyond the currently fashionable discussion of the opposition between scientific and humanistic cultures and their respective "methods." What is at stake is not some ideal fusion of the separate cultures and their modes of thought, but the right of interpretation (and implicitly all humanistic disciplines) to claim as its object genuine knowledge. The two forces that Schleiermacher perceived in interpretation and in human thinking generally are versions of two processes that are indeed comprised in every realm of thought that can lay claim to knowledge. Thus Sir Peter Medawar states:

> What are usually thought of as two alternative and indeed competing accounts of *one* process of thought are in fact accounts of the *two* successive and complementary episodes of thought that occur in every advance of scientific understanding. . . . The chief weakness of Millian induction was its failure to distinguish between the acts of mind involved in discovery and in proof. . . . Mill thought that

his process of "induction" could fulfill the same two functions; but, alas, mistakenly, for it is not the origin but only the acceptance of hypotheses that depends upon the authority of logic. . . . Obviously "having an idea" is an imaginative exploit of some kind, the work of a single mind; obviously "trying it out" must be a ruthlessly critical process to which many skills and many hands may contribute.[25]

While there is not and cannot be any method or model of correct interpretation, there can be a ruthlessly critical process of validation to which many skills and many hands may contribute. Just as any individual act of interpretation comprises both a hypothetical and a critical function, so the discipline of interpretation also comprises the having of ideas and the testing of them. At the level of the discipline these two "moments" or "episodes" can be separated in a way that they cannot be in the course of construing a text, for any written interpretation is a hypothesis implying a number of subhypotheses, all of which are open to examination. Conflicting interpretations can be subjected to scrutiny in the light of the relevant evidence, and objective conclusions can be reached. Of course, imagination is required—a divinatory talent like that needed to make interpretive guesses—simply to discover highly relevant evidence. Devising subsidiary interpretive hypotheses capable of sponsoring probability decisions is not in principle different from devising experiments which can sponsor decisions between hypotheses in the natural sciences. But although the divinatory faculty is essential even in the validating process, the essence of that process is the making of judgments on the basis of all the relevant evidence that has so far been brought forward, and such judgments can be made in the light of day.

Even the fact that some un-self-critical or fractious souls might stubbornly refuse assent to conclusions so reached does

25. "Anglo-Saxon Attitudes," *Encounter, 25* (August 1965), 54. Medawar acknowledges his debt to Karl Popper.

not exclude such conclusions from the domain of genuine knowledge. For when a scholar has said, "Here is all the relevant evidence that has been brought forward, and here are the conclusions which that evidence requires," his statement is no longer subject merely to opposition by rhetorical posturing. His claim can be shown to be false—either because he has overlooked some of the known evidence or because he has made a mistake in logic. Such an exposure of his oversight or his mistake can objectively overturn his conclusion, but nothing else can. His conclusion must stand until new evidence is brought forward.

The discipline of interpretation is founded, then, not on a methodology of construction but on a logic of validation. The principles of that logic, outlined in the preceding sections of this chapter, are essentially the principles which underlie the drawing of objective probability judgments in all domains of thought. The inevitable tendency of those logical principles is away from generalized maxims and toward an increasing particularity of relevant observations. The proper realm for generalizations in hermeneutics turns out to be the realm of principles, not of methods, for the principles underlying probability judgments require that every practical interpretive problem be solved in its particularity and not in accordance with maxims and approaches which usurp the name of theory. Nevertheless, despite its practical concreteness and variability, the root problem of interpretation is always the same—to guess what the author meant. Even though we can never be certain that our interpretive guesses are correct, we know that they *can* be correct and that the goal of interpretation as a discipline is constantly to increase the probability that they are correct. In the earlier chapters of this book, I showed that only one interpretive problem can be answered with objectivity: "What, in all probability, did the author mean to convey?" In this final chapter, I have tried to show more particularly wherein that objectivity lies. It lies in our capacity to say on firm principles, "Yes, that answer is valid" or "No, it is not."

Appendix I. Objective Interpretation

The fact that the term "criticism" has now come to designate all commentary on textual meaning reflects a general acceptance of the doctrine that description and evaluation are inseparable in literary study. In any serious confrontation of literature it would be futile, of course, to attempt a rigorous banishment of all evaluative judgment, but this fact does not give us the license to misunderstand or misinterpret our texts. It does not entitle us to use the text as the basis for an exercise in "creativity" or to submit as serious textual commentary a disguised argument for a particular ethical, cultural, or aesthetic viewpoint. Nor is criticism's chief concern—the present relevance of a text—a strictly necessary aspect of textual commentary. That same kind of theory which argues the inseparability of description and evaluation also argues that a text's meaning is simply its meaning "to us, today." Both kinds of argument support the idea that interpretation is criticism and vice versa. But there is clearly a sense in which we can neither evaluate a text nor determine what it means "to us, today" until we have correctly apprehended what it means. Understanding (and therefore interpretation, in the strict sense of the word) is both logically and psychologically prior to what is generally called criticism. It is true that this distinction between understanding and evaluation cannot always show itself in the finished work of criticism—nor, perhaps, should it—but a general grasp and acceptance of the distinction might help correct some of the most serious faults of current criticism (its subjectivism and relativism) and might even make it plausible to think of literary study as a corporate enterprise and a progressive discipline.

No one would deny, of course, that the more important issue is not the status of literary study as a discipline but the vitality of literature—especially of older literature—in the world at large.

Appendix I: Objective Interpretation

The critic is right to think that the text should speak to us. The point which needs to be grasped clearly by the critic is that a text cannot be made to speak to us until what it says has been understood. This is not an argument in favor of historicism as against criticism—it is simply a brute ontological fact. Textual meaning is not a naked given like a physical object. The text is first of all a conventional representation like a musical score, and what the score represents may be construed correctly or incorrectly. The literary text (in spite of the semimystical claims made for its uniqueness) does not have a special ontological status which somehow absolves the reader from the demands universally imposed by all linguistic texts of every description. Nothing, that is, can give a conventional representation the status of an immediate given. The text of a poem, for example, has to be construed by the critic before it becomes a poem for him. Then it is, no doubt, an artifact with special characteristics. But before the critic construes the poem it is no artifact for him at all, and if he construes it wrongly, he will subsequently be talking about the wrong artifact, not the one represented by the text. If criticism is to be objective in any significant sense, it must be founded on a self-critical construction of textual meaning, which is to say, on objective interpretation.

The distinction I am drawing between interpretation and criticism was one of the central principles in the now vestigial science of hermeneutics. August Boeckh, for example, divided the theoretical part of his *Encyclopädie* into two sections, one devoted to *Interpretation* (*Hermeneutik*) and the other to *Kritik*. Boeckh's discussion of this distinction is illuminating: interpretation is the construction of textual meaning as such; it explicates (*legt aus*) those meanings, and only those meanings, which the text explicitly or implicitly represents. Criticism, on the other hand, builds on the results of interpretation; it confronts textual meaning not as such, but as a component within a larger context. Boeckh defined it as "that philological function through which a text is understood not simply in its own terms and for its own sake, but in order to establish a relationship with something else, in such a way that the goal is a knowledge of this relationship itself." [1] Boeckh's definition is useful in emphasizing that interpretation and criticism

1. *Encyclopädie*, p. 170.

Appendix I: Objective Interpretation

confront two quite distinct "objects," for this is the fundamental distinction between the two activities. The object of interpretation is textual meaning in and for itself and may be called the *meaning* of the text. The object of criticism, on the other hand, is that meaning in its bearing on something else (standards of value, present concerns, etc.), and this object may therefore be called the *significance* of the text.

The distinction between the meaning and the significance of a text was first clearly made by Frege in his article "Über Sinn und Bedeutung," where he demonstrated that although the meanings of two texts may be different, their referent or truth-value may be identical.[2] For example, the statement, "Scott is the author of *Waverley*," is true and yet the meaning of "Scott" is different from that of "the author of *Waverley*." The *Sinn* of each is different, but the *Bedeutung* (or one aspect of *Bedeutung*—the designatum of "Scott" and "author of *Waverley*") is the same. Frege considered only cases where different *Sinne* have an identical *Bedeutung,* but it is also true that the same *Sinn* may, in the course of time, have different *Bedeutungen.* For example, the sentence, "There is a unicorn in the garden," is prima facie false. But suppose the statement were made when there *was* a unicorn in the garden (as happened in Thurber's imaginative world); the statement would be true; its relevance would have shifted. But true or false, the meaning of the proposition would remain the same, for unless its *meaning* remained self-identical, we would have nothing to label true or false. Frege's distinction, now widely accepted by logicians, is a special case of Husserl's general distinction between the inner and outer horizons of any meaning. In section A I shall try to clarify Husserl's concept and to show how it applies to the problems of textual study and especially to the basic assumptions of textual interpretation.

My purpose is primarily constructive rather than polemical. I would not willingly argue that interpretation should be practiced in strict separation from criticism. I shall ignore criticism simply in order to confront the special problems involved in construing

2. Gottlob Frege, "Über Sinn und Bedeutung," *Zeitschrift für Philosophie und philosophische Kritik, 100* (1892). The article has been translated, and one English version may be found in H. Feigl and W. Sellars, *Readings in Philosophical Analysis* (New York, 1949).

the meaning or *Sinn* of a text. For most of my notions I disclaim any originality. My aim is to revive some forgotten insights of literary study and to apply to the theory of interpretation certain other insights from linguistics and philosophy. For although the analytical movement in criticism has permanently advanced the cause of intrinsic literary study, it has not yet paid enough attention to the problem of establishing norms and limits in interpretation. If I display any argumentative intent, it is not, therefore, against the analytical movement, which I approve, but only against certain modern theories which hamper the establishment of normative principles in interpretation and which thereby encourage the subjectivism and individualism which have for many students discredited the analytical movement. By normative principles I mean those notions which concern the nature of a correct interpretation. When the critic clearly conceives what a correct interpretation is in principle, he possesses a guiding idea against which he can measure his construction. Without such a guiding idea, self-critical or objective interpretation is hardly possible. Current theory, however, fails to provide such a principle. The most influential and representative statement of modern theory is *Theory of Literature* by Wellek and Warren, a book to which I owe much. I ungratefully select it (especially Chap. 12) as a target of attack, both because it is so influential and because I need a specific, concrete example of the sort of theory which requires amendment.[3]

A. THE TWO HORIZONS OF TEXTUAL MEANING

The metaphorical doctrine that a text leads a life of its own is used by modern theorists to express the idea that textual meaning changes in the course of time.[4] This theory of a changing meaning serves to support the fusion of interpretation and criticism and, at the same time, the idea that present relevance forms the basis for textual commentary. But the view should not remain unchallenged, since if it were correct, there could be no objective knowledge about texts. Any statement about textual meaning could be valid only for the moment, and even this temporary validity could not

3. Wellek and Warren, *Theory of Literature,* Chap. 12. This chapter is by Wellek.
4. See, for example, ibid., p. 31.

be tested, since there would be no permanent norms on which validating judgments could be based. While the "life" theory does serve to explain and sanction the fact that different ages tend to interpret texts differently, and while it emphasizes the importance of a text's present relevance, it overlooks the fact that such a view undercuts *all* criticism, even the sort which emphasizes present relevance. If the view were correct, criticism would not only lack permanent validity, but could not even claim current validity by the time it got into print. Both the text's meaning and the tenor of the age would have altered. The "life" theory really masks the idea that the reader construes his own, new meaning instead of that represented by the text.

The "life" theory thus implicitly places the principle of change squarely where it belongs, that is, not in textual meaning as such, but in changing generations of readers. According to Wellek, for example, the meaning of the text changes as it passes "through the minds of its readers, critics, and fellow artists."[5] Now when even a few of the norms which determine a text's meaning are allotted to readers and made dependent on their attitudes and concerns, it is evident that textual meaning must change. But is it proper to make textual meaning dependent upon the reader's own cultural givens? It may be granted that these givens change in the course of time, but does this imply that textual meaning itself changes? As soon as the reader's outlook is permitted to determine what a text means, we have not simply a changing meaning but quite possibly as many meanings as readers.

Against such a reductio ad absurdum, the proponent of the current theory points out that in a given age many readers will agree in their construction of a text and will unanimously repudiate the accepted interpretation of a former age. For the sake of fair-mindedness, this presumed unanimity may be granted, but must it be explained by arguing that the text's meaning has changed? Recalling Frege's distinction between *Sinn* and *Bedeutung,* the change could be explained by saying that the meaning of the text has remained the same, while the significance of that meaning has shifted.[6] Contemporary readers will frequently share

5. Ibid., p. 144.
6. It could also be explained, of course, by saying that certain generations of readers tend to misunderstand certain texts.

similar cultural givens and will therefore agree about what the text means to them. But might it not be the case that they agree about the text's meaning "to them" because they have first understood its meaning? If textual meaning itself could change, contemporary readers would lack a basis for agreement or disagreement. No one would bother seriously to discuss such a protean object. The significance of textual meaning has no foundation and no objectivity unless meaning itself is unchanging. To fuse meaning and significance, or interpretation and criticism, by the conception of an autonomous, living, changing meaning does not really free the reader from the shackles of historicism; it simply destroys the basis both for any agreement among readers and for any objective study whatever.

The dilemma created by the fusion of *Sinn* and *Bedeutung* in current theory is exhibited as soon as the theorist attempts to explain how norms can be preserved in textual study. The explanation becomes openly self-contradictory: "It could be scarcely denied that there is [in textual meaning] a substantial *identity* of 'structure' which has remained the *same* throughout the ages. This *structure,* however, is dynamic: it *changes* throughout the process of history while passing through the minds of its readers, critics, and fellow artists."[7] First the "structure" is self-identical; then it changes! What is given in one breath is taken away in the next. Although it is a matter of common experience that a text appears different to us than it appeared to a former age, and although we remain deeply convinced that there *are* permanent norms in textual study, we cannot properly explain the facts by equating or fusing what changes with what remains the same. We must distinguish the two and give each its due.

A couplet from Marvell, used by Wellek to suggest how meaning changes, will illustrate my point:[8]

> My vegetable love should grow
> Vaster than empires and more slow.

Wellek grants that "vegetable" here probably means more or less what we nowadays express by "vegetative," but he goes on to sug-

7. Wellek and Warren, p. 144. My italics.
8. Ibid., pp. 166–67.

gest that we cannot avoid associating the modern connotation of "vegetable" (what it means "to us"). Furthermore, he suggests that this enrichment of meaning may even be desirable. No doubt, the associated meaning *is* here desirable (since it supports the mood of the poem), but Wellek could not even make his point unless we could distinguish between what "vegetable" probably means as used in the text and what it commonly means to us. Simply to discuss the issue is to admit that Marvell's poem probably does not imply the modern connotation, for if we could not separate the sense of "vegetative" from the notion of an "erotic cabbage," we could not talk about the difficulty of making the separation. One need not argue that the delight we may take in such new meanings must be ignored. On the contrary, once we have self-critically understood the text, there is little reason to exclude valuable or pleasant associations which enhance its significance. However, it is essential to exclude these associations in the process of interpretation, that is, in the process of understanding what a text means. The way out of the theoretical dilemma is to perceive that the meaning of a text does not change and that the modern, different connotation of a word like "vegetable" belongs, if it is to be entertained at all, to the constantly changing significance of a text's meaning.

It is in the light of the distinction between meaning and significance that critical theories like T. S. Eliot's need to be viewed.[9] Eliot, like other modern critics, insists that the meaning of a literary work changes in the course of time, but, in contrast to Wellek, instead of locating the principle of change directly in the changing outlooks of readers, Eliot locates it in a changing literary tradition. In his view, the literary tradition is a "simultaneous" (as opposed to temporal) order of literary texts which is constantly rearranging itself as new literary works appear on the public scene. Whenever a new work appears it causes a rearrangement of the tradition as a whole, and this brings about an alteration in the meaning of each component literary text. For example, when Shakespeare's *Troilus* entered the tradition, it altered not only the meaning of Chaucer's *Troilus,* but also, to some degree, the meaning of every other text in the literary tradition.

9. Eliot, "Tradition and the Individual Talent."

Appendix I: Objective Interpretation

If the changes in meaning Eliot speaks of are considered to be changes in significance, then his conception is perfectly sound. And indeed, by definition, Eliot is speaking of significance rather than meaning, since he is considering the work in relation to a larger realm, as a component rather than a world in itself. It goes without saying that the character of a component considered as such changes whenever the larger realm of which it is a part changes. A red object will appear to have different color qualities when viewed against differently colored backgrounds. The same is true of textual meaning. But the meaning of the text (its *Sinn*) does not change any more than the hue and saturation of the red object changes when seen against different backgrounds. Yet the analogy with colored objects is only partial: I can look at a red pencil against a green blotting pad and perceive the pencil's color in that special context without knowing the hue and saturation of either pencil or blotter. But textual meaning is a construction, not a naked given like a red object, and I cannot relate textual meaning to a larger realm until I have construed it. Before I can judge just how the changed tradition has altered the significance of a text, I must understand its meaning or *Sinn*.

This permanent meaning is, and can be, nothing other than the author's meaning. There have been, of course, several other definitions of textual meaning—what the author's contemporaries would ideally have construed, what the ideal present-day reader construes, what the norms of language permit the text to mean, what the best critics conceive to be the best meaning, and so on. In support of these other candidates, various aesthetic and psychological objections have been aimed at the author: first, his meaning, being conditioned by history and culture, is too confined and simple; second, it remains, in any case, inaccessible to us because we live in another age, or because his mental processes are private, or because he himself did not know what he meant. Instead of attempting to meet each of these objections separately, I shall attempt to describe the general principle for answering all of them and, in doing so, to clarify further the distinction between meaning and significance. The aim of my exposition will be to confirm that the author's meaning, as represented by his text, is unchanging and reproducible. My problem will be to show that, although textual meaning is *determined* by the psychic acts of an author and realized by those of a reader, textual meaning itself must not be *identified* with the author's or reader's psychic acts as such. To make this crucial point, I shall find it useful to draw upon Husserl's analysis of verbal meaning.

In his chief work, *Logische Untersuchungen,* Husserl sought, among other things, to avoid an identification of verbal meaning with the psychic acts of speaker or listener, author or reader, but to do this he did not adopt a strict, Platonic idealism by which meanings have an actual existence apart from meaning experiences. Instead, he affirmed the objectivity of meaning by analyzing the observable relationship between it and those very mental processes in which it is actualized, for in meaning experiences themselves, the objectivity and constancy of meaning are confirmed.

Husserl's point may be grasped by an example from visual experience.[10] When I look at a box, then close my eyes, and then reopen them, I can perceive in this second view the identical box I saw before. Yet, although I perceive the same box, the two acts of seeing are distinctly different—in this case, temporally different. The same sort of result is obtained when I alter my acts of seeing spatially. If I go to another side of the room or stand on a chair, what I actually "see" alters with my change in perspective, and yet I still "perceive" the identical box; I still understand that the *object* of my seeing is the same. Furthermore, if I leave the room and simply recall the box in memory, I still understand that the *object* I remember is identical with the object I saw. For if I did not understand that, how could I insist that I was remembering? The examples are paradigmatic: All events of consciousness, not simply those involving visual perception and memory, are characterized by the mind's ability to make modally and temporally different *acts* of awareness refer to the same *object* of awareness. An object for the mind remains the same even though what is

10. Most of my illustrations in this section are visual rather than verbal since the former may be more easily grasped. If, at this stage, I were to choose verbal examples I would have to interpret the examples before making my point. I discuss a literary text in sections B and C. The example of a box was suggested to me by Helmut Kuhn, "The Phenomenological Concept of 'Horizon,' " in *Philosophical Essays in Memory of Edmund Husserl,* ed. Marvin Farber (Cambridge, Mass., 1940).

"going on in the mind" is not the same. The mind's object therefore may not be equated with psychic processes as such; the mental object is self-identical over against a plurality of mental acts. [11]

The relation between an act of awareness and its object Husserl calls "intention," using the term in its traditional philosophical sense, which is much broader than that of "purpose" and is roughly equivalent to "awareness." (When I employ the word subsequently, I shall be using it in Husserl's sense.) [12] This term is useful for distinguishing the components of a meaning experience. For example, when I "intend" a box, there are at least three distinguishable aspects of that event. First, there is the object as perceived by me; second, there is the act by which I perceive the object; and finally, there is (for physical things) the object which exists independently of my perceptual act. The first two aspects of the event Husserl calls "intentional object" and "intentional act" respectively. Husserl's point, then, is that *different* intentional acts (on different occasions) "intend" an *identical* intentional object.

The general term for all intentional objects is meaning. Verbal meaning is simply a special kind of intentional object, and like any other one, it remains self-identical over against the many different acts which "intend" it. But the noteworthy feature of verbal meaning is its supra-personal character. It is not an intentional object for simply one person, but for many—potentially for all persons. Verbal meaning is, by definition, *that aspect of a speaker's "intention" which, under linguistic conventions, may be shared by others.* Anything not sharable in this sense does not belong to the verbal intention or verbal meaning. Thus, when I say, "The air is crisp," I may be thinking, among other things,

11. See Aaron Gurwitsch, "On the Intentionality of Consciousness," in *Philosophical Essays,* ed. Farber.

12. Although Husserl's term is a standard philosophical one for which there is no adequate substitute, students of literature may unwittingly associate it with the intentional fallacy. The two uses of the word are, however, quite distinct. As used by literary critics the term refers to a purpose which may or may not be realized by a writer. As used by Husserl the term refers to a process of consciousness. Thus in the literary usage, which involves problems of rhetoric, it is possible to speak of an unfulfilled intention, while in Husserl's usage such a locution would be meaningless.

A. The Two Horizons of Textual Meaning

"I should have eaten less at supper," and "Crisp air reminds me of my childhood in Vermont," and so on. In certain types of utterance such unspoken accompaniments to meaning may be sharable, but in general they are not, and therefore they do not generally belong to verbal meaning. The nonverbal aspects of the speaker's intention Husserl calls "experience" and the verbal ones "content." However, by content he does not mean simply intellectual content, but all those aspects of the intention—cognitive, emotive, phonetic (and in writing, even visual)—which may be conveyed to others by the linguistic means employed.[13]

Husserl's analysis (in my brief exposition) makes the following points then: Verbal meaning, being an intentional object, is unchanging, that is, it may be reproduced by different intentional acts and remains self-identical through all these reproductions. Verbal meaning is the sharable content of the speaker's intentional object. Since this meaning is both unchanging and interpersonal, it may be reproduced by the mental acts of different persons. Husserl's view is thus essentially historical, for even though he insists that verbal meaning is unchanging, he also insists that any particular verbal utterance, written or spoken, is historically determined. That is to say, the meaning is determined once and for all by the character of the speaker's intention.[14]

Husserl's views provide an excellent context for discussing the central problems of interpretation. Once we define verbal meaning as the content of the author's intention (which for brevity's sake I shall call simply the author's "verbal intention"), the problem for the interpreter is quite clear: he must distinguish those meanings which belong to that verbal intention from those which do not belong. This problem may be rephrased, of course, in a way that nearly everyone will accept: the interpreter has to distinguish what a text implies from what it does not imply; he must give the text its full due, but he must also preserve norms and limits. For hermeneutic theory, the problem is to find a *principle* for judging whether various possible implications should or should not be admitted.

13. Edmund Husserl, *Logische Untersuchungen. Zweiter Band. Untersuchungen zur Phänomenologie und Theorie der Erkenntnis. I Teil* (2d ed. Halle, 1913), pp. 96–97.
14. Ibid., p. 91.

Appendix I: Objective Interpretation

I describe the problem in terms of implication, since, for practical purposes, it lies at the heart of the matter. Generally, the explicit meanings of a text can be construed to the satisfaction of most readers; the problems arise in determining inexplicit or "unsaid" meanings. If, for example, I announce, "I have a headache," there is no difficulty in construing what I "say," but there may be great difficulty in construing implications like "I desire sympathy" or "I have a right not to engage in distasteful work." Such implications may belong to my verbal meaning, or they may not belong. This is usually the area where the interpreter needs a guiding principle.

It is often said that implications must be determined by referring to the context of the utterance, which, for ordinary statements like "I have a headache," means the concrete situation in which the utterance occurs. In the case of written texts, however, context generally means verbal context: the explicit meanings which surround the problematical passage. But these explicit meanings alone do not exhaust what we mean by context when we educe implications. The surrounding explicit meanings provide us with a sense of the whole meaning, and it is from this sense of the whole that we decide what the problematical passage implies. We do not ask simply, "Does this implication belong with these other explicit meanings?" but rather, "Does this implication belong with these other meanings *within a particular sort of total meaning?*" For example, we cannot determine whether "root" belongs with or implies "bark" unless we know that the total meaning is "tree" and not "grass." The ground for educing implications is a sense of the whole meaning, and this is an indispensable aspect of what we mean by context.

Previously I defined the whole meaning of an utterance as the author's verbal intention. Does this mean that the principle for admitting or excluding implications must be to ask, "Did the author have in mind such an implication?" If that is the principle, all hope for objective interpretation must be abandoned, since in most cases it is impossible (even for the author himself) to determine precisely what he was thinking of at the time or times he composed his text. But this is clearly not the correct principle. When I say, "I have a headache," I may indeed imply, "I would like some sympathy," and yet I might not have been explicitly conscious of such an implication. The first step, then, in discovering a principle for admitting and excluding implications is to perceive the fundamental distinction between the author's verbal intention and the meanings of which he was explicitly conscious. Here again, Husserl's rejection of psychologism is useful. The author's verbal intention (his total verbal meaning) may be likened to my "intention" of a box. Normally, when I perceive a box, I am explicitly conscious of only three sides, and yet I assert with full confidence (although I might be wrong) that I "intend" a box, an object with *six* sides. Those three unseen sides belong to my "intention" in precisely the same way that the unconscious implications of an utterance belong to the author's intention. They belong to the intention taken as a whole.

Most, if not all, meaning experiences or intentions are occasions in which the whole meaning is not explicitly present to consciousness. But how are we to define the manner in which these unconscious meanings are implicitly present? In Husserl's analysis, they are present in the form of a "horizon," which may be defined as a system of typical expectations and probabilities.[15] "Horizon" is thus an essential aspect of what we usually call context. It is an inexplicit sense of the whole, derived from the explicit meanings present to consciousness. Thus, my view of three surfaces, presented in a familiar and typically box-like way, has a horizon of typical continuations; or, to put it another way, my "intention" of a whole box defines the horizon for my view of three visible sides. The same sort of relationship holds between the explicit and implicit meanings in a verbal intention. The explicit meanings are components in a total meaning which is bounded by a horizon. Of the manifold typical continuations within this horizon the author is not and cannot be explicitly conscious, nor would it be a particularly significant task to determine just which components of his meaning the author *was* thinking of. But it is of the utmost importance to determine the horizon which defines the author's intention as a whole, for it is only with reference to this horizon, or sense of the whole, that the interpreter may distinguish those implications which are typical and proper components of the meaing from those which are not.

15. See Edmund Husserl, *Erfahrung und Urteil,* ed. L. Landgrebe (Hamburg, 1948), pp. 26–36, and Kuhn, "The Phenomenological Concept of 'Horizon.' "

Appendix I: Objective Interpretation

The interpreter's aim, then, is to posit the author's horizon and carefully exclude his own accidental associations. A word like "vegetable," for example, had a meaning horizon in Marvell's language which is evidently somewhat different from the horizon it has in contemporary English. This is the linguistic horizon of the word, and it strictly bounds its possible implications. But all of these possible implications do not necessarily belong within the horizon of the particular utterance. What the word implies in the particular usage must be determined by asking, "Which implications are typical components of the whole meaning under consideration?" By analogy, when three surfaces are presented to me in a special way, I must know the typical continuations of the surfaces. If I have never encountered a box before, I might think that the unseen surfaces were concave or irregular, or I might simply think there are other sides but have no idea what they are like. The probability that I am right in the way I educe implications depends upon my familiarity with the type of meaning I consider.

That is the reason, of course, that the genre concept is so important in textual study. By classifying the text as belonging to a particular genre, the interpreter automatically posits a general horizon for its meaning. The genre provides a sense of the whole, a notion of typical meaning components. Thus, before we interpret a text, we often classify it as casual conversation, lyric poem, military command, scientific prose, occasional verse, novel, epic, and so on. In a similar way, I have to classify the object I see as a box, a sphere, a tree, and so on before I can deduce the character of its unseen or inexplicit components. But these generic classifications are simply preliminary indications. They give only a rough notion of the horizon for a particular meaning. The aim of interpretation is to specify the horizon as far as possible. Thus, the object I see is not simply a box but a cigarette carton, and not simply that but a carton for a particular brand of cigarettes. If a paint mixer or dyer wants to specify a particular patch of color, he is not content to call it blue; he calls it Williamsburg Blue. The example of a color patch is paradigmatic for all particular verbal meanings. They are not simply *kinds* of meanings, nor are they single meanings corresponding to individual intentional acts (Williamsburg Blue is not simply an individual patch of color); they are *typical* meanings, particular yet reproducible, and the typical *components* of such meanings are similarly specific. The interpreter's job is to specify the text's horizon as far as he is able, and this means, ultimately, that he must familiarize himself with the typical meanings of the author's mental and experiential world.

The importance of the horizon concept is that it defines in principle the norms and limits which bound the meaning represented by the text. But, at the same time, the concept frees the interpreter from the constricting and impossible task of discovering what the author was explicitly thinking of. Thus, by defining textual meaning as the author's meaning, the interpreter does not, as it is so often argued, impoverish meaning; he simply excludes what does not belong to it. For example, if I say, "My car ran out of gas," I imply, typically, "The engine stopped running." Whether I also imply "Life is ironical" depends on the generality of my intention. Some linguistic utterances, many literary works among them, have an extremely broad horizon which at some points may touch the boundaries of man's intellectual cosmos. But whether this is the case is not a matter for a priori discussion; the decision must be based on a knowledgeable inference as to the particular intention being considered.

Within the horizon of a text's meaning, however, the process of explication is unlimited. In this respect Dryden was right; no text is ever fully explicated. For example, if I undertook to interpret my "intention" of a box, I could make explicit unlimited implications which I did not notice in my original intention. I could educe not only the three unseen sides, but also the fact that the surfaces of the box contain twenty-four right angles, that the area of two adjoining sides is less than half the total surface area, and so on. And if someone asked me whether such meanings were implicit in my intention of a box, I must answer affirmatively. In the case of linguistic meanings, where the horizon defines a much more complex intentional object, such determinations are far more difficult to make. But the probability of an interpreter's inference may be judged by two criteria alone—the accuracy with which he has sensed the horizon of the whole and the typicality of such a meaning within such a whole. Insofar as the inference meets these criteria, it is truly an explication of textual meaning. It simply renders explicit that which was, consciously or unconsciously, in the author's intention.

Appendix I: Objective Interpretation

The horizon which grounds and sanctions inferences about textual meaning is the "inner horizon" of the text. It is permanent and self-identical. Beyond this inner horizon any meaning has an "outer horizon"; that is to say, any meaning has relationships to other meanings; it is always a component in larger realms. This outer horizon is the domain of criticism. But this outer horizon is not only unlimited, it is also changing since the world itself changes. In general, criticism stakes out only a portion of this outer horizon as its peculiar object. Thus, for example, Eliot partitioned off that aspect of the text's outer horizon which is defined by the simultaneous order of literary texts. The simultaneous order at a given point in time is therefore the inner horizon of the meaning Eliot is investigating, and this inner horizon is just as definite, atemporal, and objective as the inner horizon which bounds textual meaning. However, the critic, like the interpreter, must construe correctly the components of his inner horizon, and one major component is textual meaning itself. The critic must first accurately interpret the text. He need not perform a detailed explication, but he needs to achieve (and validate) that clear and specific sense of the whole meaning which makes detailed explication possible.

B. DETERMINATENESS OF TEXTUAL MEANING

In the previous section I defined textual meaning as the verbal intention of the author, and this argues implicitly that hermeneutics must stress a reconstruction of the author's aims and attitudes in order to evolve guides and norms for construing the meaning of his text. It is frequently argued, however, that textual meaning has nothing to do with the author's mind but only with his verbal achievement, that the object of interpretation is not the author but his text. This plausible argument assumes, of course, that the text automatically has a meaning simply because it represents an unalterable sequence of words. It assumes that the meaning of a word sequence is directly imposed by the public norms of language, that the text as a "piece of language" is a public object whose character is defined by public norms.[16] This view is in one respect

16. The phrase, "piece of language," comes from the first paragraph of Empson's *Seven Types of Ambiguity*. It is typical of the critical school Empson founded.

B. Determinateness of Textual Meaning

sound, since textual meaning must conform to public norms if it is in any sense to be verbal (i.e. sharable) meaning; on no account may the interpreter permit his probing into the author's mind to raise private associations (experience) to the level of public implications (content).

However, this basically sound argument remains one-sided, for even though verbal meaning must conform to public linguistic norms (these are highly tolerant, of course), no mere sequence of words can represent an actual verbal meaning with reference to public norms alone. Referred to these alone, the text's meaning remains indeterminate. This is true even of the simplest declarative sentence like "My car ran out of gas" (did my Pullman dash from a cloud of Argon?). The fact that no one would radically misinterpret such a sentence simply indicates that its frequency is high enough to give its usual meaning the apparent status of an immediate given. But this apparent immediacy obscures a complex process of adjudications among meaning possibilities. Under the public norms of language alone no such adjudications can occur, since the array of possibilities presents a face of blank indifference. The array of possibilities only begins to become a more selective system of *probabilities* when, instead of confronting merely a word sequence, we also posit a speaker who very likely means something. Then and only then does the most usual sense of the word sequence become the most probable or "obvious" sense. The point holds true a fortiori, of course, when we confront less obvious word sequences like those found in poetry. A careful exposition of this point may be found in the first volume of Cassirer's *Philosophy of Symbolic Forms,* which is largely devoted to a demonstration that verbal meaning arises from the "reciprocal determination" of public linguistic possibilities and subjective specifications of those possibilities.[17] Just as language constitutes and colors subjectivity, so does subjectivity color language. The author's or speaker's subjective act is formally necessary to verbal meaning, and any theory which tries to dispense with the author

17. Vol. 1, *Language.* It is ironic that Cassirer's work should be used to support the notion that a text speaks for itself. The realm of language is autonomous for Cassirer only in the sense that it follows an independent development which is reciprocally determined by objective *and* subjective factors. See pp. 69, 178, 213, 249–50, and passim.

as specifier of meaning by asserting that textual meaning is purely objectively determined finds itself chasing will-o'-the-wisps. The burden of this section is, then, an attack on the view that a text is a "piece of language" and a defense of the notion that a text represents the determinate verbal meaning of an author.

One of the consequences arising from the view that a text is a piece of language—a purely public object—is the impossibility of defining in principle the nature of a correct interpretation. This is the same impasse which results from the theory that a text leads a life of its own, and, indeed, the two notions are corollaries since any "piece of language" must have a changing meaning when the changing public norms of language are viewed as the only ones which determine the sense of the text. It is therefore not surprising to find that Wellek subscribes implicitly to the text-as-language theory. The text is viewed as representing not a determinate meaning, but rather a system of meaning potentials specified not by a meaner but by the vital potency of language itself. Wellek acutely perceives the danger of the view:

> Thus the system of norms is growing and changing and will remain, in some sense, always incompletely and imperfectly realized. But this dynamic conception does not mean mere subjectivism and relativism. All the different points of view are by no means equally right. It will always be possible to determine which point of view grasps the subject most thoroughly and deeply. A hierarchy of viewpoints, a criticism of the grasp of norms, is implied in the concept of the adequacy of interpretation.[18]

The danger of the view is, of course, precisely that it opens the door to subjectivism and relativism, since linguistic norms may be invoked to support any verbally possible meaning. Furthermore, it is not clear how one may criticize a grasp of norms which will not stand still.

Wellek's brief comment on the problem involved in defining and testing correctness in interpretation is representative of a widespread conviction among literary critics that the most correct interpretation is the most "inclusive" one. Indeed, the view is so

18. Wellek and Warren, *Theory of Literature,* p. 144.

B. *Determinateness of Textual Meaning*

widely accepted that Wellek did not need to defend his version of it (which he calls "Perspectivism") at length. The notion behind the theory is reflected by such phrases as "always incompletely and imperfectly realized" and "grasps the subject most thoroughly." This notion is simply that no single interpretation can exhaust the rich system of meaning potentialities represented by the text. Hence, every plausible reading which remains within public linguistic norms is a correct reading so far as it goes, but each reading is inevitably partial since it cannot realize all the potentialities of the text. The guiding principle in criticism, therefore, is that of the inclusive interpretation. The most "adequate" construction is the one which gives the fullest coherent account of all the text's potential meanings.[19]

Inclusivism is desirable as a position which induces a readiness to consider the results of others, but, aside from promoting an estimable tolerance, it has little theoretical value. Although its aim is to reconcile different plausible readings in an ideal, comprehensive interpretation, it cannot, in fact, either reconcile different readings or choose between them. As a normative ideal, or principle of correctness, it is useless. This point may be illustrated by citing two expert readings of a well-known poem by Wordsworth. I shall first quote the poem and then quote excerpts from two published exegeses to demonstrate the kind of impasse which inclusivism always provokes when it attempts to reconcile interpretations and, incidentally, to demonstrate the very kind of interpretive problem which calls for a guiding principle:

> A slumber did my spirit seal;
>   I had no human fears:
> She seemed a thing that could not feel
>   The touch of earthly years.
>
> No motion has she now, no force;
>   She neither hears nor sees;
> Rolled round in earth's diurnal course,
>   With rocks, and stones, and trees.

19. Every interpretation is necessarily incomplete in the sense that it fails to explicate all a text's implications. But this kind of incomplete interpretation may still carry an absolutely correct system of emphases

Appendix I: Objective Interpretation

Here are excerpts from two commentaries on the final lines of the poem; the first is by Cleanth Brooks, the second by F. W. Bateson:

> [The poet] attempts to suggest something of the lover's agonized shock at the loved one's present lack of motion—of his response to her utter and horrible inertness. . . . Part of the effect, of course, resides in the fact that a dead lifelessness is suggested more sharply by an object's being whirled about by something else than by an image of the object in repose. But there are other matters which are at work here: the sense of the girl's falling back into the clutter of things, companioned by things chained like a tree to one particular spot, or by things completely inanimate like rocks and stones. . . . [She] is caught up helplessly into the empty whirl of the earth which measures and makes time. She is touched by and held by earthly time in its most powerful and horrible image.

> The final impression the poem leaves is not of two contrasting moods, but of a single mood mounting to a climax in the pantheistic magnificence of the last two lines. . . . The vague living-Lucy of this poem is opposed to the grander dead-Lucy who has become involved in the sublime processes of nature. We put the poem down satisfied, because its last two lines succeed in effecting a reconciliation between the two philosophies or social attitudes. Lucy is actually more alive now that she is dead, because she is now a part of the life of Nature, and not just a human "thing."[20]

If we grant, as I think we must, that both the cited interpretations are permitted by the text, the problem for the inclusivist is to reconcile the two readings.

---

and an accurate sense of the whole meaning. This kind of incompleteness is radically different from that postulated by the inclusivists, for whom a sense of the whole means a grasp of the various possible meanings which a text can plausibly represent.

20. Cleanth Brooks, "Irony as a Principle of Structure," in *Literary Opinion in America,* ed. M. D. Zabel (2d ed. New York, 1951), p. 736; F. W. Bateson, *English Poetry: A Critical Introduction* (London, 1950), pp. 33, 80–81.

B. *Determinateness of Textual Meaning*

Three modes of reconciliation are available to the inclusivist: (1) Brooks' reading includes Bateson's; it shows that any affirmative suggestions in the poem are negated by the bitterly ironical portrayal of the inert girl being whirled around by what Bateson calls the "sublime processes of Nature." (2) Bateson's reading includes Brooks'; the ironic contrast between the active, seemingly immortal girl and the passive, inert, dead girl is overcome by a final unqualified affirmation of immortality. (3) Each of the readings is partially right, but they must be fused to supplement one another. The very fact that the critics differ suggests that the meaning is essentially ambiguous. The emotion expressed is ambivalent and comprises both bitter regret and affirmation. The third mode of reconciliation is the one most often employed and is probably, in this case, the most satisfactory. A fourth type of resolution, which would insist that Brooks is right and Bateson wrong (or vice versa), is not available to the inclusivist, since the text, as language, renders both readings plausible.

Close examination, however, reveals that none of the three modes of argument manages to reconcile or fuse the two different readings. Mode 1, for example, insists that Brooks' reading comprehends Bateson's, but although it is conceivable that Brooks implies all the meanings which Bateson has perceived, Brooks also implies a pattern of emphasis which cannot be reconciled with Bateson's reading. While Bateson construes a primary emphasis on life and affirmation, Brooks emphasizes deadness and inertness. No amount of manipulation can reconcile these divergent emphases, since one pattern of emphasis irrevocably excludes other patterns, and, since emphasis is always crucial to meaning, the two constructions of meaning rigorously exclude one another. Precisely the same strictures hold, of course, for the argument that Bateson's reading comprehends that of Brooks. Nor can mode 3 escape with impunity. Although it seems to preserve a stress both on negation and on affirmation, thereby coalescing the two readings, it actually excludes both readings and labels them not simply partial, but wrong. For if the poem gives equal stress to bitter irony and to affirmation, then any construction which places a primary stress on either meaning is simply incorrect.

The general principle implied by my analysis is very simple. The submeanings of a text are not blocks which can be brought together additively. Since verbal (and any other) meaning is a *structure* of component meanings, interpretation has not done its job when it simply enumerates what the component meanings are. The interpreter must also determine their probable structure and particularly their structure of emphases. Relative emphasis is not only crucial to meaning (perhaps it is the most crucial and problematical element of all), it is also highly restrictive; it excludes alternatives. It may be asserted as a general rule that whenever a reader confronts two interpretations which impose different emphases on similar meaning components, at least one of the interpretations must be wrong. They cannot be reconciled.

By insisting that verbal meaning always exhibits a determinate structure of emphases, I do not, however, imply that a poem or any other text must be unambiguous. It is perfectly possible, for example, that Wordsworth's poem ambiguously implies both bitter irony and positive affirmation. Such complex emotions are commonly expressed in poetry, but if that is the kind of meaning the text represents, Brooks and Bateson would be wrong to emphasize one emotion at the expense of the other. Ambiguity or, for that matter, vagueness is not the same as indeterminateness. This is the crux of the issue. To say that verbal meaning is determinate is not to exclude complexities of meaning but only to insist that a text's meaning is what it is and not a hundred other things. Taken in this sense, a vague or ambiguous text is just as determinate as a logical proposition; it means what it means and nothing else. This is true even if one argues that a text could display shifting emphases like those magic squares which first seem to jut out and then to jut in. With texts of this character (if any exist), one need only say that the emphases shift and must not, therefore, be construed statically. Any static construction would simply be wrong. The fundamental flaw in the "theory of the most inclusive interpretation" is that it overlooks the problem of emphasis. Since different patterns of emphasis exclude one another, inclusivism is neither a genuine norm nor an adequate guiding principle for establishing an interpretation.

Aside from the fact that inclusivism cannot do its appointed job, there are more fundamental reasons for rejecting it and all other interpretive ideals based on the conception that a text represents a system of meaning possibilities. No one would deny that

B. Determinateness of Textual Meaning

for the interpreter the text is at first the source of numerous possible interpretations. The very nature of language is such that a particular sequence of words can represent several different meanings (that is why public norms alone are insufficient in textual interpretation). But to say that a text *might* represent several structures of meaning does not imply that it does in fact represent all the meanings which a particular word sequence can legally convey. Is there not an obvious distinction between what a text might mean and what it does mean? According to accepted linguistic theory, it is far more accurate to say that a written composition is not a mere locus of verbal possibilities, but a record (made possible by the invention of writing) of a verbal actuality. The interpreter's job is to reconstruct a determinate actual meaning, not a mere system of possibilities. Indeed, if the text represented a system of possibilities, interpretation would be impossible, since no actual reading could correspond to a mere system of possibilities. Furthermore, if the text is conceived to represent all the *actual* structures of meaning permissible within the public norms of language, then no single construction (with its exclusivist pattern of emphases) could be correct, and any legitimate construction would be just as incorrect as any other. When a text is conceived as a piece of language, a familiar and all too common anarchy follows. But, aside from its unfortunate consequences, the theory contradicts a widely accepted principle in linguistics. I refer to Saussure's distinction between *langue* and *parole*.

Saussure defined *langue* as the system of linguistic possibilities shared by a speech community at a given point in time.[21] This system of possibilities contains two distinguishable levels. The first consists of habits, engrams, prohibitions, and the like derived from past linguistic usage; these are the "virtualities" of the *langue*. Based on these virtualities, there are, in addition, sharable meaning possibilities which have never before been actualized; these are the "potentialities." The two types of meaning possibilities

21. This is the "synchronic" as opposed to the "diachronic" sense of the term. See Ferdinand de Saussure, *Cours de linguistique générale* (Paris, 1931). Useful discussions may be found in Stephen Ullman, *The Principles of Semantics* (Glasgow, 1951), and W. v. Wartburg, *Einführung in die Problematik und Methodik der Sprachwissenschaft* (Halle, 1943).

taken together constitute the *langue* which the speech community draws upon. But this system of possibilities must be distinguished from the actual verbal utterances of individuals who draw upon it. These actual utterances are called *paroles;* they are uses of language and actualize some (but never all) of the meaning possibilities constituting the *langue.*

Saussure's distinction pinpoints the issue: does a text represent a segment of *langue* (as modern theorists hold) or a *parole?* A simple test suffices to provide the answer. If the text is composed of sentences, it represents *parole,* which is to say, the determinate verbal meaning of a member of the speech community. *Langue* contains words and sentence-forming principles, but it contains no sentences. It may be represented in writing only by isolated words in disconnection (*Wörter* as opposed to *Worte*). A *parole,* on the other hand, is always composed of sentences, an assertion corroborated by the firmly established principle that the sentence is the fundamental unit of speech.[22] Of course, there are numerous elliptical and one-word sentences, but wherever it can be correctly inferred that a text represents sentences and not simply isolated words, it may also be inferred that the text represents *parole,* which is to say, actual, determinate verbal meaning.

The point is nicely illustrated in a dictionary definition. The letters in boldface at the head of the definition represent the word as *langue,* with all its rich meaning possibilities. But under one of the subheadings, in an illustrative sentence, those same letters represent the word as *parole,* as a particular, selective actualization from *langue.* In yet another illustrative sentence, under another subheading, the very same word represents a different selective actualization. Of course, many sentences, especially those found in poetry, actualize far more possibilities than illustrative sentences in a dictionary. Any pun, for example, realizes simultaneously at least two divergent meaning possibilities. But the pun is nevertheless an actualization from *langue* and not a mere system of meaning possibilities.

The *langue-parole* distinction, besides affirming the determinateness of textual meaning, also clarifies the special problems posed

22. See, for example, Cassirer, *Symbolic Forms,* Vol. 1, *Language,* p. 304.

by revised and interpolated texts. With a revised text, composed over a long period of time (*Faust,* for example), how are we to construe the unrevised portions? Should we assume that they still mean what they meant originally or that they took on a new meaning when the rest of the text was altered or expanded? With compiled or interpolated texts, like many books of the Bible, should we assume that sentences from varied provenances retain their original meanings or that these heterogeneous elements have become integral components of a new total meaning? In terms of Saussure's distinction, the question becomes: should we consider the text to represent a compilation of divers *paroles* or a new unitary *parole* "respoken" by the new author or editor? I submit that there can be no definitive answer to the question, except in relation to a specific scholarly or aesthetic purpose, for in reality the question is not, "How are we to interpret the text?" but, *"Which* text are we to interpret?" Is it to be the heterogeneous compilation of past *paroles,* each to be separately considered, or the new, homogeneous *parole?* Both may be represented by the written score. The only problem is to choose, and having chosen, rigorously to refrain from confusing or in any way identifying the two quite different and separate "texts" with one another. Without solving any concrete problems, then, Saussure's distinction nevertheless confirms the critic's right in most cases to regard his text as representing a single *parole.*

Another problem which Saussure's distinction clarifies is that posed by the bungled text, where the author aimed to convey a meaning which his words do not convey to others in the speech community. One sometimes confronts the problem in a freshman essay. In such a case, the question is, does the text mean what the author wanted it to mean or does it mean what the speech community at large takes it to mean? Much attention has been devoted to this problem ever since the publication in 1946 of Wimsatt's and Beardsley's essay on "The Intentional Fallacy."[23] In that essay the position was taken (albeit modified by certain qualifications) that the text, being public, means what the speech community takes it to mean. This position is, in an ethical sense, right (and language, being social, has a strong ethical aspect): if the author has bungled

23. See Chap. 1, n. 11.

so badly that his utterance will be misconstrued, then it serves him right when people misunderstand him. However, put in linguistic terms, the position becomes unsatisfactory. It implies that the meaning represented by the text is not the *parole* of an author, but rather the *parole* of the speech community. But since only individuals utter *paroles*, a *parole* of the speech community is a nonexistent, or what the Germans call an *Unding*. A text can represent only the *parole* of a speaker or author, which is another way of saying that meaning requires a meaner.

However, it is not necessary that an author's text represent the *parole* he desired to convey. It is frequently the case, when an author has bungled, that his text represents no *parole* at all. Indeed, there are but two alternatives: either the text represents the author's verbal meaning or it represents no determinate verbal meaning at all. Sometimes, of course, it is impossible to detect that the author has bungled, and in that case, even though his text does not represent verbal meaning, we shall go on misconstruing the text as though it did, and no one will be the wiser. But with most bungles we are aware of a disjunction between the author's words and his probable meaning. Eliot, for example, chided Poe for saying "My most immemorial year," when Poe "meant" his most *memorable* year.[24] We all agree that Poe did not mean what speakers of English generally mean by the word "immemorial"—and so the word cannot have the usual meaning. (An author cannot mean what he does not mean.) The only question, then, is: does the word mean more or less what we convey by "never to be forgotten" or does it mean nothing at all? Has Poe so violated linguistic norms that we must deny his utterance verbal meaning or content?

The question probably cannot be answered by fiat, but since Poe's meaning is generally understood, and since the single criterion for verbal meaning is communicability, I am inclined to describe Poe's meaning as verbal.[25] I tend to side with the Poes

24. T. S. Eliot, "From Poe to Valéry," *Hudson Review, 2* (1949), 232.
25. The word is, in fact, quite effective. It conveys the sense of "memorable" by the component "memorial," and the sense of "never to be forgotten" by the negative prefix. The difference between this and jabberwocky words is that it appears to be a standard word occurring in a context of standard words. Perhaps Eliot is right to scold Poe, but he cannot properly insist that the word lacks a determinate verbal meaning.

and Malaprops of the world, for the norms of language remain far more tolerant than dictionaries and critics like Eliot suggest. On the other hand, every member of the speech community, and especially the critic, has a duty to avoid and condemn sloppiness and needless ambiguity in the use of language, simply in order to preserve the effectiveness of the *langue* itself. Moreover, there must be a dividing line between verbal meanings and those meanings which we half-divine by a supra-linguistic exercise of imagination. There must be a dividing line between Poe's successful disregard of normal usage and the incommunicable word sequences of a bad freshman essay. However, that dividing line is not between the author's meaning and the reader's, but rather between the author's *parole* and no *parole* at all.

Of course, theoretical principles cannot directly solve the interpreter's problem. It is one thing to insist that a text represents the determinate verbal meaning of an author, but it is quite another to discover what that meaning is. The very same text could represent numerous different *paroles,* as any ironic sentence discloses ("That's a *bright* idea?" or "That's a bright *idea!*"). But it should be of some practical consequence for the interpreter to know that he does have a precisely defined task, namely, to discover the author's meaning. It is therefore not only sound but necessary for the interpreter to inquire, "What in all probability did the author mean? Is the pattern of emphases I construe the author's pattern?" But it is both incorrect and futile to inquire, "What does the language of the text say?" That question can have no determinate answer.

C. VERIFICATION

Since the meaning represented by a text is that of another, the interpreter can never be certain that his reading is correct. He knows furthermore that the norms of *langue* by themselves are far too broad to specify the particular meanings and emphases represented by the text, that these particular meanings were specified by particular kinds of subjective acts on the part of the author, and that these acts, as such, remain inaccessible.[26] A less self-

26. To recall Husserl's point, a particular verbal meaning depends on a particular species of intentional act, not on a single, irreproducible act.

critical reader, on the other hand, approaches solipsism if he assumes that the text represents a perspicuous meaning simply because it represents an unalterable sequence of words. For if this perspicuous meaning is not verified in some way, it will simply be the interpreter's own meaning, exhibiting the connotations and emphases which he himself imposes. Of course, the reader must realize verbal meaning by his own subjective acts (no one can do that for him), but if he remembers that his job is to construe the author's meaning, he will attempt to exclude his own predispositions and to impose those of the author. However, no one can establish another's meaning with certainty. The interpreter's goal is simply this—to show that a given reading is more probable than others. In hermeneutics, verification is a process of establishing relative probabilities.

To establish a reading as probable it is first necessary to show, with reference to the norms of language, that it is possible. This is the criterion of *legitimacy:* the reading must be permissible within the public norms of the *langue* in which the text was composed. The second criterion is that of *correspondence:* the reading must account for each linguistic component in the text. Whenever a reading arbitrarily ignores linguistic components or inadequately accounts for them, the reading may be presumed improbable. The third criterion is that of *generic appropriateness:* if the text follows the conventions of a scientific essay, for example, it is inappropriate to construe the kind of allusive meaning found in casual conversation. [27] When these three preliminary criteria have been satisfied, there remains a fourth criterion which gives significance to all the rest, the criterion of plausibility or *coherence.* The three preliminary norms usually permit several readings, and this is by definition the case when a text is problematical. Faced with alternatives, the interpreter chooses the reading which best meets the criterion of coherence. Indeed, even when the text is not problematical, coherence remains the decisive criterion, since the meaning is "obvious" only because it "makes sense." I wish, therefore, to focus attention on the criterion of coherence and shall take for granted the demands of legitimacy, correspondence, and

27. This third criterion is, however, highly presumptive, since the interpreter may easily mistake the text's genre.

generic appropriateness. I shall try to show that verification by the criterion of coherence, and ultimately, therefore, verification in general, implies a reconstruction of relevant aspects in the author's outlook. My point may be summarized in the paradox that objectivity in textual interpretation requires explicit reference to the speaker's subjectivity.

The paradox reflects the peculiar nature of coherence, which is not an absolute but a dependent quality. The laws of coherence are variable; they depend upon the nature of the total meaning under consideration. Two meanings ("dark" and "bright," for example) which cohere in one context may not cohere in another.[28] "Dark with excessive bright" makes excellent sense in *Paradise Lost,* but if a reader found the phrase in a textbook on plant pathology, he would assume that he confronted a misprint for "dark with excessive blight." Coherence depends on the context, and it is helpful to recall our definition of context: it is a sense of the whole meaning, constituted of explicit partial meanings plus a horizon of expectations and probabilities. One meaning coheres with another because it is typical or probable with reference to the whole (coherence is thus the first cousin of implication). The criterion of coherence can be invoked only with reference to a particular context, and this context may be inferred only by positing the author's horizon, his disposition toward a particular type of meaning. This conclusion requires elaboration.

The fact that coherence is a dependent quality leads to an unavoidable circularity in the process of interpretation. The interpreter posits meanings for the words and word sequences he confronts, and, at the same time, he has to posit a whole meaning or context in reference to which the submeanings cohere with one another. The procedure is thoroughly circular; the context is derived from the submeanings and the submeanings are specified and rendered coherent with reference to the context. This circularity makes it very difficult to convince a reader to alter his construction, as every teacher knows. Many a self-willed student continues to insist that his reading is just as plausible as his instructor's, and, very often, the student is justified; his reading does make good

28. Exceptions to this are the syncategorematic meanings (color and extension, for example) which cohere by necessity regardless of the context.

sense. Often, the only thing at fault with the student's reading is that it is probably wrong, not that it is incoherent. The student persists in his opinion precisely because his construction *is* coherent and self-sustaining. In such a case he is wrong because he has misconstrued the context or sense of the whole. In this respect, the student's hardheadedness is not different from that of all self-convinced interpreters. Our readings are too plausible to be relinquished. If we have a distorted sense of the text's whole meaning, the harder we look at it the more certainly we shall find our distorted construction confirmed.

Since the quality of coherence depends upon the context inferred, there is no absolute standard of coherence by which we can adjudicate between different coherent readings. Verification by coherence implies therefore a verification of the grounds on which the reading is coherent. *It is necessary to establish that the context invoked is the most probable context.* Only then, in relation to an established context, can we judge that one reading is more coherent than another. Ultimately, therefore, we have to posit the most probable horizon for the text, and it is possible to do this only if we posit the author's typical outlook, the typical associations and expectations which form in part the context of his utterance. This is not only the one way we can test the relative coherence of a reading, but it is also the only way to avoid pure circularity in making sense of the text.

An essential task in the process of verification is, therefore, a deliberate reconstruction of the author's subjective stance to the extent that this stance is relevant to the text at hand.[29] The im-

29. The reader may feel that I have telescoped a number of steps here. The author's verbal meaning or verbal intention is the object of complex intentional acts. To reproduce this meaning it is necessary for the interpreter to engage in intentional acts belonging to the same species as those of the author. (Two different intentional acts belong to the same species when they "intend" the same intentional object.) That is why the issue of "stance" arises. The interpreter needs to adopt sympathetically the author's stance (his disposition to engage in particular kinds of intentional acts) so that he can "intend" with some degree of probability the same intentional objects as the author. This is especially clear in the case of *implicit* verbal meaning, where the interpreter's realization of the author's stance determines the text's horizon.

portance of such psychological reconstruction may be exemplified in adjudicating between different readings of Wordsworth's "A Slumber Did My Spirit Seal." The interpretations of Brooks and Bateson, different as they are, remain equally coherent and self-sustaining. The implications which Brooks construes cohere beautifully with the explicit meanings of the poem within the context which Brooks adumbrates. The same may be said of Bateson's reading. The best way to show that one reading is more plausible and coherent than the other is to show that one context is more probable than the other. The problem of adjudicating between Bateson and Brooks is therefore, implicitly, the problem every interpreter must face when he tries to verify his reading. He must establish the most probable context.

Now when the *homme moyen sensuel* confronts bereavement such as that which Wordsworth's poem explicitly presents, he adumbrates, typically, a horizon including sorrow and inconsolability. These are for him components in the very meaning of bereavement. Sorrow and inconsolability cannot fail to be associated with death when the loved one, formerly so active and alive, is imagined as lying in the earth, helpless, dumb, inert, insentient. And since there is no hint of life in Heaven but only of bodily death, the comforts of Christianity lie beyond the poem's horizon. Affirmations too deep for tears, like those Bateson insists on, simply do not cohere with the poem's explicit meanings; they do not belong to the context. Brooks' reading, therefore, with its emphasis on inconsolability and bitter irony, is clearly justified not only by the text but by reference to universal human attitudes and feelings.

However, the trouble with such a reading is apparent to most Wordsworthians. The poet is not an *homme moyen sensuel;* his characteristic attitudes are somewhat pantheistic. Instead of regarding rocks and stones and trees merely as inert objects, he probably regarded them in 1799 as deeply alive, as part of the immortal life of nature. Physical death he felt to be a return to the source of life, a new kind of participation in nature's "revolving immortality." From everything we know of Wordsworth's typical attitudes during the period in which he composed the poem, inconsolability and bitter irony do not belong in its horizon. I think, however, that Bateson overstates his case and that he fails to emphasize properly the negative implications in the poem ("No motion has she now, no force"). He overlooks the poet's reticence, his distinct unwillingness to express any unqualified evaluation of his experience. Bateson, I would say, has not paid enough attention to the criterion of correspondence. Nevertheless, in spite of this, and in spite of the apparent implausibility of Bateson's reading, it remains, I think, somewhat more probable than that of Brooks. His procedure is also more objective. Even if he had botched his job thoroughly and had produced a less probable reading than that of Brooks, his method would remain fundamentally sound. Instead of projecting his own attitudes (Bateson is presumably not a pantheist) and instead of positing a "universal matrix" of human attitudes (there is none), he has tried to reconstruct the author's probable attitudes so far as these are relevant in specifying the poem's meaning. It is still possible, of course, that Brooks is right and Bateson wrong. A poet's typical attitudes do not always apply to a particular poem, although Wordsworth is, in a given period, more consistent than most poets. Be that as it may, we shall never be certain what any writer means, and since Bateson grounds his interpretation in a conscious construction of the poet's outlook, his reading must be deemed the more probable one until the uncovering of some presently unknown data makes a different construction of the poet's stance appear more valid.

Bateson's procedure is appropriate to all texts, including anonymous ones. On the surface, it would seem impossible to invoke the author's probable outlook when the author remains unknown, but in this limiting case the interpreter simply makes his psychological reconstruction on the basis of fewer data. Even with anonymous texts it is crucial to posit not simply some author or other, but a particular subjective stance in reference to which the construed context is rendered probable. That is why it is important to date anonymous texts. The interpreter needs all the clues he can muster with regard not only to the text's *langue* and genre, but also to the cultural and personal attitudes the author might be expected to bring to bear in specifying his verbal meanings. In this sense, all texts, including anonymous ones, are "attributed." The objective interpreter simply tries to makes his attribution explicit, so that the grounds for his reading are frankly acknowledged. This opens the way to progressive accuracy in interpretation, since it is possible then to test the assumptions behind a reading as well as the coherence of the reading itself.

The fact that anonymous texts may be successfully interpreted does not, however, lead to the conclusion that all texts should be treated as anonymous ones, that they should, so to say, speak for themselves. I have already argued that no text speaks for itself and that every construed text is necessarily attributed. These points suggest strongly that it is unsound to insist on deriving all inferences from the text itself. When we date an anonymous text, for example, we apply knowledge gained from a wide variety of sources which we correlate with data derived from the text. This extrinsic data is not, however, read into the text. On the contrary, it is used to verify that which we read out of it. The extrinsic information has ultimately a purely verificative function.

The same thing is true of information relating to the author's subjective stance. No matter what the source of this information may be, whether it be the text alone or the text in conjunction with other data, this information is extrinsic to verbal meaning as such. Strictly speaking, the author's subjective stance is not part of his verbal meaning even when he explicitly discusses his feelings and attitudes. This is Husserl's point again. The intentional object represented by a text is different from the intentional acts which realize it. When the interpreter posits the author's stance he sympathetically reenacts the author's intentional acts, but although this imaginative act is necessary for realizing meaning, it must be distinguished from meaning as such. In no sense does the text represent the author's subjective stance: the interpreter simply adopts a stance in order to make sense of the text, and, if he is self-critical, he tries to verify his interpretation by showing his adopted stance to be, in all probability, the author's.

Of course, the text at hand is the safest source of clues to the author's outlook, since men do adopt different attitudes on different occasions. However, even though the text itself should be the primary source of clues and must always be the final authority, the interpreter should make an effort to go beyond his text wherever possible, since this is the only way he can avoid a vicious circularity. The harder one looks at a text from an incorrect stance, the more convincing the incorrect construction becomes. Inferences about the author's stance are sometimes difficult to make even when all relevant data are brought to bear, and it is self-defeating to make the inferential process more difficult than it need be. Since these inferences are ultimately extrinsic, there is no virtue in deriving them from the text alone. One must not confuse the result of a construction (the interpreter's understanding of the text's *Sinn*) with the *process* of construction or with a validation of that process. The *Sinn* must be represented by and limited by the text alone, but the processes of construction and validation involve psychological reconstruction and should therefore be based on all the data available.

Not only the criterion of coherence but all the other criteria used in verifying interpretations must be applied with reference to a psychological reconstruction. The criterion of legitimacy, for example, must be related to a speaking subject, since it is the author's *langue,* as an internal possession, and not the interpreter's which defines the range of meaning possibilities a text can represent. The criterion of correspondence has force only because we presume that the author meant something by each of the linguistic components he employed, and the criterion of generic appropriateness is relevant only so far as generic conventions are possessed and accepted by the author. The fact that these criteria all refer ultimately to a psychological construction is hardly surprising when we recall that to verify a text is simply to establish that the author probably meant what we construe his text to mean. The interpreter's primary task is to reproduce in himself the author's "logic," his attitudes, his cultural givens, in short, his world. Even though the process of verification is highly complex and difficult, the ultimate verificative principle is very simple—the imaginative reconstruction of the speaking subject.[30]

The speaking subject is not, however, identical with the subjectivity of the author as an actual historical person; it corresponds, rather, to a very limited and special aspect of the author's total subjectivity; it is, so to speak, that "part" of the author which

30. Here I purposefully display my sympathies with Dilthey's concepts, *Sichhineinfühlen* and *Verstehen.* In fact, my whole argument may be regarded as an attempt to ground some of Dilthey's hermeneutic principles in Husserl's epistemology and Saussure's linguistics.

C. Verification

specifies or determines verbal meaning.[31] This distinction is quite apparent in the case of a lie. When I wish to deceive, my secret awareness that I am lying is irrelevant to the verbal meaning of my utterance. The only correct interpretation of my lie is, paradoxically, to view it as being a true statement, since this is the only correct construction of my verbal intention. Indeed, it is only when my listener has *understood* my meaning (presented as true) that he can *judge* it to be a lie. Since I adopted a truth-telling stance, the verbal meaning of my utterance would be precisely the same, whether I was deliberately lying or suffering from the erroneous conviction that my statement was true. In other words, an author may adopt a stance which differs from his deepest attitudes in the same way that an interpreter must almost always adopt a stance different from his own.[32] But for the process of interpretation, the author's private experiences are irrelevant. The only relevant aspect of subjectivity is that which determines verbal meaning or, in Husserl's terms, content.

In a sense all poets are, of course, liars, and to some extent all speakers are, but the deliberate lie, spoken to deceive, is a borderline case. In most verbal utterances, the speaker's public stance is not totally foreign to his private attitudes. Even in those cases where the speaker deliberately assumes a role, this mimetic stance is usually not the final determinant of his meaning. In a play, for example, the total meaning of an utterance is not the intentional object of the dramatic character; that meaning is simply a component in the more complex intention of the dramatist. The speaker himself is spoken. The best description of these receding

---

31. Spranger aptly calls this the "cultural subject." See Eduard Spranger, "Zur Theorie des Verstehens und zur geisteswissenschaftlichen Psychologie," in *Festschrift Johannes Volkelt zum 70. Geburtstag* (Munich, 1918), p. 369. It should be clear that I am here in essential agreement with the American anti-intentionalists (term used in the ordinary sense). I think they are right to exclude private associations from verbal meaning. But it is of some practical consequence to insist that verbal meaning is that aspect of an author's meaning which is interpersonally communic*able*. This implies that his verbal meaning is that which, under linguistic norms, one *can* understand, even if one must sometimes work hard to do so.

32. Bally calls this "dédoublement de la personalité." See his *Linguistique générale et linguistique française,* p. 37.

levels of subjectivity was provided by the scholastic philosophers in their distinction between "first intention," "second intention," and so on. Irony, for example, always entails a comprehension of two contrasting stances (intentional levels) by a third and final complex intention. The speaking subject may be defined as the final and most comprehensive level of awareness determinative of verbal meaning. In the case of a lie, the speaking subject assumes that he tells the truth, while the actual subject retains a private awareness of his deception. Similarly, many speakers retain in their isolated privacy a self-conscious awareness of their verbal meaning, an awareness which may agree or disagree, approve or disapprove, but which does not participate in determining their verbal meaning. To interpretation, this level of awareness is as irrelevant as it is inaccessible. In construing and verifying verbal meaning, only the speaking subject counts.

A separate exposition would be required to discuss the problems of psychological reconstruction. I have here simply tried to forestall the current objections to extrinsic biographical and historical information by pointing, on the one hand, to the exigencies of verification and, on the other, to the distinction between a speaking subject and a "biographical" person. I shall be satisfied if this part of my discussion, incomplete as it must be, will help revive the half-forgotten truism that interpretation is the construction of *another's* meaning. A slight shift in the way we speak about texts would be highly salutary. It is natural to speak not of what a text says, but of what an author means, and this more natural locution is the more accurate one. Furthermore, to speak in this way implies a readiness (not notably apparent in recent criticism) to put forth a wholehearted and self-critical effort at the primary level of criticism—the level of understanding.

(First published in *PMLA*, September 1960)

APPENDIX II.

GADAMER'S THEORY OF INTERPRETATION

Under the somewhat ironic title *Wahrheit und Methode* (Tübingen, 1960), Hans-Georg Gadamer has published the most substantial treatise on hermeneutic theory that has come from Germany in this century. In scope, length, and learning it bears comparison with Boeckh's *Encyclopädie* (Leipzig, 1877), and it is precisely in such a comparison that the deliberate irony of Professor Gadamer's title appears, for this is a polemic against that nineteenth-century preoccupation with objective truth and correct method of which Boeckh's work was representative and its full title symptomatic—*Encyclopädie und Methodologie der philologischen Wissenschaften.* Against this preoccupation Gadamer protests that there can be no *Methodologie* of textual interpretation because interpretation is not, after all, a *Wissenschaft* whose aim is objective and permanent knowledge. Truth cannot reside, as Boeckh thought, in the genuine re-cognition of an author's meaning (*"das Erkennen des Erkannten"*), for this unrealizable ideal naïvely disregards the fact that every putative re-cognition of a text is really a new and different cognition in which the interpreter's own historicity is the specifica differentia. The historicity of understanding (*"die Geschichtlichkeit des Verstehens"*) is what the nineteenth century overlooked. No method can transcend the interpreter's own historicity, and no truth can transcend this central truth.

What is new in Gadamer's theory is not this central thesis, which is widely held and probably has more adherents than critics, but his mode of presentation.[1] He introduces new concepts and gives old words new meanings. *Vorurteil,* for example, is not to be

1. One very important critic has been Emilio Betti whose *Teoria generale della interpretazione* is by far the most significant recent

avoided but welcomed; interpretation does not require the neutralization of one's personal horizon but involves a process of *Horizontverschmelzung;* the history of interpretation is a history of application—a *Wirkungsgeschichte.* In addition to these concepts, Gadamer presents a detailed criticism of earlier hermeneutic theories, a series of extremely valuable excursuses into the history of ideas, and an illuminating theory of art as *Spiel.* Quite apart from its theoretical argument, *Wahrheit und Methode* is a book of substance that has begun to radiate an influence far beyond Germany. In America, James M. Robinson has observed that "in the present situation Dilthey and increasingly Heidegger are being superseded by the Heidelberg philosopher Hans-Georg Gadamer, a former pupil of Heidegger and Bultmann, whose *magnum opus* grounds the humanities in a hermeneutic oriented not to psychologism or existentialism, but rather to language and its subject matter."[2]

Gadamer's book extends and codifies the main hermeneutical concepts of Bultmann, Heidegger, and their adherents and can be considered a summa of what Robinson calls "The New Hermeneutic." *Wahrheit und Methode* has been welcomed by Robinson and other theologians and by continental literary critics as a philosophical justification for "vital and relevant" interpretations that are unencumbered by a concern for the author's original intention. On this point "The New Hermeneutic" reveals its affinities with "The New Criticism" and the newer "Myth Criticism." All three have impugned the author's prerogative to be the determiner of textual meaning. Gadamer, however, grounds his anti-intentionalism partially in aesthetics (like the New Critics) and not at all in the collective unconscious (like the Myth Critics), but primarily in the radical historicism of Martin Heidegger.

Gadamer owes much of the vocabulary and context of his exposition to Heidegger. "Distance in time could only be thought of in its hermeneutical productiveness after Heidegger had lent an

---

treatise in the tradition of Schleiermacher and Dilthey. In a later booklet, *Die Hermeneutik als allgemeine Methodik der Geisteswissenschaften* (Tübingen, 1962), he takes sharp issue with Gadamer, Bultmann, and their followers.

2. See "Hermeneutic Since Barth," in *The New Hermeneutic,* eds. J. M. Robinson and J. B. Cobb, Jr. (New York, 1964), p. 69.

existential sense to the idea of understanding" (p. 281).[3] But despite the modesty with which Gadamer dedicates his work to "the new aspect of the hermeneutical problem disclosed by Heidegger's existential analysis of human being" (p. 245), the theory he puts forward belongs in many of its features to a skepticism regarding historical knowledge that long predated *Sein und Zeit.* Still, Gadamer does owe to Heidegger the positive embracing of historically distorted knowledge as something "real" and "phenomenal" in contrast to academic pseudo-knowledge which is "abstract" and "constructed." For "in view of the historicity of our being, the rehabilitation of (a text's) original conditions is a futile undertaking. What is rehabilitated from an alien past is not the original. In its continued alienation it has a merely secondary existence" (p. 159).

That is the flavor of Gadamer's attack on the philological tradition in Germany and its "naïve" aspirations to objectivity. From the start it had been a dead and spiritless enterprise that lacked validity, vitality, and *humane Bedeutung.* However, the new hermeneutics Gadamer offers to replace the tradition of Schleiermacher, Humboldt, Droysen, Boeckh, Steinthal, Dilthey, and Simmel may be more destructive in its implications than he had reckoned. In any case, his theory contains inner conflicts and inconsistencies which not one of the above masters would have allowed to pass into print.

A. TRADITION AND THE INDETERMINACY OF MEANING

Although the nature of textual meaning is a crucial subject for hermeneutic theory. Gadamer does not devote a substantial discussion to it. His primary concern is to attack the premise that textual meaning is the same as the author's meaning. To suppose that a text means what its author meant is to Gadamer pure romantic *Psychologismus,* for a text's meaning does not lie in mental processes, which are in any case inaccessible, but in the subject matter or thing meant, the *Sache,* which, while independent of author and reader, is shared by both. Thus, the motto to the

3. The page references throughout are to Gadamer, *Wahrheit und Methode.* The translations are mine.

central section of Gadamer's book is Luther's dictum, *"Qui non intellegit res, non potest ex verbis sensum elicere."* The *res,* not the author, is the determiner of meaning.

Luther's point as I understand it is firmly valid. It is impossible to elicit the sense of the word "railroad" unless one knows what a railroad is. However, Luther carefully distinguishes, as Gadamer does not, between *res* and *sensus.* Indeed, Gadamer identifies meaning and subject matter—as though meaning were an autonomous entity quite independent of consciousness—which is a repudiation not simply of psychologism but of consciousness itself. It will not do to invoke Husserl as an ally on this point (p. 211), since Husserl's repudiation of psychologism consisted in distinguishing between mental acts, meanings, and things, not in abolishing the former two. Husserl describes meaning as distinct from, yet dependent on, mental acts, and for him the author alone is the determiner of a text's meaning.[4] While Gadamer is right to reject the loose identification of mental processes and meanings in Schleiermacher and Dilthey, his exposition appears to imply that textual meaning can somehow exist independently of individual consciousness.

He finds sanction for this supposed independence in the nature of written language: "It seems to us to be the distinguishing feature and dignity of literary art that in it language is not speech. That is to say, while remaining independent of all relation of speaking, or being addressed, or being persuaded, it still possesses meaning and form" (p. 177). Accordingly, a written text is not to be considered as recorded speech, but as an independent piece of language. "Actually the condition of being written down is central to the hermeneutic phenomenon because the detachment of a written text from the writer or author as well as from any particular addressee or reader gives it an existence of its own" (p. 369). The text, being independent of any particular human consciousness, takes on the autonomous being of language itself. As Heidegger inimitably put the case:

> Der Mensch spricht nur, indem er der Sprache entspricht.
> Die Sprache spricht.
> Ihr Sprechen spricht für uns im Gesprochenen.[5]

4. See *Logische Untersuchungen,* pp. 91–97.
5. Heidegger, *Unterwegs zur Sprache.*

A. Tradition and the Indeterminacy of Meaning

But the matter can be put another way. If the language of a text is not speech but rather language speaking its own meaning, then whatever that language says to us is its meaning. It means whatever we take it to mean. Reduced to its intelligible significance, the doctrine of the autonomy of a written text is the doctrine of the indeterminacy of textual meaning.

The implications of that doctrine are not altogether shirked by Gadamer. "The meaning of a text goes beyond its author not just sometimes but always. Understanding is not a reproductive but always a productive activity" (p. 280). Furthermore, "the winning of the true sense contained in a text or artistic work never comes to an end. It is an infinite process" (p. 282). Thus *the* meaning of the text is a never-exhausted array of possible meanings lying in wait for a never-ending array of interpreters. But if this is so, it follows that no single interpretation could ever correspond to the meaning of the text, for no actual interpretation could ever be the same as an array of possible meanings. By no magical road could an actual interpretation or even an infinite series of them ever be made identical with a locus of possibilities. Quite clearly, to view the text as an autonomous piece of language and interpretation as an infinite process is really to deny that the text has *any* determinate meaning, for a determinate entity is what it is and not another thing, but an inexhaustible array of possibilities is an hypostatization that is nothing in particular at all.

Though he has not clearly defined the issue, Gadamer may have wished to avoid this disconcerting consequence by conceiving of a text's meaning as changing in time, yet determinate at any given point in time. This concept of a historically changing meaning preserves the infinite productiveness of interpretation without relinquishing the idea of a determinate meaning, for it is only when a text does mean something and not just anything that interpretation is a plausible enterprise. But here a problem arises. Suppose, as it often happens, two readers disagree about the meaning of a text at exactly the same moment of time. What principle would they have for determining who is more nearly right? They could not measure their interpretations against what the text had meant in the past, since it no longer means what it meant before. Apparently there is no way of determining what a text means at a given moment. So again, under this hypothesis, the meaning is indeterminate, since we cannot distinguish even in principle, much less in practice, between what it means and what it does not mean.

It is, perhaps, to avoid this nihilistic conclusion that Gadamer introduces the concept of tradition: "The substance of literature is not the dead persistence of an alien being that exists simultaneously with the experienced reality of a later time. Literature is rather a function of spiritual conservation and tradition, and therefore carries into every present its hidden history" (p. 154). I take this to mean that the changing substance of a text is determined by the widespread cultural effects and manifestations it has passed through, and that this wider significance is commonly understood and accepted within any present culture. "In truth, the important thing is to recognize distance in time as a positive and productive possibility of understanding. It is not a yawning abyss, but is filled out through the continuity of its coming hither and by that tradition in whose light shines everything that comes down to us" (p. 281).

The idea of tradition is essential to Gadamer because it points to a principle for resolving disagreements between contemporary readers. The reader who follows the path of tradition is right, and the reader who leaves this path is wrong. The determinate meaning of a text at a given point in time is what a present culture would generally take that meaning to be. The principle seems analogous to legal pragmatism in which a law means what the judges take it to mean, but in law there is a hierarchy of judges, and a papal-like authority accrues to the highest judge. Gadamer's concept of tradition lacks this hierarchical structure and therefore cannot in fact save the day. For the concept of tradition with respect to a text is no more or less than the history of how a text has been interpreted. Every new interpretation by its existence belongs to and alters the tradition. Consequently, tradition cannot really function as a stable, normative concept, since it is in fact a changing, descriptive concept. (It is a notable characteristic of theories which reject the prerogative of the author that they attempt illicitly to convert neutral, descriptive concepts into normative ones.) The futility of performing this legerdemain appears when we observe that the original problem has not disappeared but has cropped up again in another form. For the problem of determining the true character of a changing tradition is the same as the problem of determining the true character of a changing meaning.

B. *Repetition and the Problem of Norms*

Without a genuinely stable norm we cannot even in principle make a valid choice between two differing interpretations, and we are left with the consequence that a text means nothing in particular at all.

B. REPETITION AND THE PROBLEM OF NORMS

As the foregoing makes clear, the problem of norms is crucial. If we cannot enunciate a principle for distinguishing between an interpretation that is valid and one that is not, there is little point in writing books about texts or about hermeneutic theory. Gadamer himself, when he argues against the most extreme form of non-normative theory, faces squarely up to this:

> If a work is not complete in itself how can we have a standard against which to measure the validity of our perception and understanding? A fragment arbitrarily broken off from a continuing process cannot contain a compelling norm. And from this it follows that all must be left to the perceiver to make what he can out of what lies before him. One way of understanding the form is as legitimate as another. There is no criterion of validity. Nor does the poet himself possess one (even the aesthetic of "genius" confirms that), rather, each encounter with the work ranks as a new creation. This seems to me an untenable hermeneutic nihilism. (p. 90)

What is the compelling norm that vanquishes this nihilism? Gadamer's most precise statements are those which declare what the norm is not: "Norm concepts like the meaning of the author or the understanding of the original reader represent in truth mere empty blanks that are filled up by understanding from occasion to occasion" (p. 373). In that case what is left? There is left the assertion that a text, despite the fact that its meaning changes, nevertheless does represent a stable and repeatable meaning. Gadamer rightly perceives that without this there can be no norm and no valid interpretation, although his acceptance of the exigency is grudging:

> The meaning of a written sign is in principle identifiable and repeatable. Only that which is identical in each repetition is

that which was really laid down in the written sign. Yet it is at once clear that here "repetition" cannot be taken in a strict sense. It does not mean a referring back to some primal original in which something was said or written. The understanding of a written text is not repetition of something past, but participation in a present meaning. (p. 370)

This seems to say that the meaning of the text is self-identical and repeatable and, in the next breath, that the repetition is not really a repetition and the identity not really an identity. This kind of reasoning stands as eloquent testimony to the difficulties and self-contradictions that confront Gadamer's theory as soon as one asks the simple question: What constitutes a valid interpretation? Gadamer's most sustained attempt to solve this problem is now to be examined.

C. EXPLICATION AND THE FUSION OF HORIZONS

If an interpreter cannot overcome the distorting perspective of his own historicity, no matter how hard he tries, then it follows that "one understands differently when one understands at all" (p. 280). An apparent confirmation of this doctrine has been observed by all teachers who read student examinations. Experience has taught them that the student who expresses an idea in his own words has probably understood the idea, while the one who merely repeats the lecturer's words probably has not. We seem to be led to the skeptical and psychologistic conclusion that each man, being different, has to understand differently in order to understand at all.

But is this a correct inference from the phenomenon? The example of the lecturer and his students really points in the opposite direction. The indication that a student has understood the lecturer is not merely that he has expressed himself in different words, for he would also plausibly do that if he had misunderstood the speaker. The sign that he has understood the lecturer's meaning is that he has expressed a similar or equivalent meaning even though his words are different. If the meaning had not been translated into a new idiom with some success we would have no grounds for inferring that the student had understood. That which he has understood is, after all, a meaning, not an expression, and this is

C. Explication and the Fusion of Horizons

precisely why the lecturer may begin to feel uneasy when he finds merely his own expression repeated.

It follows that the proper form of Gadamer's dictum is that one tends to *express* a meaning differently when one understands at all. It is literally nonsense to state that one understands only when one does not understand. However, Gadamer attempts to salvage this apparent contradiction by equating understanding with explication: "In the last analysis, understanding and explication are the same" (p. 366). This remarkable assertion is defended by the following argument: "Through explication the text is to be brought to speech. But no text and no book can speak when it does not speak a language that reaches others. And so explication must find the right language if it would really make the text speak" (p. 375). A past text cannot be understood until it has been explicated in the idiom of the present day. Thus, the speaking of the mute text can occur only in and through a modern commentary. Since the being understood or speaking of the text is effected by an explication, it follows that explication and understanding are "in the last analysis" the same.

With this highly insubstantial argument Gadamer has set out to topple one of the firmest distinctions in the history of hermeneutic theory, that between the *subtilitas intelligendi* and the *subtilitas explicandi*—the art of understanding a text and the art of making it understood by others. Attempting to efface this distinction results only in logical embarrassment before the simplest questions, such as, "What does the explicator understand before he makes his explication?" Gadamer's difficulty in coping with this basic question is quite apparent when he comes to describe the process of interpretation. He cannot say that the interpreter understands the original sense of the text, since that would be to disregard the historicity of understanding. He cannot say, on the other hand, that the interpreter understands his own subsequent explication, since that would be patently absurd.

His solution is to opt for a compromise: "The real meaning of a text as it addresses itself to an interpreter . . . is always *codetermined* by the historical situation of the interpreter" (p. 280, my italics). Thus, what an interpreter understands is neither wholly the result of his own perspective nor wholly that of the original perspective. It is rather the product of a fusion between these two, which Gadamer calls a *Horizontverschmelzung*. "In the process of understanding there always occurs a true fusion of perspectives in which the projection of the historical perspective really brings about a sublation of the same" (p. 290). Thus, the perspective and idiom of the interpreter are always partly constitutive of his understanding.

Once again Gadamer's attempted solution turns out, on analysis, to exemplify the very difficulty it was designed to solve. How can an interpreter fuse two perspectives—his own and that of the text —unless he has somehow appropriated the original perspective and amalgamated it with his own? How can a fusion take place unless the things to be fused are made actual, which is to say, unless the original sense of the text has been understood? Indeed, the fundamental question which Gadamer has not managed to answer is simply this: how can it be affirmed that the original sense of a text is beyond our reach and, at the same time, that valid interpretation is possible?

Gadamer is much more conciliatory to the ideal of valid interpretation than his assumptions warrant. If he were true to his assumption of radical historicity, that which he calls a fusion of historical perspectives could not be affirmed at all. If the interpreter is really bound by his own historicity, he cannot break out of it into some halfway house where past and present are merged. At best he can only gather up the leftover, unspeaking inscriptions from the past and wring from them, or impose on them, some meaning in terms of his own historical perspective. For once it is admitted that the interpreter can adopt a fused perspective different from his own contemporary one, then it is admitted in principle that he *can* break out of his own perspective. If that is possible, the primary assumption of the theory is shattered.

D. THE HISTORICITY OF UNDERSTANDING

I have examined the three principal concepts by which Gadamer has tried to salvage the idea of valid interpretation from the ruins of historicity—tradition, quasi-repetition, and horizon-fusion. All three ideas have this interesting common feature: they each constitute an attempt to fuse together the past and the present while still acknowledging their incompatible separateness. This inner contradiction has been the focus of my attack on Gadamer's theory. On the other hand, I recognize the validity of Gadamer's insistence that a vital, contemporary understanding of the past is the only understanding worth having and his rightness in insisting on the differentness in the cultural givens and shared attitudes between a past age and the present one. What is wanted is to preserve these truths without committing contradictions and abolishing logically necessary distinctions.

The fundamental distinction overlooked by Gadamer is that between the meaning of a text and the significance of that meaning to a present situation. It will not do to say in one breath that a written text has a self-identical and repeatable meaning and in the next that the meaning of a text changes. Instead of reproducing this paradox in a concept like quasi-repetition, Gadamer should have tried to resolve it by observing that the word "meaning" has been given two distinct senses. There is a difference between the meaning of a text (which does not change) and the meaning of a text to us today (which changes). The meaning of a text is that which the author meant by his use of particular linguistic symbols. Being linguistic, this meaning is communal, that is, self-identical and reproducible in more than one consciousness. Being reproducible, it is the same whenever and wherever it is understood by another. However, each time this meaning is construed, its meaning to the construer (its significance) is different. Since his situation is different, so is the character of his relationship to the construed meaning. It is precisely because the meaning of the text is always the same that its relationship to a different situation is a different relationship. This is surely what Gadamer wishes to call attention to by his insistence on vitality and change. It is what he means or should have meant by the concept of *Horizontverschmelzung*. He could have avoided self-contradiction by perceiving that this melting or fusing always involves two processes that are separate and distinct no matter how entangled they may be in a given instance of understanding. One process is the interpreter's construing and understanding of textual meaning. This act of construing is prior to everything else. But the interpreter also finds a way to relate this construed meaning to himself and, in the case of written criticism, to recast it in his own idiom. This recasting *could* be called a fusion of horizons, but it would be more accurate to call it a perception of the relevance assumed by the text when its meaning is related to a present situation.

This resolution of Gadamer's contradictions does, of course, disregard the historicity of understanding, since it assumes that an interpreter can construe the original meaning of a past text. Gadamer found himself in contradictions precisely because he disallowed this possibility. Now, by what right do I return to a pre-Heideggerian naïveté and allow it? First, I would point out that my account by no means abandons the concept of historicity —assuming that the word is taken to represent a fundamental differentness between past and present cultures. What I deny is not the fact of difference but the asserted impossibility of sameness in the construing of textual meaning.

On what grounds is this impossibility asserted by Gadamer? He does not argue the case but assumes that it has been established by Heidegger. Heidegger, on Gadamer's interpretation, denies that past meanings can be reproduced in the present because the past is ontologically alien to the present. The being of a past meaning cannot become the being of a present meaning, for being is temporal and differences in time are consequently differences in being. If this is the argument on which Gadamer wishes to found his doctrine of historicity, he should acknowledge that it is ultimately an argument against written communication in general and not just against communication between historical eras. For it is merely arbitrary, on this argument, to hold that a meaning fifty years old is ontologically alien while one three years or three minutes old is not. It is true that Heidegger introduces the concept of *Mitsein* which corresponds to the idea of cultural eras, but this does not solve the problem. The ontical character of time does not in itself require the arbitrary slicing up of time into homogeneous periods.

But the doctrine of radical historicity might, after all, be true. It states that all present acts of understanding fail to re-cognize past meanings. This seems to be a statement like "All swans are white," that is, a statement which could be falsified. However, it is really not that kind of empirical statement at all, since there is no way of being certain in *any* act of understanding (much less in all such acts) that the author's meaning has or has not been reproduced. The doctrine of radical historicity is ultimately a dogma, an idea

D. The Historicity of Understanding

of reason, an act of faith. So, of course, is the contrary doctrine: *not* all acts of understanding fail to re-cognize past meanings. While neither dogma could be falsified, one may very well be more probable than the other.

The less skeptical position is more probable primarily because it coheres with the rest of experience while the radically historicistic position does not. If we believe from experience that linguistic communication through texts past or present has *ever* occurred, then the dogma of radical historicity is rendered improbable. The historicist dogma is not really a dogma about the ontological nature of time, since it does not deny the possibility of written communication between persons living in the "same" period, inhabiting the "same" milieu, and speaking the "same" language. However, this sameness is an illicit abstraction which conceals the fact that each moment is a different period, a different milieu, and even a different language. If the historicist wishes to emphasize the possibility of communication within a given period, he had better not insist that time itself is the decisive differentiating factor that distinguishes one "period" from another.

If time is not the decisive differentiating factor, the following consequence ensues. To say that men of different eras cannot understand each other is really to say that men who exist in significantly different situations and have different perspectives on life cannot understand each other. If it is right to think that all men exist in situations that are significantly different from one another and that all have different perspectives, then the historicist dogma reduces to simple psychologism: men in general, being different from one another, cannot understand the meanings of one another. The saving concepts of *Mitsein* and *Tradition* are mirages. Even though there are always shared elements in a culture which constitute its very substance, *all* men in a culture do not share the same general perspective on life, the same assumptions; they do not always speak the same idiom. It is a naïve abstraction to consider any period in the past or the present as having this kind of homogeneity.

Indeed, the great insight of historicism, as Meinecke has shown, is not that various cultural eras are uniform in themselves and different from one another, but that men are significantly different from one another. Differences of culture are manifestations of this root possibility of differences among men. The Heideggerian version of the historicist insight renders itself meaningless if it denies the ontological status of individuality and uniqueness among men who live in the same culture. Indeed, the concept of a homogeneous present culture is empirically false and cannot suffice to bridge the gap between persons of the same period. That is the real ontological gap—the one that subsists between persons, not the one that subsists between historical eras. If the former can be bridged, as Gadamer and Heidegger admit, then so can the latter, for the historicity of understanding is, in its fundamental significance, merely an instance of the multiplicity of persons.

E. PREJUDICE AND PRE-UNDERSTANDING

The firmest conception and most powerful weapon in Gadamer's attack on the objectivity of interpretation is not the doctrine of historicity but the doctrine of prejudice (*Vorurteil*). This concept is Gadamer's version of a hermeneutic principle that was first clearly perceived by Schleiermacher, then fully elaborated by Dilthey and Husserl, and finally given an existential turn by Heidegger. It will be my purpose in this final section to turn my critique of Gadamer's book to good account by showing how the concept of *Vorurteil* has a significance far more positive than that given it in *Wahrheit und Methode*. I shall suggest, though by necessity briefly, the methodological importance of the doctrine for conducting all forms of textual interpretation.

The doctrine of prejudgment is briefly as follows. The meaning of a text (or anything else) is a complex of submeanings or parts which hang together. (Whenever the parts do not cohere, we confront meaninglessness or chaos, not meaning.) Thus the complex of parts is not a merely mechanical collocation, but a relational unity in which the relations of the parts to one another and to the whole constitute an essential aspect of their character as parts. That is, the meaning of a part as a part is determined by its relationship to the whole. Thus, the nature of a partial meaning is dependent on the nature of the whole meaning to which it belongs. From the standpoint of knowledge, therefore, we cannot perceive the meaning of a part until after we have grasped the meaning of the whole, since only then can we understand the function of the part within the whole. No matter how much we may emphasize the quasi-independence of certain parts or the priority of our encounter with parts before any sense of the whole arises, still we *cannot* understand a part as such until we have a sense of the whole. Dilthey called this apparent paradox the hermeneutic circle and observed that it was not vicious because a genuine dialectic always occurs between our idea of the whole and our perception of the parts that constitute it. Once the dialectic has begun, neither side is totally determined by the other.

The doctrine of pre-understanding is logical or phenomenological rather than empirical, and it would no doubt be very difficult to devise an empirical test for it. Nevertheless, we might take as an example a sentence like "He words me Gyrles" (*Antony and Cleopatra,* Act V). How do we know (if we do know) that "words" is a verb unless we have already dimly grasped the sentence as a whole? We might say something about normal syntax and the grammatical exigencies of "he," "me," and the terminal "s," but that is possible only because we have submerged the normal function of "words."[6] It is conceivable to misread the sentence: "He says 'Gyrles' to me" or "He, that is Gyrles, words me," and such misreadings would imply different preliminary guesses about the nature of the whole. Though it is right to argue that some words of a sentence are always less variable and dependent than others, these are still, at best, simply clues or possibilities that do not become determinate until they fall into place within the whole —no matter how vaguely that whole may be perceived. In fact, this preliminary perception is always vague since it is by necessity, without parts, unarticulated. It is an adumbration, a pre-apprehension rather than an articulated understanding. A close analogy is the dim adumbration of an answer that we must always project in order to ask a question in the first place.

Gadamer's argument for the necessity of *Vorurteil* in interpretation is accomplished by transforming the concept of pre-apprehension into the word "prejudice," for if our understanding of a text is always governed by a pre-understanding, it follows that this preliminary adumbration must come from ourselves since it does

6. These grammatical exigencies are, in any case, components of pre-understanding.

not and cannot come from the as yet indeterminate text. What we supply by way of pre-understanding must therefore be constituted by our own expectations, attitudes, and predispositions, in short, from our own prejudices. This is by no means a troublesome conclusion in Gadamer's view. The fact that our interpretations are always governed by our prejudices is really the best guarantee that texts will have significance for us. Instead of trying to overcome our prejudices—an attempt which cannot succeed and can result only in artificial, alien constructions—we should welcome them as the best means of preserving the vitality of our inheritance and our tradition.[7]

The argument is powerful, but clearly its validity depends on the truth of its major premise that pre-apprehensions are identical with or composed of prejudices. If that is so, then the principle tenet of all perspectivistic, psychologistic, and historicistic theories must be true. In fact, however, the substitution of "predisposition" or "prejudice" for "pre-understanding" hides an illicit and false equation. The word "predisposition" or "prejudice" connotes the idea of a preferred or habitual stance, making the equation imply that an interpreter cannot alter his habitual attitudes even if he wants to. But this is false, since interpreters have been known to alter their view of a text's meaning, rare as this occurrence may be. If, on the other hand, prejudice is taken to mean not just the interpreter's habitual attitudes, but the whole array of attitudes that he can adopt, then certainly a pre-apprehension must be a prejudice; however, this becomes an empty tautology since any stance I adopt must ipso facto be possible for me, and the word "prejudice" loses its desired connotations. One could, of course, reply that an interpreter's possible stances are limited by his historicity even though he may to some extent alter his habitual ones, but this again is an assertion that has nothing to do with the logical necessity of pre-understanding. It is merely a repetition of the historicist dogma that we cannot re-cognize past meanings. The notion of *Vorurteil* adds nothing to this previously assumed dogma except to give it a misleading flavor of logical rigor.

---

7. Such arguments invariably use the monolithic "we" and "our" and so assume the existence of a nonexistent unanimity and homogeneity.

E. Prejudice and Pre-Understanding

The doctrine of pre-understanding is in fact altogether neutral with respect to historicity and prejudice. Ultimately it is no more or less than the doctrine of the logical priority of the hypothesis. The preliminary grasp of a text that we must have before we can understand it is the hermeneutical version of the hypothesis we must have about data before we can make sense of them. (The claim that hypotheses are induced from or generated out of data has lost favor, not least because it fails to explain how differing hypotheses can be generated from the same data.) Pre-understanding is not, of course, a neat and simple model for the hypothetico-deductive process, since the data it explains are constituted to a large extent by the hypothesis itself. That is to say, the contours of the words in a sentence are determined very substantially by our pre-apprehension of the form and meaning of the sentence, whereas in a perfect model the data would act as they chose regardless of our hypothesis about them. This highly constitutive character of hermeneutic hypotheses explains why they tend to be self-confirming and why it is hard to convince anyone to change his interpretation of a text.

However, as Dilthey saw, the hermeneutic hypothesis is not completely self-confirming since it has to compete with rival hypotheses about the same text and is continuously measured against those components of the text which are least dependent on the hypothesis. Thus, one further indication that preliminary hermeneutic hypotheses (pre-apprehensions) are not the same as prejudices is that hypotheses in general cannot be reduced to habitual attitudes or modes of thought. If that were true, new hypotheses could not appear. In fact, nobody knows just how hypotheses arise. Certainly to equate them with predispositions is to reduce all new ideas about data to old prejudices—a strange destiny for a notion like the special theory of relativity, for example. [8]

Since a pre-understanding is a vague hypothesis that is constitutive of understanding, and since understanding is therefore partly dependent on pre-understanding, the problem of achieving a valid

8. The best discussion of hypotheses in interpretation is to be found in R. S. Crane, *The Languages of Criticism and the Structure of Poetry* (Toronto, 1953), pp. 176–80. Crane implicitly connects the concepts of genre and hypothesis (see pp. 146, 167).

pre-apprehension of the text is a crucial problem in interpretation. What is a valid pre-apprehension? Bluntly stated, it is a correct preliminary grasp of the author's meaning. But how unsatisfactory this answer is! There is no way of knowing in advance just what the author may be getting at, and there are so many possible preliminary guesses that the chance of hitting on the right one is extremely slim—so slim, apparently, that a deep skepticism regarding the likelihood of valid interpretation seems warranted.

However, the probability appears less slim, as indeed it is, if we formulate the problem more accurately. To speak individualistically simply in terms of an inaccessible authorial intention is to misrepresent the problem. Our chances of making a correct preliminary guess about the nature of someone's verbal meaning are enormously increased by the limitations imposed on that meaning through cultural norms and conventions. A single linguistic sign can represent an identical meaning for two persons because its possible meanings have been limited by convention. By the same token, the larger linguistic configurations which an interpreter confronts also have this conventional and normative character. This is what makes correct pre-apprehension reasonably likely to occur, for not just words, but sentences, and not just sentences, but utterances as long as *War and Peace* are partly governed by the norms and conventions deposited by previous usages.[9] That is to say, all communicable speech acts, written or spoken, belong to a limited number of genres. Now, a genre is a kind and shape of utterance whose norms and conventions have been partly fixed through past usage. Every communicable utterance belongs to a genre so defined, and in communicated speech there can be no such thing as a radically new genre, for so-called new genres are always, by linguistic and social necessity, extensions and variations of existing norms and conventions. The most primitive and fundamental genres are the sentences—the smallest units of communicable speech—but every larger utterance

9. Saussure makes an elegant and helpful distinction between "actualities" and "virtualities" in language, the former being usages which have already been realized, and the latter extensions of meaning made possible by the former. Every time a virtuality is actualized, new virtualities are thereby created. See Saussure, *Cours de linguistique générale.*

also possesses with varying degrees of rigidity the normative and conventional character of single-sentence utterances.

This is what gives the interpreter's pre-understanding a good chance of being correct, for the author's meaning has a shape and scope that is governed by conventions which the interpreter can share as soon as he is familiar with those conventions.[10] In the process of interpretation, therefore, a preliminary guess or pre-apprehension with respect to a text is really a guess about the genre to which the text belongs, and the most appropriate form of the question, "What is the nature of a valid pre-apprehension?" is the question, "To what genre does this text belong?" Indeed, this is the most important question an interpreter could ask about a text, since its answer implies the way the text should be understood with respect to its shape and emphasis as well as the scope and direction of its meanings.

Schleiermacher, whose aphorisms on interpretation are among the most profound contributions to hermeneutics, deserves credit for first laying bare the fundamental importance of genre. "Uniqueness in speech," he said, "shows itself as a deviation from the characteristics that determine the genre," for in every case of understanding, "the whole is apprehended as genre—*Das Ganze wird ursprünglich verstanden als Gattung.*"[11] In this insight Schleiermacher laid the foundation for that ideal discipline which impelled his thinking on hermeneutics—a truly general theory of interpretation. For the concept of genre cuts through all particular varieties of biblical, poetical, historical, and legal interpretation of texts because the notion of genre in itself determines an intrinsic mode of proceeding. To be concerned with the precise genre of a text is to give every text its due and to avoid the external imposition of merely mechanical methods and canons of interpretation.

Finally, the concept of genre calls attention to the necessity of self-critical thinking in interpretation, for there can be no apodictic certainty that our preliminary guess regarding a text's genre is correct. Yet that guess governs and constitutes what we subsequently say about the text. Thus our self-confirming pre-under-

10. This is not circular, since the probable conventions under which a text was written may be discovered by studying other texts and other authors within his culture.
11. *Hermeneutik*, pp. 46, 47.

standing needs to be tested against all the relevant data we can find, for our idea of genre is ultimately a hypothesis like any other, and the best hypothesis is the one that best explains all the relevant data. This identity of genre, pre-understanding, and hypothesis suggests that the much-advertised cleavage between thinking in the sciences and the humanities does not exist. The hypothetico-deductive process is fundamental in both of them, as it is in all thinking that aspires to knowledge.

(First published in *The Review of Metaphysics,* March 1965)

APPENDIX III. AN EXCURSUS ON TYPES

A. SELF-IDENTITY OF TYPES

Since the word "type" has been a focal point of this essay, it will be useful to bring together the principal conceptions which serve to define the word as I use it. Inevitably I can only hint at or ignore some of the philosophical problems that are raised by a general theory of types—problems which ultimately embrace the whole field of epistemology. By way of orientation I shall discuss only those aspects which are most relevant to hermeneutic theory. This will require a description that goes beyond merely ostensive definition but falls short of a fully developed theory of types.

I consider a type to be a mental object or, if one prefers, an idea. The essential feature of a type idea is its ability to subsume more than one experience and therefore to represent more than one experience. The subsumptive and representational function of type ideas is, of course, essential and fundamental to language, for if such a function did not exist, no one could subsume or represent two different entities by the same word. Thus, if the word "tree" can subsume or represent more than one tree or tree experience, it follows that the meaning of "tree" when it serves this function must be a type idea.

How is it possible for a type, which is but one thing, to subsume and represent more than one thing? Although this question lies at the heart of all knowing and thinking, it has never, I think, been adequately answered. The attempt to reject such questions on the part of Wittgenstein and his adherents is entirely unsatisfactory, since no matter how far an analysis proceeds and no matter how many concessions are made to the inherent "vagueness" of thought, it must be admitted that we can perceive a region of precise identity in two different experiences. Nor is the paradox adequately resolved by the old abstraction theory, under which two different entities are identified by abstracting the traits that are the same

265

and ignoring those that are different. No doubt this kind of process can and does occur, but the theory does not explain how two traits (from two different entities) are *judged* to be the same.[1] The *Identitätsproblem* was confronted directly by Brentano and Husserl and was carried very far by the latter, but while Husserl transforms the vocabulary of the problem in an illuminating way, the paradox remains. Somehow, consciousness is capable of identifying two different experiences. In fact, this seems to be a fundamental function of consciousness, and the degree to which the mind is capable of performing this miraculous feat is a very important measure of intelligence.

The clearest and, no doubt, most elementary form of typification is exemplified in any act of recognition or memory. One experiences an object—say, an old dirty schoolcap. At some later time (ten seconds or ten years) one recognizes that same dirty old cap, but how does one know it is the same cap? In fact, one does not know it at all, since the cap might not be the same. Furthermore, it is obvious that the experience of memory or recognition is a different experience from the original one. Thus, the act of identification must depend on some remembered tertium quid that bridges the two experiences, and this must be a type idea. Of course, in this case the type idea embraces not two different entities but two different experiences of the same entity. However, this sameness is often not a matter of certainty, and the fact that a person can be tricked into believing that two different objects are the same suggests that a typifying function is at work every time a recognition occurs—whether it be true or false.

In an act of recognition, the entity which is recognized or remembered is not normally considered to be a mere instance of a type, because the two instances are identified completely. No difference whatever is perceived between them, only between the two experiences of the instance. In normal usage, we first begin to speak of a type when we identify two entities which we know to be different in some respects. A dirty old schoolcap and a clean new one are different entities that can be subsumed under the same type, namely, schoolcap. In this kind of typification the subsumption of the two instances is made possible because certain

1. See Peter Geach, *Mental Acts: Their Content and Their Objects* (London, 1957), pp. 18–44.

aspects can be identified: for instance, both entities have the same shape or the same function. These identical traits may be vague or abstract, and they may be arbitrarily invented, but without this precise identity at the level of the type, the subsumption by the type would be impossible. As in the example of recognition, the type idea here unifies more than one instance by virtue of a partial identification of the instances. The identification is not judged to be complete, as it is in recognition, but it is only by virtue of an identification at some level that the two instances belong to the same type.

Is it possible that two instances can belong to the same type if they have merely similarities or "family resemblances" but are in no respect identical? This reduces to the question, can there be similarity without there being at some level an identity which grounds the similarity? Although we may say that the following two curves are similar, $\curlyvee$ Λ , it is obvious that the curves themselves are in no way congruent. They are judged to be similar only because certain prior judgments have been made—that is, they are judged to be curves and to have whatever traits distinguish curves from other entities. If that type identification of curves had not been made, the subsequent judgment of similar curves could not have been made. More particularly, the curves might both be judged to be similar to a sine curve, $\frown\smile$, that is, the judgment of similarity might be made by reference to the similarity of both to something else. However, to leave the matter there is to plunge into the abyss of an infinite regress, since the similarity of each curve to a sine curve presents precisely the same problem as the similarity of the curves to one another. In fact, we can only say that the two curves are similar because they are, at some level of abstraction or typification, identical. They both belong to the same type because they both have the traits that define the type. It is by virtue of these identical type traits that they are judged to be similar.

But are there not types which are founded not on a partial identity of traits but on a range of instances which exist in a continuum? For example, we call a color red if it falls somewhere in the range of colors between purple and orange. Yet, oddly enough, between any two different colors falling within this range there does not exist any conceivable identity which grounds their similarity: the two red colors are different and perfectly homogeneous. It would be artificial to dissect their homogeneity into a purely red "moment" common to both and a non-red "moment" which distinguishes them. The colors are seen all at once, and they are judged to be similar. How is this judgment made? This example proves that there may be similarity without identity and that this similarity can be the basis of a type.

This kind of example forces us to perceive an aspect of types that was partly hidden in the preceding examples, namely, that sometimes the judgment of similarity is not the basis of a typification, but, on the contrary, a typification is often the basis of a similarity judgment. For in what respect is an orange-red similar to a purple-red? As particular color patches nothing about them is the same or similar; they are, in fact, incommensurable until they are understood to be moments in a continuum and, more precisely, moments in a type within a continuum of types. Is it not astonishing that a rainbow is perceived not simply as a continuum of colors but as bands of colors? Yet how can a continuum be divided into bands; where are the divisions to be made? Apparently here typification is a function of perception itself.[2] The infinite number of different colors is embraced by a few finite color types, and the judgment of similarity is made on the basis of that typification. From the standpoint of knowledge, two patches are judged to be similar because they belong to a type, not vice versa. Typification precedes similarity judgments; the type enforces a prior identification of the two instances, despite their incommensurability as particular colors. Whatever the underlying physiological mechanism may be, the two reds are seen to be similar only because they are seen to be reds. The judgment does not proceed the other way round, from similarity to redness, but from redness (i.e. identity) to similarity. The task of placing different instances in a continuum is subsequent to this typification.

This conclusion is confirmed by the threshold effect of similarity judgments. Two colors may lie very close to one another on the rainbow, but one of them will be judged red, the other orange (or purple). Yet the proximity of the red to the purple on the continuum may be just as great as that between two reds which are

2. In this case the function has a physiological basis.

judged to have greater similarity. If the colors are not compared but are simply judged by themselves, this threshold effect is even greater. The same kind of effect obtains with sounds. Two pairs of vocal noises may be equally close to one another in a continuum, yet one pair may be identified as two "r's," the other pair as an "r" and a "w." This disparity in similarity judgments suggests that they are preceded or constituted by typifications, and that the typification which identifies or fails to identify the two instances is the basis for a judgment of similarity or dissimilarity. It may be argued that this prior typification could not occur unless there were a proximity or similarity judgment prior to that. But apparently, what happens is not that one instance is perceived as close to another, but that they are perceived as the same, namely, as "red" or as "r." The differentiations are subsequent to this. Thus, even in the case of two different "homogeneous" experiences, the ground of a similarity is an identity, and the root function of a type idea remains that of identifying different instances.

B. VERBAL MEANINGS AS TYPES

How do type-ideas arise? A Lockean would insist that they arise entirely from experience. To gain the type represented by a use of the word "tree," it is necessary to have had an experience of an actual or depicted tree. From previous experience one gains the types that subsume later experiences. But this account, while it may be demonstrably true for some types, such as tree, cannot be valid for the typifications that cause a rainbow to be seen as bands (or types) of colors. Furthermore, types are constitutive of all meaningful experience, and therefore typification must be an element in the very first experience of a tree, just as much as in the first experience of a rainbow. Although this qualification of the Lockean account is necessary, it is not, from the standpoint of hermeneutic theory, highly important. At the level of verbal meaning, all types, regardless of their earliest provenance, are learned types—that is, they are type ideas which derive from previous experience and can subsume later experience.

What is the nature of this subsumption? To call a newly experienced object a tree is to recognize that it has traits identical to those in previous tree experiences. But the subsumption is not simply a process of identifying certain explicit traits; it also entails a structure of expectations by virtue of which one believes that many of the unexamined or unattended traits in the new experience will be the same as traits characteristic of previous experience. This structure of inexplicit expectations is always a component of a type, since it is by virtue of them that a new instance can be subsumed before it is completely known.

Thus a type always has a dimension of vague expectations by virtue of which more than one concrete instance can be subsumed without compelling an alteration of the type. If this dimension were precise and altogether explicit, the expectations could not be fulfilled by different explicit traits. Yet the vagueness of the expectations is not complete: they may be fulfilled by different entities, but not by any and all entities. A tree is not an herb or a bush, by which we may infer that the range which an type can subsume is limited by other learned types having some traits in common with it. However, we would never know that a particular instance was a bush and not a tree if we had not learned the type represented by "bush." The phoneme "r" subsumes a fairly wide range of sounds, yet the range is certainly limited by "w" and "l." Another way in which the inherent and necessary vagueness of a type may be limited is by increasing the number of its explicit traits, thereby changing the range of inexplicit ones. Thus, "bonsai tree" has more explicit traits than "tree" and changes the range of inexplicit expectations. As the number of explicit traits rises, the area of vagueness diminishes so that fewer different instances can be subsumed by the type. But no matter how explicit the type becomes, it cannot altogether conquer the area of vagueness, since an altogether explicit type could be subsumed by only one instance and would be, from the standpoint of knowledge, what we usually name an "individual," not a "type."

While the learning of types and the subsumption of instances is a feature of all disciplines, the nature of types has been a subject of particular interest to those concerned with the methods of psychology and sociology. In one respect this fact is ironic, since these disciplines frequently have particularizing rather than typifying goals, unlike disciplines such as physics or logic, which try to subsume all possible instances under the fewest possible types. But this irony is only apparent. The subsumption of instances is a problem that becomes increasingly complex as one narrows the range of the type. It is then that one is compelled to examine the nature and function of types, for as they begin to multiply, they take on greater interest and complexity. A type that covers all instances (say, "Being") may be of interest in itself but does not usually breed interest in such types as "tree," "bush," and "bonsai," or their complex relations to one another.

Those who have most deeply considered the methodological function of types (I am thinking particularly of Dilthey, Weber, Stern, and Kretschmer) are in accord on one point: type concepts are indispensable in all attempts to understand an individual entity in its particularity. That such particularizing or "idiographic" knowledge is a primary aim of textual interpretations should be self-evident, but it is far from self-evident that an individual entity can be known only through a type. That conception seems to abandon the ideal of particularity from the start and to accept uncritically Dilthey's motto, *Individuum est ineffabile.* However, Dilthey's conclusion is inescapable.

Take the example of coming to know another person. First we encounter traits and gestures which already have a physiognomic significance because we assume that they belong to a person and not to a robot or some other type of thing. Our first encounter is thus necessarily with a type—that is, with a *person,* though our earliest discernible typification is likely to be far narrower than that. Since we know explicitly only the few traits we have observed, why are these explicit traits connected to one another in a meaningful way? Why are they not simply discrete observations having no connection with each other and no physiognomic significance? Their interconnections and meaningfulness arise from the fact that they are understood to be traits *of* a person—that is, they are understood to be explicit aspects of something whose general character we have learned from past experience. This type idea, which consists of conditioned expectations, is the ground or background which connects the traits we have observed with a notion of the whole person. It is this unifying ground alone which lends coherence to our scattered explicit observations.

This example, which is paradigmatic for coming to know any and all particular things, shows the indispensable heuristic func-

271

tion of type ideas. Whenever we encounter something, we always encounter it partially, because our knowing is temporal (we experience clusters of traits successively) and because it is selective (we cannot attend to everything explicity all at once). Our less-than-divine intellect is, as Augustine observed, time-ridden. Some traits of a thing always lie outside our explicit awareness, either because we have not yet experienced those traits or because we are not at the moment attending to them. These unattended or unknown traits constitute a penumbra which may be called a "unifying background." It has also been called a "field" or "ground," or "substrate" or "horizon," but whatever it is called, it is always present and gives our experience the quality of a type idea. It is a type experience precisely because it embraces inexplicit expectations which, by virtue of their inexplicitness (or vagueness), could be fulfilled by different concrete traits. If these expectations did not have some degree of vagueness or tolerance, the background would be explicit like the foreground, and we would know all the traits all at once—an impossibility for our time-ridden consciousness. Thus, at every stage of coming to know anything in particular, we are brought to our knowledge by virtue of type ideas. And no matter how particularized our knowledge becomes, the temporal and attentional limitations of consciousness ensure that a penumbra of greater or lesser extent always remains, so that we can never completely relinquish the type by which we have come to know the particular.

Since our idea of a particular thing is always a type idea of greater or lesser explicitness, it must follow that types have not only an indispensable heuristic function but also an inescapable constitutive function. It is perfectly true that we do not always preserve the original type by means of which we first came to know something in particular; our expectations may be tolerant, but they are not always fulfilled by experience, and this may cause us to alter the heuristic type. A book can turn out to be a cigarette box; a column can be a clever trompe d'oeil; a nice chap can turn out to be a cad. But whatever stage of explicitness we reach, there always remains something inexplicit, something expected or anticipated rather than attended to, so that the latest stage of knowledge remains governed by the latest type idea through which it was reached. No matter how much the heuristic type may have been altered in the process of knowing, it is, at its last stage, constitutive as well as heuristic.

To point out the constitutive character of types is merely to extend a Kantian insight into the realm of ordinary experience. The ultimate categories by which we structure and constitute experience may be reducible to ten or twelve, but in their unreduced variety they are as numerous as the countless type ideas through which we come to know the particulars of experience, and these type ideas are no less constitutive of experience than time, space, and causality. But there is this one immense distinction: the fundamental categories of experience are, no doubt, immutable, whereas the everyday types by which we constitute experience are open to revision. The noumenal world beyond the categories is to us inaccessible, but the phenomenal world through which we learn our types is also the world which can teach us to revise them.

Since the temporal and attentional limitations of consciousness give every conception of a particular thing the character of a type, we are frequently compelled to recognize that our conception may be inadequate to the thing. Most of us have this clear-sighted humility with respect to our conception of another person; we realize that something in the penumbra of our conception might in fact turn out to be contrary to our expectations. We may not, of course, reveal this becoming humility with respect to a cigarette or an acorn or a paper clip, though it would be warranted all the same. On the other hand, the incongruity between the complete explicitness of things and the incomplete explicitness of our conceptions about them does not necessarily obtain when the thing we are concerned to know is a verbal meaning. Here full congruity is possible because meanings, being themselves types, are capable of being fully known. Someone else's conception or type, because it is a conception and not in the ordinary sense a thing, can be identical with my own conception or type. This is another way of stating Vico's insight that the human realm is genuinely knowable while the realm of nature is not, or (to recall a more venerable ancestry) it is a version of the pre-Socratic doctrine that only like can know like.

This distinction between knowledge of meanings and knowledge of things raises an interesting point with respect to the heuristic and constitutive function of types in the process of interpretation.

Appendix III: An Excursus on Types

In knowledge of things, our conception of the thing is always con-stituted by the last and most explicit stage of the heuristic type through which we came to know the thing. Thus, there is always something provisional in our conception—an expectation that might not be fulfilled. This is not necessarily the case in coming to know meanings. It is true that the last stage of the heuristic type is also constitutive, but this constitutive type can and ultimately should cease to be heuristic at all, for knowledge of meaning (in Boeckh's phrase, "knowledge of the known") cannot be more explicit than its object permits. There is nothing vague about a thing, but there is always something vague about a meaning. At some point, therefore, an inexplicit adumbration must remain just that, since to make it explicit would be to entertain a different meaning, not the one which is to be known. Verbal meaning is not to be treated like an acorn, a cigarette, or a paper clip, as though it were capable of unlimited explicitness. In confronting a meaning (that is, a type) there comes a point when the type is the thing. When the process of knowing has been carried this far, when there is no longer a heuristic and provisional element, we can say that the particular type we know is the particular type we wanted.[3]

3. Thus, while I can understand what someone means by "lyric poetry," "satire," or "the novel," I can criticize his meaning by asserting that the identity of traits among the instances represented by these types has no consistent basis in fact. Wittgenstein is too willing to rest content with the vague family types of ordinary speech. In extraordi-nary discourse these family types can be rejected in favor of strict types that represent instances having precisely specified identical traits.

274

INDEX

275

Index